The Emancipation of the Jews of Alsace

Jewish Communities in Alsace

The Emancipation of
the Jews of Alsace

ACCULTURATION AND TRADITION

IN THE NINETEENTH CENTURY

Paula E. Hyman

YALE UNIVERSITY PRESS

NEW HAVEN AND LONDON

Parts of this book appeared in different form in *Assimilation and Community: The Jews in Nineteenth-Century Europe,* ed Jonathan Frankel and Steven Zipperstein, Cambridge University Press, 1991, *Jewish Settlement and Community in the Modern Western World,* ed. Ronald Dotterer, Deborah Dash Moore, and Steven M Cohen, Susquehanna University Press, 1991, and *Umah v'Toldoteha,* ed Shmuel Ettinger, Merkaz Shazar, 1984.

Set in Berkeley Old Style type by Keystone Typesetting, Inc , Orwigsburg, Pennsylvania Printed in the United States of America by Lightning Source.

Library of Congress Cataloging-in-Publication Data
Hyman, Paula, 1946–
The emancipation of the Jews of Alsace, acculturation and tradition in the nineteenth century / Paula E Hyman
p   cm
Includes bibliographical references (p   ) and index
ISBN 0-300-04986-2 (alk paper)
1 Jews—France—Alsace—History—19th century   2 Alsace (France)—Ethnic relations   I Title
DS135 F85A474   1991
944' 383004924—dc20   91-12389
ISBN-13: 978-0-300-04986-2   CIP

The paper in this book meets the guidelines for permanence and durability of the Committee on Production Guidelines for Book Longevity of the Council on Library Resources

Contents

Preface

Although a scholar's work is often solitary, many individuals and institutions contribute to the research and writing of a book. In my study of the impact of emancipation on a traditional, nonurban Jewish population, I benefited from both the financial assistance and the helpful advice available within the community of scholars.

My first trips to Alsace and Paris to collect data for a quantified study of Jewish social mobility were funded by summer grants from the National Endowment for the Humanities and Columbia University's Council for Research in the Social Sciences. A fellowship from the American Council of Learned Societies enabled me to analyze and write my initial findings. As I expanded my project and methodology, I was fortunate to receive a fellowship from the National Endowment for the Humanities and grants from the Abbell Research Fund of the Jewish Theological Seminary of America and the Memorial Foundation for Jewish Culture. A Lady Davis Fellowship permitted me to write the first draft of this book in the stimulating atmosphere of Jerusalem, while a senior faculty fellowship from Yale University enabled me to apply the finishing touches to the manuscript free from the responsibilities of teaching and administration. I am grateful to all of these institutions for their important contribution to this book

I also wish to thank the staffs of the many libraries and archives in France, the United States, and Israel where I pursued my interest in the Jews of Alsace. My task was greatly eased by their courtesy and professionalism. I particularly appreciate the generosity of Moche Catane of Jerusalem, who graciously permitted me to read and take notes on his private collection of the letters of his great-grandfather.

I am grateful to colleagues at Columbia University, the Jewish Theological Seminary, the Hebrew University, and Yale University with whom I discussed my project over the years and particularly to all those who read and commented on various drafts of this book. Steven M. Cohen introduced me to the complexities of quantified research and guided me in my initial interpretation of my data Freddy Raphael provided a warm welcome to Strasbourg and generously shared his vast knowledge of Alsatian Jewry with me. Vicki Caron, Richard Cohen, Debórah Dwork, Marion Kaplan, and Deborah Dash Moore read the entire manuscript and offered valuable suggestions for clarification of my argument and for stylistic revision that improved this book. Our dialogue on various aspects of modern Jewish history has enriched my thinking as a historian, as has the vibrant intellectual community at Yale.

My family has shared in the intellectual adventure and in much of the travel necessary to prepare this book. My daughters, Judith and Adina, have been delightful companions on research trips and have compelled me to formulate my research findings with clarity. My husband, Stanley Rosenbaum, has provided emotional support, a listening ear, and partnership in debate throughout our life's journey together. It is to him that I dedicate this book.

The Emancipation of the Jews of Alsace

ONE

Introduction

Modern Jews emerged in Europe during the nineteenth century. In the years between the outbreak of the French Revolution and the dawn of the twentieth century, the political and economic status of European Jews changed dramatically. During this period all Jews living west of the Elbe achieved civil emancipation. They were no longer tolerated aliens subject to discriminatory taxation and economic and residential restrictions, but rather equal citizens, enjoying all the rights and bearing all the responsibilities of their Gentile compatriots. Taking advantage of new economic and educational opportunities, European Jews gradually acculturated and became integrated into the economic, social, and institutional life of their respective nations. Their formerly autonomous, largely self-governing corporate communities, limited and restructured in the course of emancipation, gave way to more or less voluntary communities devoted to religious and philanthropic concerns.[1]

Cultural and religious developments within these Jewish communities, stimulated by intellectual and economic elites living in major cities, signaled a radical break with the past. Many Jews now discovered their individuality and embarked on a journey of self-definition freed from the constraints of a collective identity. Formulating new educational priorities for themselves, they subordinated the study of rabbinic culture to the acquisition of secular knowledge. Attuned to the norms and values of the larger society, they adapted Jewish religious practices—particularly in the aesthetic realm—to the standards governing the emerging middle classes. They embraced new ideologies, such as the universalism, civic patriotism, and political liberalism of the Enlightenment, that promised them social acceptance as well as opportunities for individual achievement.

1

The extent of social change among at least the most visible Jews in the nineteenth century can be judged in part by the reactions of Gentile observers. During the last decades of the eighteenth century, when European intellectuals and bureaucrats conducted a lively debate on the admissibility of Jews into civil society, Jews were attacked, even by their supporters, as economically retrograde, socially backward, and culturally laggard. The Abbé Henri Grégoire, the liberal French cleric who promoted Jewish emancipation during the French Revolution, could only marvel at the prevalence of Jewish superstition: Jews were "attached not only to the Mosaic law, but to superimposed chimeras, which feed upon blind credulity."[2] Less than a century later, Jews often appeared to many to be in the vanguard of currents of change—more successful manipulators of the capitalist system and more enamored of and adapted to urban living than any other group. The new anti-Semites of the time successfully exploited these socioeconomic characteristics of Jews in their propaganda. From Paul de Lagarde, who scourged Jewish propagation of materialism and liberalism, to Maurice Barrès, who regretted their disproportionate representation in positions of economic and political power, critics of modern capitalist society fixed upon the Jew as an agent of capitalism and a symbol of all the ills that had followed the erosion of traditional economic and social patterns.

The changing perception of the nature of the "Jewish danger" reflected the new economic and cultural behavior of European Jews. In this century of urbanization, industrialization, and emancipation, significant numbers of Jews appeared in the liberal professions, in the arts and journalism, and, most important, in the middle and upper ranks of commercial enterprise. Secular Jewish intellectuals, articulate and prolific, became influential in the urban cultural centers of Europe.

In spite of the enormous social, cultural, and psychological transformation experienced by Jews in the century following the French Revolution, historians have paid scant attention to the processes (rather than the end product) of social change among this most significant of Western and European minority groups. Yet it is crucial to examine how Jews accommodated to changed political and economic conditions in order to understand their new relation to the larger society, as well as their development of modern communal institutions and new forms of Jewish culture. For the most part, historians of Europe and of Jewish culture have not investigated the various responses, in different social contexts, of the masses of Jews to the circumstances they confronted in the nineteenth century. Jews whose exploits were singled out by the anti-Semites or who had public roles have dominated the historical accounts of the emergence of modern Jewry. Those Jews who lived in obscurity, who disappeared into the socially constructed stereotype of "the Jew," have scarcely become visible in historical reconstructions of the transformation of Jewish social, cultural, and economic life.

Modern Jewish historiography has been intoxicated with the struggle to achieve emancipation. Not surprisingly, it has focused on the legal, institutional, and ideological components of Jewish integration into European societies. By stressing ideological programs, political strategy, and institutional developments, modern Jewish historians have inevitably studied the proclamations and activity of Jewish elites, mainly urban ones With this focus, they have transferred to both secular intellectuals and the politically and economically prominent the attention that classical Jewish history has lavished upon the rabbinic elite. By the early nineteenth century, secular urban elites constituted the most visible, though far from the largest, segment of Jewish society and took central stage in the campaigns to acquire emancipation and shape the modern Jew. Bourgeois Jewish leaders, self-conscious and articulate, first internalized the critique of traditional Jewish society offered by both proponents and opponents of Jewish emancipation and impressed upon their constituents the need for change and self-improvement.

Examining the struggle for emancipation from the vantage point of Jewish elites has had certain consequences Most important, it has led to an emphasis on the discontinuities in Jewish experience and the rapidity of cultural change in the years following the French Revolution—for the elites were the first Jews to perceive, and benefit from, the opportunities offered by modern Western societies. It has also promoted a concentration by historians on metropolitan centers of political and economic power, where elites were most influential in determining policy and in offering themselves as the model of the modern Jew.

Only in the past two decades have there emerged a handful of studies addressing the socioeconomic developments of Jews within a variety of contexts, both urban and rural, in Western and Central Europe.[3] Shifting focus to examine the lives of ordinary Jews—most of whom, in 1800 and later, were living in villages rather than large cities—brings to the fore the responses of the masses to new opportunities.[4] This grass-roots approach permits an assessment of the impact of ideologies on the masses and corrects the distortions inevitably produced by looking primarily at the advanced minority of European Jews. How rapid was social change among the majority of Jews living in Western and Central Europe? Which aspects of social behavior were most susceptible to change? Where can one locate the agents of change within Jewish communities? Did the ideological statements of Jewish notables belie a continuity in practice among their less prominent constituents? Local and comparative studies concerned with these questions have begun to integrate the Jewish masses into our portrait of the emergence of Jewish modernity and to indicate that the process of assimilation was much more uneven and complicated than earlier histories have suggested. Legal change and social reality, after all, do not necessarily march in a chronological lockstep.

The social history approach also challenges accepted notions of when the rupture with traditional patterns of Jewish life occurred. The ideological and political focus of much of Jewish historiography has led historians from Salo Baron and Jacob Katz to Michael Meyer and David Sorkin to conclude that the crucial period of change in the West was from 1775 to 1830.[5] In those years thinkers and statesmen of the Enlightenment first addressed the Jewish question and proposed emancipation and assimilation. Also in those years Jewish intellectuals and members of the upwardly striving bourgeoisie began their passionate acquisition of European culture and proclaimed themselves eager to integrate into society. The German Jewish historian Isaak Markus Jost shaped an enduring popular historical conception when he remarked in 1833, "All of us who were still children thirty years ago can testify to the incredible changes that have occurred both within and outside us We have traversed, or better still, flown through a thousand-year history."[6]

The view from the masses of Continental European Jewry is different. It suggests that cultural change was a far more gradual process and that the crucial period for most Western Jews occurred two generations later, from 1848 to 1870 Like most French peasants who did not become conscious of themselves as French until the decades just before World War I, most Jews living in France, though not peasants, had not become "israélites français" until the second half of the nineteenth century.[7]

If Jewish historiography has focused too exclusively upon the pleasures and pains of an articulate elite, European historiography has been absorbed in the sufferings of Jews as a victimized minority. For European historians Jews represent an important and hitherto untapped resource for comparative investigation. They can serve as a test case for measuring socioeconomic change and opportunity, as well as the possibilities for and contours of ethnic minority identification within European societies. Yet European historians have studied Jews primarily as victims of anti-Semitism or as bellwethers to diagnose the state of liberalism in particular nations. They have been far more interested in the image of the Jews, and its political usage, than in the Jews themselves Even students of European social mobility have overlooked the Jews, either because their sample populations include few Jews or because they choose to examine social mobility in a working-class industrial context (in which Jews rarely figured before the mass migration from Eastern Europe). A nonpeasant group in all European countries, Jews continued to differ in several economic, cultural, and demographic indices from the larger population in the nineteenth and twentieth centuries, in spite of their unflagging efforts at social integration. Even as they acculturated, they did not become undistinguishable from their compatriots. Because of their persistent differentness as a minority group, they provide a means for exploring the effects of discrimination, both past and ongoing, on social change and economic and cultural behavior. They likewise offer an opportunity to investigate the influence of traditional social patterns, structural features, and cultural values on socioeconomic and demographic behavior. Understanding what advantages—and liabilities—Jews enjoyed in the nineteenth-century European city and its environs also enables us to examine the nature of European economic development from the perspective of a nonpeasant minority.

This book studies the pace and processes of social change among the inarticulate Jewish masses by focusing on nineteenth-century Alsatian Jewry, an ideal vehicle for such a study. Unlike the Jews of Bordeaux or Paris, or the *maskilim* (secular intellectuals of the Jewish Enlightenment) of Berlin, who have attracted attention beyond what their numbers merit, the Jews of Alsace on the eve of the French Revolution and thereafter were a traditional population largely untouched by secular culture. Alsatian Jews were not an atypical Western Jewry. Indeed, they were more like the masses of Jews in the south German states and east Prussia than were the Jews of Berlin or Hamburg. They were religiously observant, spoke their own Yiddish dialect, and lived in villages and small towns in the Alsatian countryside. In fact, until emancipation, Jews were not permitted to reside in the largest cities of Alsace, including both Strasbourg and Colmar. The 22,500 Jews living in Alsace constituted more than half of the French Jewish population in 1789. Because of their location within France and their conservative social and religious patterns, they were the first large traditional Jewish community to experience the benefits, and the challenges, of emancipation.[8] As pioneers on the path that all other traditional Jews of Western and Central Europe would follow, they offer an opportunity to investigate the impact of the pivotal change in Jewish legal status in modern Europe upon a sizable group of traditional Jews.

Jews had lived in Alsace since the Middle Ages As a frontier region on the crossroads of trade routes to the German states and the Low Countries, Alsace had cultural as well as economic connections that transcended national boundaries. It is not surprising, then, that on the eve of the French Revolution, the Jews of Alsace had much in common with their Jewish neighbors across the Rhine. Together they formed the cultural orbit of Western Ashkenazi Jewry Alsatian Jews purchased sacred books published in Germany, imported rabbinic leaders from Germany, and sent their native-born rabbis to study in German and other Central European *yeshivot* (academies of advanced Torah study). The Alsatian Jewish marriage market extended more often to the east than to the west.[9] With the Revolution, France conferred a civic status upon the Jews of Alsace for which their cousins across the Rhine had to wait another eighty years. It also promoted forms of behavior and identity considered consonant with citizenship.

Although Alsatian Jews remained the heartland of French Jewry until 1871, even as they sent their young to Paris and abroad throughout the century, they produced few local luminaries. In this the social historian is perhaps fortunate, for figures of the stature of a Moses Mendelssohn or his disciples in the Berlin *Haskalah* (Jewish Enlightenment movement) so dwarf their contemporaries that it is easy to overlook the activity of their less illustrious fellow Jews. The Jews of Alsace were distinctly ordinary people who sought to improve their personal fortune, increase their security in a region plagued by sporadic anti-Semitic incidents, and explore new economic and social opportunities that would allow them both to attain integration into French society and to retain a distinctive Jewish identity.

The inarticulate and unexceptional are often difficult to study: they give us few specific indications of their motivations and ideological predispositions. But they often do leave behind, in the course of their daily routine, records of their behavior that, when carefully examined, can reveal as much as ideological pronouncements, although they focus on different issues. The Jews of Alsace emerge at mid-century from local manuscript censuses, which list addresses, occupations, household size and composition, and occasionally place of birth. Their communal tax rolls, available through 1831, give some indication of wealth. Their choice of marriage partners, migratory patterns, intergenerational social mobility, and growing literacy in French can all be studied through civil marriage records. Local notarial records show the kinds of wealth acquired by the more successful Jews at mid-century. And finally, Jews figure prominently in the commercial court records of Strasbourg; although they constituted some

3 percent of the Alsatian population, Jews appear in approximately 25 percent of the cases of the Strasbourg court from the 1820s through the 1860s. From this litigation, the economic activity of otherwise anonymous Jewish cattle dealers, small merchants, and wholesale businesspeople is available for investigation. Thus the methods used and sources tapped by European social historians can be employed to reach the types of Jews who are otherwise absent from more traditional documents.

For information on the Jews of Alsace, this book draws upon manuscript censuses and marriage records of the entire Jewish population of Strasbourg and of three smaller communities, Bischheim, Niederroedern, and Itterswiller, which are of different sizes and are located in different areas of the department of the Lower Rhine. It also uses scattered census data and marriage records from other towns and villages in both Alsatian departments When supplemented by governmental reports, records of the Jewish consistories, newspaper accounts, minute books of *hevrot* (confraternities for study and philanthropy), memoirs, and literary writing, the bare bones of quantifiable data yield a flesh and blood portrait of a community in transition from the status of westernmost outpost of traditional Ashkenazi Jewry to a nationally defined, acculturated modern Jewry.

The Jews of Alsace provoke a number of critical questions about the dynamics of Jewish acculturation and modernization as we study how they took advantage of the opportunities made available by their emancipation. How did the different social contexts of village and city affect the religious, cultural, and economic adaptation of Alsatian Jews to the new conditions of a post-emancipation society? What roles did Jewish elites, acting through the official communal institutions of the consistories, and government bodies play in transforming the Jewish masses into good citizens and modern Jews? In focusing upon one specific Jewish population, this book aims to explore issues appropriate to other similarly constituted Jewish groups and to illuminate the broader subject of social change among nineteenth-century Western European Jewry as a whole.

To understand the process of social change, I have chosen to examine the social, political, and cultural forces that maintained continuity and stability before turning to those economic and political factors that undermined the pre-emancipation Jewish way of life. This division, of course, is artificial; countervailing forces were at work throughout the nineteenth century, although the factors that promoted change ultimately prevailed.

The viability of traditional Jewish society in a post-emancipation political setting emerges from an examination of the culture and economic and domestic reality of the lives of the Jews living in the Alsatian countryside The first half of the book illustrates the interplay between the economic roles and public perception of the Jews in Alsace, their limited steps toward acculturation, occupational change, and social integration, and their retention of a traditional Jewish popular culture. Any assessment of the impact of political emancipation on a Jewish population, after all, must consider the local status of the Jews in fact as well as in law and their perception of their opportunities for social mobility and integration as measured against the security offered by a known way of life. Despite the early emancipation of the Jews in France and the protection of Jewish rights proffered by the central government, the economic role of the Jews in Alsace and the relations between Jews and Gentiles were slow to change. Local popular anti-Semitism had an impact on the social and economic integration of the Jews of Alsace The "Jewish question," much of it revolving around the issue of purported Jewish usury, continued to perturb public opinion in Alsace and shape the Jewish response to emancipation throughout the nineteenth century. I examine how the Jews perceived and acted on the economic opportunities of an expanding capitalist economy and the ways this retarded the economic assimilation that Jewish as well as Gentile leaders had promoted as a goal of emancipation. Finally, I demonstrate how the structural features of Alsatian Jewish communities enabled Alsace to become the seat of organized resistance to institutional reforms imposed from Paris. In doing so we retrieve a discourse that ran counter to that of the urban Jewish elites who championed significant changes in Jewish culture.

The second half of this book examines the elements that reshaped the pre-emancipation patterns of Alsatian Jewish life: the contracting role of Jews in the rural economy, the impact of migration and urbanization, the introduction of modern primary schools, the policies of acculturated urban Jewish leaders in both Paris and Alsace, and state intervention. It analyzes the paths of acculturation and social mobility that Alsatian Jews followed as they entered bourgeois occupations in increasing numbers and adopted the urban bourgeoisie as their model of behavior. It also illustrates the ways Jews adapted their religious tradition to bourgeois standards and disseminated new models of Jewish culture from city to countryside. In spite of the persistence of Jewish poverty in Alsace, the majority of Jews improved their living conditions in the course of the nineteenth century, forging a bourgeois lifestyle that challenged the cultural conservatism of traditional Jewish society in the countryside. Exploring the dimensions of social change among the Jews of Alsace and its acceleration in the period after 1848 suggests general social and political factors that must be investigated in any analysis of Jewish accommodation to modern western societies and highlights the specific features of the Alsatian Jewish experience. The role of the state in fostering acculturation is an example of the former; the proliferation in Alsace of publicly subsidized confessional primary schools as a result of the Guizot Law of 1833 is an example of the latter

The structure of the Jewish community in nineteenth-century France is crucial in understanding the patterns of social change among the Jews of Alsace (as well as the rest of French Jewry). Although emancipation destroyed the self-governing Jewish corporate communities under whose jurisdiction Jews had lived for centuries, in 1808 Napoleon established a centralized, hierarchical system of consistories for Jews, parallel to the institutional structure for Protestants A departmental consistory, with its seat in the city with the largest Jewish population, was created in each department with at least two thousand Jews. Local Jewish communities were under the control of the departmental consistory, which in turn was under the jurisdiction of a Central Consistory located in Paris. The Central Consistory reported to the Ministry of Cults, which supervised its activities

The consistories were oligarchic in nature. During the course of the century, the power of laymen in the consistories was strengthened, and lay-rabbinic tension was a regular phenomenon in French Jewish life. Following the practice prevalent in the French polity, the franchise was limited to a group of notables. Until the 1840s the three lay and rabbinic members of the departmental consistories were chosen by twenty-five notables, who were selected by the government from among the wealthiest and most respected men in the department. Since the masses were disenfranchised and the government favored notables likely to promote Jewish acculturation and religious reform, conditions were set in place for conflict between an acculturated elite minority, generally administering the consistories, and the Jewish masses. After the expansion of male suffrage following the Revolution of 1848, however, this conflict between urban elites and the Jewish masses in Alsace was often played out in consistorial elections, and progressive domination of the consistories of Alsace, especially that of the Upper Rhine, was by no means a forgone conclusion.[10]

Several factors thus combined to shape the processes of accommodation of Alsatian Jews to the French version of modernity. In forming a new French Jewish identity—in dealing with questions of reform, communal priorities, and group self-perception—communal institutions interacted with and attempted to modify the behavior of individual Jews. Progressive Jewish elites, within the departmental consistories as well as the Central Consistory, called upon the representatives of state power to buttress their efforts to effect change among the masses of Jews in Alsace. Their policies, and the responses they provoked from the Jewish masses, determined the pace of Jewish acculturation in Alsace. The penetration of new ideas into the Alsatian countryside was a necessary step in the transformation of traditional Jewish cultural patterns, but the erosion of the village Jewish economy after mid-century was a more powerful agent of social change. Together they gradually reshaped the contours of Jewish life.

Shaking off their former constraints, yet never entirely free from the marks of Jewishness, imposed both internally and externally, nineteenth-century European Jews remade themselves—became "new men" in an age open to new men. To understand the inordinate attention paid to Jews by their contemporaries in nineteenth- and twentieth-century Europe and to understand the evolution of a modern Jewish identity in the West, we must explore the dimensions of the acculturation and socioeconomic mobility of Jews, as well as their attempts to maintain or refashion their tradition, as they emerged from their castelike status as aliens in the villages of Western and Central Europe. Such an exploration is also necessary to elucidate their roles in European economic and cultural life as well as their changing sense of self vis-à-vis the surrounding environment. To assess the nature of continuity in a period generally characterized as one of social upheaval and to comprehend the processes of Jewish accommodation to new conditions, we must be sensitive to the ways ordinary Jews perceived their own society. How were their perceptions of, and reactions to, new opportunities mediated by the legacy of past discrimination, previously learned skills, and religio-cultural traditions? How did they reconcile Jewish needs for a measure of particularism with French demands for universalism? The answers to these questions are intended to contribute to an understanding of the relations of minority and majority groups in industrializing societies, as well as to the making of the modern Jew.

TWO

The Status of
Jews in Alsace

Looking back from their vantage point as citizens and successful members of the bourgeoisie, European Jews hailed the French Revolution. As a result of its purposeful destruction of the corporate structure of the ancien régime, the Revolution of 1789 had, for the first time in Europe, conferred the rights of citizenship upon an entire Jewish population and had declared civic equality an essential feature of the modern nation-state. To be sure, the Jews so emancipated were seen as lamentably backward, but it was thought that their new political status would hasten their regeneration as productive members of the body politic.[1]

The overwhelming majority of Jews first emancipated in 1790–91 lived in the provinces of Alsace and Lorraine, most of which France had acquired at the conclusion of the Thirty Years' War through the Treaty of Westphalia in 1648. As the westernmost segment of the Ashkenazi Jewish population of Central and Eastern Europe, the Jews of Alsace had much in common with their brethren further east. Yiddish-speaking village Jews, they lived in the small towns and hamlets that dotted the hills and plain of Alsace.[2] They ordered their lives according to the rhythm of the Jewish calendar and governed themselves with rabbinic law. Subject to numerous economic disabilities, they played a vital, though much despised, role in the local economy.

Emancipation changed their legal status, but their economic role and social and religious practices, as well as their actual position within Alsatian society, proved resistant to political decrees originating in Paris. Local conditions—social, economic, cultural, and political—governed the pace of social change among Alsatian Jews and doomed the optimistic forecasts of rapid assimilation predicted by the promoters of Jewish emancipation. The traditional Jewish culture of Alsatian Jewry was no slate ready to be wiped clean by enlightened leaders, nor could the relations of minority group and majority population be regulated by legal fiat. To analyze the processes of acculturation and integration of the Jews of Alsace in the course of the nineteenth century and the evolution of Jewish-Gentile relations in the province, it is important to understand the situation of the Jews on the eve of the French Revolution and the stability of their social roles thereafter

The census of 1784 revealed 19,624 Jews lived in 183 localities in Alsace. More than 80 percent of the communes in Alsace, though, had no Jewish residents. In Strasbourg, Colmar, and Mulhouse, which as cities had the right to ban the residence of Jews, Jewish merchants and peddlers whose commercial activities were tolerated during the day were expelled at nightfall.[3] Although they constituted just 3 percent of the population of Alsace, Alsatian Jews accounted for approximately half of France's total Jewish population, with the Jews of neighboring Lorraine making up much of the rest Alsatian Jews lived in small communities, typically containing from one hundred to three hundred Jews. Since the villages where they lived were small, the Jews often constituted a sizable minority. Although in many locales Jews were 5–10 percent of the population, in at least twenty-one Alsatian villages they comprised 15–25 percent of the inhabitants.[4] The small size of the communities created close bonds and ensured rigid communal constraints. There were no secrets among Jews living in the same village.

The Jews were limited to a narrow range of economic pursuits. They could neither own land nor manage retail businesses or inns, and they were excluded from the artisan guilds. Most Alsatian Jews therefore supported themselves through peddling and dealing in secondhand clothing and merchandise. Given the difficulty of rural transportation in the ancien régime, most peasants had little direct contact with the market. The Jewish peddler with his variety of wares found ready customers in the villages and the countryside. The peddler also brought news and acted as intermediary in the marketing of peasants' crops Setting out on Sunday, his sack over his shoulder, the peddler followed his regular route throughout the week, returning home only for the Sabbath. As one Jewish writer noted, "It was Friday evening that these unfortunate peddlers whom one saw the entire week, staff in hand and back bent under a *ballot* of merchandise, running through hills and valleys and living on water and black bread, it was that evening, you could be sure that they would have their *barches* (white Sabbath loaves), their wine, their beef, and their fish."[5]

Though his life was difficult, the Jewish peddler was viewed with ambivalence by his customers. The goods he brought—matches, pins, and notions—were appreciated. Yet peddling was not considered real work, because the peddler produced nothing. And the Jewish peddler drove a hard bargain. Jews also supported themselves as brokers of grain and as cattle dealers (a modest trade) and horse dealers (a more substantial one). The most successful horse dealers, like Naftali (Herz) Cerf Berr, wealthy syndic and *shtadlan* (political intercessor) of Alsatian Jewry, served as contractors for the king's armies.[6]

Jews of all ranks lent money at interest, and in so doing performed a useful function. Few other credit facilities in Alsace served the peasantry until the mid-nineteenth century. The peasant who needed a loan had to borrow from a Jew or a Christian notary. He often preferred the Jew because such loans could be more easily kept secret. For the Jewish moneylender security was precarious. Interest rates were not fixed, and collection of debts was not assured. Since Jews could not own land, should landed property fall into their hands through default on a loan, they had to sell it within a year. A contemporary writer noted in the 1780s that "this commerce does not yield them much."[7] Nonetheless, on the eve of the Revolution it was widely believed that one-third of all mortgages in Alsace were in Jewish hands.[8] The Jews, some feared, were coming to dominate the economic life of the province.

Economic and political conditions conspired to ensure significant social distance between Jews and Gentiles in Alsace. The presence of both Catholics and Protestants in Alsace seems not to have mitigated tensions between Jewish and Christian Alsatians. Under the ancien régime Jews were subject to a humiliating body tax that was also levied on animals, and they paid a variety of special taxes to the king and the local noblemen. They could own no property, including their houses, and could not run public shops.[9] The exclusion of Jews from the guilds reinforced their social distance from Gentiles as well as served to maintain their occupational distinctiveness. Most contacts between the two groups were utilitarian and instrumental; the peasant was the customer of the Jewish cattle dealer, of the Jewish peddler, of the Jewish moneylender (who was often the cattle dealer or peddler including a loan in his transaction). The Jew was the customer of the local Christian artisan. To the growing local bourgeoisie, the Jewish merchant was also a competitor.

Jews were identified politically with the interests of the king and nobility, who benefited from taxing Jews for the right to reside on their land. Noble patrons found Jews invaluable, especially in wartime, when as purveyors of agricultural products they supplied horses, grain, and ready cash. In 1784 Louis XVI issued letters patent which affirmed royal control over the Jews. Asserting his authority vis-à-vis the local nobility, the king took responsibility for the Jews' protection and reserved the right to make decisions about the application or elimination of restrictions on them. The letters patent of 1784 attempted to rationalize government policy toward the Jews by casting off traditional restrictions in order that the Jews might abandon petty commerce and contribute more effectively to the French economy. To realize these goals the legislation eliminated the body tax on Jews traveling from place to place and lifted the ban on Jewish participation in industrial enterprise and in landhold-ing [10] Those classes most hostile to royal authority found in the new privileges accorded the Jews a ready symbol of the king's abuse of power.

Popular hostility toward the Jews on the part of both peasantry and bour-geoisie erupted in the last years of the ancien régime and during the Revolution. In 1777 anti-Jewish leaders in Alsace and Lorraine flooded the provinces with false receipts for peasant debts owed to Jews [11] In 1789 Alsatian peasants sought stricter regulation of loans in their *cahiers*. The cahiers of both Colmar and Metz even suggested that priests be permitted to lend at interest to prevent the people from becoming debtors of the Jews.[12] In July 1789, with the outbreak of revolution, Alsatian peasants staged anti-Jewish riots in seventy localities, during which they damaged Jewish property and destroyed the records of money lent to them.[13]

The Alsatian bourgeoisie was equally hostile to the Jewish populace, though it relied on law rather than violence to achieve its aims. Throughout the ancien régime—the last appeal was made in 1786—merchants applied to local *parle-ments* to restrict the commerce of Jews.[14] The cahiers of the third estate in Alsace and Lorraine expressed opposition to the commercial competition of Jews and to their unrestricted admission into the provinces.[15] In Thionville, for example, the third estate sought protection against Jewish moneylending and called for the dispersion of the Jews in the kingdom and colonies. In Haguenau the third estate demanded that the number of Jewish families allowed to reside in the area be limited.[16] Even after the Revolution had begun its work, the Alsatian bourgeoisie was unwilling to extend the concepts of *égalité* and *frater-nité* to the Jews of the province. On October 10, 1790, the Municipal Council of Strasbourg called for the prohibition of peddling by Jewish merchants in the city.[17] Moreover, the Jacobin deputy from Alsace, Jean-François Rewbell, vig-

orously opposed the emancipation of the Jews and secured a companion piece
of legislation to the bill emancipating the Jews of Alsace-Lorraine on September 27, 1791. The decree sponsored by Rewbell was issued the following day.
It called for a report on loans owed to Jews and solicited advice from the district directors as to how these debts could best be liquidated.[18]

The revolutionary years brought little change among the Jews of Alsace.
Emancipation had taken them by surprise. In their own cahiers they had sought
only an end to special taxation, petitioning for fiscal assimilation and for the
rights of free residence and travel. Initially they had asked to retain their
communal autonomy. Only after they became aware of the cahiers of the Jews
of Paris, submitted on August 26, 1789, which declared the willingness of the
small group of Jews in the capital to renounce corporate separateness, did the
Jews of Alsace-Lorraine bow to the new political reality and make a similar
declaration.[19]

In pre-emancipation Europe, Jewish communities, to which all Jews were
subject, had sweeping powers, including the right of taxation and the right to
adjudicate disputes within the community according to Jewish law. Although
Jewish communities lost the right of self-regulation with emancipation, they
did not disappear. Compulsory taxation of Jews to pay the salaries of their
religious functionaries continued until September 1, 1795, for example.[20]
Since the debts of former Jewish communities were not included in the law of
August 15, 1793, by which the government nationalized the debts of disbanded corporations, including religious communities, those Jewish communities in debt—the "Nation Juive" of Alsace and Metz—had to maintain an
administrative structure to levy and collect taxes.[21] Jews also preserved their
communities on a voluntary basis to provide for their religious needs. Indeed, it
was as religious bodies that Jewish communities suffered under the anti-religious zeal of the Terror. Synagogues and religious schools were ordered
closed, and ritual objects of silver and gold were confiscated. In addition, Jews
were required to work on the Sabbath and were forbidden to light Sabbath
candles.[22]

The Jews made use of their particular economic and social situation to
weather the turbulent years of the Revolution. The demand for army purveyors
and for credit was high. Peasants eager to purchase nationalized land thronged
to Jews for loans. Many Jews became impoverished in this period, however,
because speculation on public property and the depreciation of currency made
moneylending an especially precarious occupation. In addition, the emigration
of wealthy nobles deprived many Jews of a source of livelihood. Export prohibi-

tions were also damaging to Jewish commerce. Still, between 1784 and 1808–10 the officially recognized Jewish population of Alsace grew by 24 percent through a combination of immigration and natural increase. Although Jews constituted only 3 percent of the Alsatian population, they were becoming more visible. They had migrated to Strasbourg and Colmar, where they were now permitted to live, and had also dispersed, dwelling in 15 percent more communes than in 1784.[23]

By 1806 protests arose in Alsace about the Jewish domination of the province. Bourgeois interests, seeking land to enlarge their estates, sought to restrict competition to keep prices down. Wealthy members of the bourgeoisie and affluent peasants were eager to prevent the breakup of large tracts of nationalized lands, which occurred when poorer peasants bought small plots. The General Councils in Alsace, composed of proprietors, notables, and wealthy bourgeois, denounced Jews to the authorities and proposed restrictions on their economic activities. In 1806 the Council of Strasbourg declared that the Jews "are a different and distinct nation" into whose hands Alsace was falling.[24] After the battle of Austerlitz a delegation of bourgeois from Strasbourg received an audience with Napoleon at which they complained that Alsace was being strangled by Jewish debts and declared that they feared the dispossession of the peasants.[25] It was commonly believed that Jews held mortgage debts of 35 to 44 million francs. As speculators they appear to have actually controlled about 10 percent of the nationalized land in the Department of the Lower Rhine in the years 1789–1811, but they kept only 20 percent of the land they acquired for their own use.[26] The prefectural reports, sympathetic to the interests of powerful bourgeois and peasants, supported the anti-Jewish charges. Although Christians also lent money at interest, and some were reported to have "inspired such terror in their victims that debtors dare not lodge complaints," traditional anti-Jewish prejudice served to frame the question as a Jewish rather than an economic one.[27]

In response to accusations leveled against the Jews and an anti-Jewish report issued by the minister of justice, in 1806 Napoleon declared a one-year moratorium on debts owed to Jews. Napoleon shared the anti-Jewish prejudices of his time and bore a strong aversion to commerce in general and moneylending in particular.[28] A recently published book on the evils of Jewish usury and the impossibility of assimilating the Jews, as well as an article repudiating Jewish emancipation by the Viscount Louis de Bonald, described as "a theoretician of counter-revolution," had also deeply impressed him. In 1806 Napoleon referred to the Jews as "a debased and degraded nation."[29] He was also sensitive to economic complaints, for he needed popular support to conduct his military campaigns. The Jews, politically defenseless and traditional scapegoats, were an ideal group to regulate as an indication of Napoleon's concern for the plight of the people. During the year's moratorium on payments of debts owed to Jews, the minister of the interior received individual petitions requesting new delays. The complaints received against non-Jewish moneylenders were routinely ignored.[30]

After studying the problem and convening, with great theatricality, a Sanhedrin to discuss the new relation of Jews to France, on March 17, 1808, Napoleon issued what the Jews came to call the "Infamous Decree."[31] Since the departments of the Gironde, the Seine, Livourne, and the Pyrenees, as well as sixteen other departments, were exempt from the provisions of the decree, which were to last ten years, they fell primarily on the Jews of Alsace-Lorraine.[32] According to the decree Jews had to adopt surnames, refrain from the use of Hebrew in commercial affairs, and register their occupations. When drafted, unlike other Frenchmen, they could not find a substitute but had to serve in the army. No foreign Jews were permitted in France unless they owned property, established a business, or performed military service. No new Jewish settlements could be established in Alsace, and individual Jews were deprived of the right of mobility within Alsatian departments unless they acquired landed property and engaged in agriculture. Most important, Jewish commercial activity was severely restricted. Jews were not allowed to extend loans to minors, to married women without their husbands' permission, or to soldiers without their officers' consent. All loans had to be notarized at full value, and interest could not exceed 5 percent. Any loans previously contracted that did not meet these newly imposed conditions could be nullified. Finally, each Jewish merchant had to apply for a special patent from the prefect in order to conduct business. These patents were dependent on certificates of good conduct issued by the local municipal council and the consistory, the administrative organ of the Jewish community created by Napoleon and supervised by the state.

According to the statistics cited by Moche Catane, who studied the applications for patents throughout the Department of the Lower Rhine, slightly less than half of the heads of families succeeded in acquiring the patents, as many Jew chose not to subject themselves to the complicated application process. Only 169 heads of family were formally denied a patent.[33]

Designed to channel the Jews from petty commerce and moneylending into crafts and agriculture and to hasten their fusion with the general population, the Infamous Decree of 1808 was a retreat from the principles of emancipation and equal treatment before the law. Through lack of enforcement, it failed to achieve its goals. Under the new government of the Restoration, the decree was allowed to lapse in 1818 despite pleas from the General Councils of Alsace to renew its provisions.[34]

Popular hostility to Jews remained high in Alsace because of the Jews' economic role and the propagation of anti-Jewish attitudes by the church, the local councils, and the press. In 1810 the Central Consistory cited "the heredity of religious hatred still subsisting" in Alsace, which it attributed to a lack of civilization and to Christian religious instruction. "The Revolution," it declared, "made no difference in the opinion toward Jews in this land; the same hatred is shown to them. . . . It is very rare to see a Jew, no matter how well educated or how honest, fulfilling municipal functions or serving on the jury. The most ignorant of villagers is preferred. . . . When the Imperial decree of March 17, 1808, was promulgated, many mayors published this law with an undue display and many times to the sound of a tambour."[35] Symbolic of the social inferiority of the Jews in the first decades of the nineteenth century is Erckmann's and Chatrian's statement in their novel *Le Blocus* (1867), set in Alsace: "Christians, at that time, customarily addressed Jews, even the elderly, with the familiar 'tu.'"[36]

Thirty years after Jewish emancipation, in the 1820s, the Jewish question again received both popular and official attention Public demands to renew the provisions of the restrictive decree of 1808 were not settled until after 1823. Credit-hungry peasants, suffering from the economic crisis that accompanied the downfall of Napoleon, had become increasingly indebted to Jews. According to the historian Paul Leuilliot, Jewish loans nearly doubled in the five years following 1818 in the Altkirch region of the Upper Rhine In 1822 a number of men traversed that *arrondissement* "announcing that the government intended to destroy an impious race, exciting the citizens to denounce all the debts which they had contracted to Jews." Although the instigators of this activity were arrested, peasants became aroused and held anti-Jewish meetings in a number of Alsatian villages to discuss how debts owed to Jews could be annulled. In Durmenach peasants ran through the streets, threatening the local Jews and breaking into the homes of their creditors to demand the return of their notes.[37] In Altkirch a judge of the tribunal established a registry to record peasant complaints about Jews. The Jewish notables of the Upper Rhine protested that in court cases concerning Jewish moneylending, court functionaries often expressed blanket anti-Jewish statements on the order of "in Alsace where the plague of Judaism reigns with all its calamities."[38] In 1823 both Alsatian departments formally deliberated whether the renewal of the 1808 decree was necessary to stamp out "Jewish usury" and demanded information from the mayors on the economic activity of the Jews of their communes. One report from Wintzenheim (Upper Rhine) summed up the popular antipathy toward the Jews with the comment, "'We now see the mistake' of granting them the rights of citizens; 'the law of the state is merely a means for them to secure domination.'"[39] In spite of the many expressions of anti-Jewish sentiment, the government did not renew the discriminatory legislation of 1808.

Public debate on the Jewish question flourished in the 1820s. Renewed discussion of the "Jewish question" in enlightened circles was legitimated when the Society of Sciences, Agriculture, and Arts of Strasbourg sponsored an essay contest in 1824 to address, more than thirty years after the emancipation of the Jews, disparaging questions about their behavior. As in the noted Metz essay contest of 1785, the Strasbourg sponsors sought practical suggestions on how to enable the Jews of Alsace to enjoy the benefits of civilization. They also asked contestants to consider whether the social estrangement of the Jews in Alsace resulted from the Jews' superstitious practices and obstinate persistence in following ancient customs, deemed (by the contest's sponsors) inappropriate to the times and the political situation Accepting the premises of these questions, the participants submitted several essays and suggested various strategies for improving Jewish behavior, including recourse to exceptional legislation.[40]

In the wake of this contest several books on the "Jewish Question" were published The first, *Considérations sur l'état des juifs dans la société chrétienne et particulièrement en Alsace*, published in 1824, was written by Michel Betting de Lancastel, the secretary general of the prefecture of the Upper Rhine [41] Betting de Lancastel accepted much of the liberal argument for Jewish emancipation, with its negative critique of traditional Judaism and of Jewish economic activity and social characteristics, but he rejected the claim that Jewish behavior was the result of persecution. He expressed his deep disappointment that the Jews had not yet reformed their behavior and accepted the obligations of citizenship Although he reaffirmed that Jewish faults were correctable, cited the potential benefits of education, and asserted that Jewish law in itself was not an obstacle to the amelioration of the Jews, he also criticized the exploitative nature of Jewish commerce and moneylending and the prevalence of filth and vagabond-age among the Jews of Alsace. Rejecting exceptional legislation aimed at Jews as both unjust and unworkable, he suggested that the strict application of general legislation could prevent the damage to society that the Jews caused in Alsace.

Finally, he tied the right of Jews to the state's legal protection to their acceptance of the decisions of the Napoleonic Sanhedrin, which subordinated Jewish law to French civil law. Such an acceptance he found lacking in Alsace. To address the real social problems that had provoked outbursts of anti-Jewish feeling among the populace, always more prone to persecute the Jews than the sovereign power, he recommended strict enforcement of laws against usury and surveillance of Jewish and Gentile usurers alike, the establishment of *monts-de-piété* (state-owned pawnshops) to compete with Jewish moneylenders, the elimination of ignorant rabbis from office, and the use of common law to expel Jewish immigrants who were not "useful" to society. Written by a liberal, albeit highly critical, government functionary in Alsace, Betting de Lancastel's book revealed the limits of official tolerance of Jews and lent an aura of respectability to such popular notions as the perniciousness of Jewish commercial activity and the antisocial nature of the Talmud. In the generation that had elapsed since the Revolution little had changed in enlightened opinion of the Jews

Another work, Amédée Tourette's *Discours sur les juifs d'Alsace,* published as a pamphlet the following year, was similar in scope. Written by a member of the Society of Sciences, Agriculture, and Arts of the Department of the Lower Rhine, it lamented the Jews' continuing distinctiveness in their customs, dress, and language and their tendency to superstitious religious practices—that is, the practices of traditional Judaism. Tourette's solution was one often proposed by contemporary writers: the promotion of agriculture and useful crafts among the Jews [42]

Although Jewish rights were never curtailed after the 1808 decree lapsed in 1818, the situation of the Jews in Alsace was by no means comfortable. In spite of protests by Jewish authorities that anti-Jewish remarks by government officials or in public courtroom proceedings violated the spirit of equal justice for all citizens, these remarks remained a regular feature of Alsatian life into the 1860s. Public denigration of the Jews, however, was not uniform. The central government and its representatives generally treated the Jews fairly, yet local authorities, as well as newspapers, were hostile to Jews. Because the central government, often through the prefect, imposed adherence to the law upon recalcitrant local authorities, Jews in Alsace identified the French state as the guarantor of their rights.

The prefect of the Lower Rhine, for example, in a confidential report of June 18, 1843, to the minister of the interior hailed the impact of emancipation upon the Jews of the department.[43] "[Its] influence has been immense," enthused the prefect. "It has made disappear that measure of contempt that their civil and political incapacity attached [even] to those Israelites who were the most rich and enlightened and has led to a prompt fusion of that class and the part of the Christian population whose social situation was materially analogous. It has created among the Jews a middle class which promptly . . rid itself of the vices with which its coreligionists were rightly reproached . . The existence of this sort of third estate is the most active cause of the improvement evidenced in the private life of the Jews." Although he noted that the situation of the Jews in the countryside was less deserving of favorable comment, the prefect conceded that they, too, "have lifted their heads. . . . They too feel more worthy, shake off a part of their abject status and enter upon the path of progress."[44] This favorable attitude on the part of authorities of the central state was reflected in actions such as the 1843 authorization issued by the minister of public instruction that Jewish schools in Alsace be granted communal status.[45] Similarly, in 1858 the Garde des Sceaux of the Ministry of Justice promised the Central Consistory that the use of abusive anti-Jewish expressions in the nation's courtrooms would be met with "prompt repression." Several months thereafter, Achille Ratisbonne, president of the Strasbourg Consistory, referred to this promise in his complaint to the editor of Le Droit, which regularly identified certain arrested individuals as Jews while, Ratisbonne noted with sarcasm, inadvertently omitting the religious identification of other arrested persons.[46]

Instances of local expression of anti-Jewish hostility abound in historical documents. For example, a legal brief filed in 1832 on behalf of the community of Bergheim (Upper Rhine), which was being sued for not protecting the property of a Jewish resident from a mob, resonated with anti-Semitism. Its author, M. Yves, claimed that the persecution of the Jews was a result of their own cupidity. Moreover, he charged the Jews with cowardice for having fled the mob.[47] Throughout this period court officials and newspaper articles alluded to the religious affiliation of Jewish defendants. As late as 1863 the Archives israélites, one of France's two major Jewish newspapers, complained that a recent Gazette des tribuneaux included repeated references to the defendant in a court case as "that Jew."[48] The following year the Consistory of the Upper Rhine, supported by the Central Consistory, lodged a protest with the minister of justice about the magistrates' habit of identifying Jews in court cases by their religion. The Central Consistory called attention to "the outrageous proceedings to which our coreligionists of Alsace are often exposed in the very sanctuary of justice and on the part of those . . who are called upon to see that the laws are respected and to set an example of tolerance."[49]

Other local government institutions persisted in viewing the Jews in Alsace as second-class citizens. Although the Guizot Law of 1833 mandated financial support for primary schools for citizens of each faith when there were sufficient numbers to warrant such a school, many municipal councils in Alsace were reluctant to vote subsidies for Jewish schools, even when pressured by the state. Another instance of discrimination occurred in 1853 when the Imperial Lycée of Strasbourg refused to announce publicly the names of Jewish students who had won prizes. Instead, their prizes were awarded privately. The Strasbourg Consistory delegated Rabbi Arnaud Aron, the grand rabbi of Strasbourg, to lodge a protest with the rector of the Academy of Strasbourg.[50]

Jewish teachers even encountered discrimination at the highest levels of the school system. In 1849, for example, the communal collège of Haguenau (Lower Rhine) refused to accept a Jewish teacher of mathematics and relented only after political pressure was brought to bear.[51] The following year Jérôme Aron, a professor of history in the Strasbourg lycée with an unblemished record, was dismissed from his position, according to the *Democrate du Rhin* because he was a Jew.[52]

Although anti-Jewish discrimination was most blatant in the courts and schools, it reared its head elsewhere. In 1837 the mayor of Stotzheim denied Jews the use of their new temple on the pretext that they had not previously practiced their cult publicly in the town—a ban that the prefect of the Lower Rhine dismissed with the comment that since Judaism was an officially recognized state religion, its adherents needed no special governmental authorization.[53] In the mid-1850s the president of the Imperial Court of Colmar formally denied a Jewish lawyer's application for the post of magistrate, stating that "the spirit of the populace in Alsace did not permit, for the near future, the admission of a Jewish magistrate, and a wise administration would not offend existing prejudices."[54]

The Alsatian press routinely expressed antipathy to local Jews, who were portrayed as uncultured, isolated, and exploitative of the peasantry. The *Courrier du Haut-Rhin* was particularly vituperative. In 1842 the paper characterized the Jews as the "plague" of Alsace and regularly used the word *Jew* as synonymous with usurer.[55] During a hotly contested consistorial election in 1845 the *Courrier du Haut-Rhin* saw little to recommend in either party. The "candidates of progress," it suggested, were too lenient toward Jewish economic activity: "The Jewish usurers will still be able to sleep in security; their lucrative maneuvers will not be unveiled by the consistory of progress. . . . This proves . . . that the slogan of moral and intellectual reform is only a scarecrow

for the Jews; this proves how much this sect is still perverted and backward."
The "retrograde party," on the other hand, distributed a circular in Hebrew
(probably Yiddish), that the paper characterized as "a work of fanaticism, of
extravagant hatred against the Christians. . . . Usury is their life, their existence. . . . It is well known what the religion of these enriched and ignorant
secondhand dealers is. Deceiving the Christians and earning lots of money, that
is their dogma, that is their God, that is their religion."[56] The *Courrier du Bas-
Rhin,* a moderately liberal paper generally restrained in its treatment of Jews,
was nonetheless unsympathetic to the attempt of a Jewish lawyer and consistorial activist, Michel Hemerdinger, to defend the Jews against the charges
leveled by the *Courrier du Haut-Rhin.* The resentment of the Jewish usurer
found expression in other papers as well. On July 31, 1851, the *Républicain
alsacien* published a diatribe against the Jewish usurer.[57]

Anti-Semitism in Alsace found popular expression primarily in the countryside. Urban elites, as we have seen, looked with scorn upon traditional Jews,
and possibly upon the socially aspiring members of the Jewish bourgeoisie as
well, but their social prejudice had few consequences for most Alsatian Jews.
But the resentment harbored by Alsatian peasants toward Jews, upon whom
they depended for loans, easily erupted into violence in periods of political
tension or economic deprivation. This resentment was more than the debtor's
hostility toward his creditor. The church's teaching of contempt for Jews persisted throughout the nineteenth century, reinforced by sermons and church
domination of primary education. Religious teaching alone, though, cannot
explain the patterns of popular anti-Semitism in Alsace. The anti-Judaism of the
church was a constant, and popular demonstrations of anti-Semitism, which
indulged in primarily nonreligious rhetoric, were sporadic. Christian doctrine
prepared the ground for viewing Jews—the Other—as the nefarious agents of
social change, but the socioeconomic tensions of nineteenth-century Alsace
were the immediate cause.

Peasants who feared the changes brought by capitalism were easily roused to
anger against the Jewish commercial agent, cattle dealer, and moneylender. In
periods of economic distress, which were frequent in the late 1810s, 1830s,
and 1840s, the burden of debts owed to Jews were a great hardship. Further,
the political turmoil of revolutionary days was often channeled against the
Jews, who were seen as allies of the central authorities. Jews were also the
peasants' contact with the market, so mysterious in its workings and so capable
of bringing impoverishment. Jews thus symbolized a new political and economic order of dubious merit from the peasants' point of view.

This vision of the Jew as capitalist representative and bearer of dangerous new ways emerges clearly in the 1861 novel *Maître Daniel Rock,* written by Erckmann and Chatrian. They portrayed the rural Jewish commercial broker, Elias Bloum, and the suspicion—well founded as it happens—he aroused in the simple blacksmith Daniel Rock· "The exorbitant sum which Elias had just offered him for the ruins and the uncultivated land beside them inspired the grimmest apprehensions in Master Daniel. He had no doubt that the Jew planned to establish in the very midst of the mountainside factories, mills, quarries, and other such enterprises, which would soon bring about the loss of the old customs, the abandonment of cultivation, scorn for the most respectable ways."[58]

These factors—the legacy of Christian anti-Judaism, the economic role of the Jews in Alsace, and peasant resentment of capitalist inroads in agriculture—form the backdrop to periodic violent anti-Semitic incidents. The politically turbulent years of 1819 and into the 1820s, of the early 1830s, and of 1848 provided opportunities for local resentment of the Jews to erupt into violence, although the representatives of the central government in Paris and local authorities strove to protect the Jews and maintain order. In 1819 attacks on Jews in the regions around Mulhouse and Ribeauvillé mimicked the far more widespread anti-Jewish "Hep-Hep riots" that occurred in several German states that year Durmenach (Upper Rhine) and Ingwiller and Marmoutier (both Lower Rhine) were sites of anti-Jewish violence in 1823 and 1824. During the Revolution of 1830 popular violence flared against the Jews in Wintzenheim.[59] The severe food crisis of 1832 provoked attacks on Jews in Bergheim and Ribeauvillé (both Upper Rhine). Realizing that a disturbance of public order could ultimately undermine the government, the prefects were vigilant in tracking down rumors of planned anti-Jewish attacks In 1832 the extensive correspondence of the subprefect of the arrondissement of Sélestat and the prefect of the Lower Rhine discussed precautions to take should the anti-Jewish violence that had occurred in nearby villages of the Upper Rhine spread to Sélestat. An anonymous letter warned that Jewish houses would be burned and demanded that the subprefect treat the inhabitants of the village "as a father" and return their old rights as a free city (which presumably would enable its residents to ban the entry of Jews).[60] In response to the violence in the Upper Rhine the prefect ordered that troops in the area be reinforced, for the National Guard, composed of locals, could not be counted on to protect the Jews.[61] Now, he requested the archbishop of Strasbourg to refrain in his sermons "not only from any offensive word against the Jews but even from any insinuation against them."[62]

The letters of the subprefect and the detailed police reports sent by the prefect to the Ministry of the Interior are confidential official assessments of the situation of the Jews in Alsace. The subprefect attributed the responsiveness of "the people" to anti-Jewish agitation to the "high cost of living."[63] In his evaluation the prefect cited the profound hatred of the Jews prevalent among Christians. He found the source of this was Jewish usury, through which the Jews had become the real owners of much of the land in Alsace, as well as the Jews' ubiquitous role as commercial middlemen in the countryside.[64] A fifteen-page report of July 31 cited the "bad faith which [the Jews] have always shown in their relations with Christians" and noted that "usury was, among them, an endemic vice; it is second nature for them." Although the Constituent Assembly, in conferring emancipation on the Jews, had anticipated that the Jews would abandon their old habits, "experience has proved too well how that Assembly was mistaken. . . . The moral and social state of the Jews has not changed at all through their emancipation." The prefect added that Christians, too, were to blame for their prejudice against the Jews, their exclusion of the Jews from positions of public service, their jealousy of the wealth some Jews had accumulated through hard work and industry, and the lack of local support for Jewish schools. "Reciprocal hatred," stirred up by priests, pastors, and rabbis alike, characterized the relations of Jews and Gentiles in Alsace, according to this "evenhanded" report.[65]

This hatred burst forth during the Revolution of 1848. Beginning in the last week of February and continuing sporadically through the elections of April, incidents occurred in no fewer than nineteen towns and villages in the Upper Rhine and, with less severity, in twenty-five communes in the Lower Rhine, or in more than 20 percent of the Jewish communities in the two departments.[66] In Saverne (Lower Rhine) the rabbi reported that "a band of more than 150 persons, most of them youths, at the head of which were two young men of fine family, dressed in red, ran through the town singing anti-Jewish slogans at the top of their lungs." By the following evening the crowd had swelled to four hundred, and the chanting gave way to the breaking of shutters and windows in Jewish houses. The pillaging of Jewish homes by bands of peasant youths forced some Jews to flee across the Swiss border from several Upper Rhine communities. In Altkirch peasants sacked the synagogue and looted stores owned by Jews.[67]

The violence was particularly severe in the Upper Rhine village of Dur-menach, which had both a Jewish majority and a Jewish mayor. On February 28, after the mayor had fled the town, rioters destroyed more than seventy-five Jewish homes. A *mohel* (ritual circumciser) named Raphael Brunschwig noted in his newly purchased instruction book that he "had lost all my utensils and accessories in the pillage of February 28–29 and March 1, 1848."[68] Although some have claimed that the violence was directed only against well-to-do Jews, the court case brought by 111 Jews suing the town for damages included a cross section of Durmenach Jewry. 35 property owners, 10 merchants and 3 horse dealers, 19 cattle dealers, 9 peddlers, 8 day laborers, 8 widows with no property, 4 artisans, 4 servant girls, 2 teachers, and the local *ministre-officiant*.[69]

Even in communes where no violence occurred, the events of 1848 inspired fear. Alarmed by the incidents that had occurred in several villages and antic-ipating violence in his own town, the rabbi of Mutzig (Lower Rhine) sent a pastoral letter to all Jewish communities in his jurisdiction calling for the public recitation of psalms. In Rosheim (Lower Rhine) the Jews did so for a week. On Friday, April 7, the rabbi sent a letter to the Jewish community of Rosheim to excuse his absence on that Sabbath when he was scheduled to preach in their synagogue. In the letter he predicted a massacre in Mutzig that night and informed the community that he had fasted that Friday and had ordained the recitation of penitential prayers, as on Yom Kippur, for the following Monday. According to a local Jew who recorded the events on the inside cover of his Passover Haggadah in a combination of German and Yiddish, on that Monday morning all the Jews "as one came to the synagogue and prayed for three hours. . . . [A]t three o'clock Rabbi Jehudah [of Mutzig] arrived and preached for two hours so that all wept, . . . fasted, and gave charity. . . . [A]fter all nothing happened. . . . We could, thanks to God, celebrate Passover in 'complete peace.'"[70]

Although troops were called out to restore order in several communes and bourgeois citizens in Altkirch took up arms against the marauding peasants, the Jews had few supporters among the local population. Republican papers in the cities generally condemned the anti-Jewish violence, but because of popular sentiment most of the peasants arrested in the rioting were acquitted in jury trials. At least six towns and villages were compelled to pay damages to Jewish victims of the disorders [71]

The reestablishment of order did not end anti-Jewish antipathy at the local level. Throughout the 1850s the regional authorities continued to report that Jewish usury was a prime cause of the anti-Semitic unrest that erupted in several isolated instances. In the years immediately following the Revolution of 1848, the anti-usury campaign became a rallying cry of socialist activists Indeed, the fears of the authorities were confirmed when a local socialist leader proclaimed, shortly before the coup d'état of December 2, 1851, "Now . . . it will soon burst forth. . . . We'll give it to the factory owners and the Jews."[72] The traditional anti-Semitic conception of Jews and their role in the countryside is expressed most dramatically in the reports of the procuror general of the court of Colmar in those years: "The greatest part of the Jews of Alsace seem to form a people apart in the midst of our populations. Retaining the cachet of their origin, without roots in our territory to which they refuse to become attached through . . . agriculture, they exploit the poor inhabitants of our countryside through the most hostile trafficking."[73]

In spite of the persistence of public demonstrations of anti-Jewish feeling, during the Second Republic and especially during the Second Empire the social environment became more favorable for Jews. It was a period of commercial and industrial expansion, and the role of the Jew as capitalist middleman was no longer reprehensible. In addition some Jews were prospering in the middle and higher ranks of commerce and displaying bourgeois attributes. Signs of integration of the Jewish bourgeoisie appeared in both towns and cities. Even during the Revolution of 1848 Grand Rabbi Aron joined the bishop of Strasbourg and Protestant clergy to bless liberty trees and praise the Republic In 1849 Jonas Ennery, the director of the Jewish school in Strasbourg, was elected to the National Assembly, and Jews served in the National Guard. In the 1850s and 1860s Jews in public posts were no longer rare. In Strasbourg, Bischwiller, Haguenau, and Quatzenheim (all in Lower Rhine), and Ribeauvillé and Thann (both in Upper Rhine) Jews served on the municipal council [74] In 1864 a Jew was elected mayor of the Lower Rhine village of Schirhoffen, which had a Jewish majority.[75]

During this period talented Jewish professionals began to receive the accolades appropriate to their status. In 1860 a Jewish lawyer was appointed as a judge on the tribunal of first instance in Strasbourg, and at the end of the decade another Jew was reelected as a judge in the civil tribunal of Colmar. A prominent Jewish doctor active in consistorial circles, Mathieu Hirtz, was nominated professor of pathology at the Faculty of Medicine of Strasbourg, the highest academic position occupied by a Jewish doctor. In 1864 the conference of lawyers at the Imperial Court of Paris chose a young Jewish lawyer, Alphonse Bloch of Soultz (Upper Rhine), to share the Prix Paillet Jewish teachers in Alsace garnered their share of government awards. A speaker at the Prize

Assembly of the Jewish Ecole des Arts et Métiers in Strasbourg in 1864 boasted of yet another mark of social integration—"the presence of Christian students on the benches of a Jewish school."[76] Even the municipal councils, which had been reluctant to provide financial support for Jewish religious and educational institutions proportional to that offered Christian churches and schools, now opened their purses more generously.[77] Finally, in a display of understanding for the needs of its Jewish citizens, in 1866 the city of Strasbourg suspended the blue laws and permitted the fish market to open for two hours on the three Sundays preceding the Jewish fall festivals so that Jews could purchase fish for their holiday meals.[78]

In government circles concern with Jewish usury seems to have declined in the 1860s. When a government investigation of agriculture was conducted in Alsace in 1866, its depositions included not only the standard complaints about Jewish exploitation of the simple Alsatian peasant but also some understanding of the historical factors involved in the Jew's role as intermediary in the countryside. The commission noted the particular qualities that made the Jewish broker so valuable. The commission reported:

> One cannot fail to recognize the important role which the Jew has played in the upward mobility displayed among day laborers and rural workers .. It is his intervention, without doubt, which has facilitated for many of them the access to property .. It is thanks to these brokers that cultivators large and small can make their purchases and sales at home, dispense with running to fairs and markets while losing much time and much money, and devote all their time and care to their cultivation. It is difficult to admit that such a spirit of business, if it has had unfortunate consequences, has also brought advantages and has rendered real services to the country [79]

Where once Jewish brokerage and moneylending had been deprecated as unproductive and exploitative, it was now accepted as a positive factor in economic growth. Where once the Jews were chastised for having disappointed the hopes of their emancipators, by 1866 Xavier Mossmann, the Gentile archivist of the city of Mulhouse, could write in his *Etude sur l'histoire des juifs à Colmar*, "The most sullen spirits must recognize today that the Revolution was not mistaken. In spite of the shadow of the past which for ten years, from 1808 to 1818, was projected upon them, the Jews of Alsace have made . . . surprising progress. The elite has marched at the head. You can recognize them everywhere, these men ahead of their time and who precede their coreligionists, in letters, in the arts, in education, in the sciences, in industry, in finance, in the magistracy, in the army, at the bar."[80]

In the 1850s and 1860s these signs of acceptance coexisted with lingering expressions of prejudice and, in some cases, the exclusion of Jews in bourgeois circles, which had not previously had to contend with Jews seeking admission as social equals. A prosperous Jew in Mulhouse was barred, because of his origins, from the Casino de la Bourse in 1861. In the same year, a popular almanac, written in the Alsatian dialect, carried a story about a dishonest Jew who enriched himself through deceit and usury.[81]

The social, economic, and religio-cultural transformation of the traditional Jews of Alsace occurred in a complex environment. The negative image of the Jew, long conditioned by religious and economic factors, continued to affect Jewish prospects for integration for many years. The anti-Jewish stereotype was sustained in the nineteenth century by the continuity of Alsatian Jews' economic activity and occupational distribution.

The distinctive role that the Jews of Alsace played in the regional economy in the ancien régime persisted, particularly in the countryside, until the last third of the nineteenth century, when the development of railroad lines, better roads, and credit facilities began to undermine the Jews' role as commercial and financial middlemen. Even then, however, the Jewish economic structure in the countryside remained remarkably similar to the pattern that had existed during the ancien régime, though the numbers of Jews able to support themselves in traditional village occupations dwindled markedly. This economic stasis in the villages, more than any other factor, provided the material and social context for Jewish cultural and religious developments in Alsace in the nineteenth century and largely accounted for the criticism of Alsatian Jews as backward and exploitative.

THREE

The Economic Matrix

The economic activity of Jews in Alsace was rooted in their demographic dispersion in the province—a dispersion that derived from patterns of settlement laid down in the ancien régime. On the eve of the Revolution the Alsatian population was distributed throughout the countryside, in 1,150 communes, most of them villages and small market towns. Some nestled in the foothills of the Vosges Mountains, Alsace's natural border to the west. Others were scattered on the plains, where, in the words of one geographer, "picturesque villages glittered among the orchards."[1] Alsatian villages supported themselves through farming, cultivating grapes, and using the products of the forest. With their agricultural land distributed in small parcels in the open field system, the communes gathered their half-timbered houses together in clusters or rows around the church.[2]

Jews lived in about 16 percent of the communes in Alsace. All the cities and many of the bourgs, particularly in Upper Alsace, exercised the right of not admitting Jews. The Jewish communities were relatively small; Bischheim in the Lower Rhine, the largest, had 473 Jewish residents in the census of 1784. In Upper Alsace the Jews formed mid-size communities of 100 to 400 individuals, most located in a crescent south of Colmar or on the Swiss border. Six Jewish settlements had a population greater than 200. In Lower Alsace, by contrast, where three-quarters of Alsatian Jews lived in 1784, the Jews were scattered throughout the province in 129 communities, 87 of which had fewer than 100 Jewish residents. Only Bischheim, on the outskirts of Strasbourg, Haguenau, and Mutzig had Jewish populations larger than 300.[3] Although Jewish communities were small in size, Jews constituted a sizable minority in the villages where they lived.

TABLE 3 1

Date Jewish Communities in Lower Rhine Reached Largest Size (in percentages)

	1808	1833	1840	1854	1863	N
Communes under 2,000	9 8	9.8	7.2	55.1	16 3	98
Communes over 2,000	—	6.5	16 1	51 6	25.8	31

After their emancipation in 1791 when they were granted the right to settle wherever they chose, Jews began moving to the cities. By 1808 small new communities had emerged in Colmar and Mulhouse (188 and 163 Jews, respectively); Strasbourg was the undisputed urban focus of Alsatian Jewry with 1,476 Jewish residents.[4] There was a great deal of regional migration; marriage records from 1820 to 1862 reveal that about 20 percent of Jews migrated within the province. Except for those who developed the new urban communities, most moved to communes that had traditionally hosted a Jewish population. Only eleven tiny new Jewish settlements were established in the Department of the Upper Rhine between 1808 and 1851 and only twelve in the Lower Rhine between 1808 and 1854.[5]

In spite of the regular agricultural crises in Alsace in the first half of the century and the cries of rural overpopulation, the Jewish population in the countryside, like the general population, grew until the mid-1850s, even though there was considerable migration of Alsatians of all religious backgrounds to local cities, Paris, provincial cities, and abroad. (See table 3.1.)

The population growth continued through the 1860s in the urban centers of Strasbourg, Mulhouse, and Colmar, but the communes in the countryside did not follow this pattern.[6] In the Lower Rhine 102 of 129 Jewish communities decreased in size—by an average of 16 percent—between 1854 and 1863, losing 2,810 residents. The 27 that grew increased by only 865 persons, with Strasbourg accounting for half the increase. This decline in population was linked to the pauperization of Jewish communities in the countryside, a situation that led the Strasbourg Consistory in 1853 to form the Committee for the Amelioration of the Jews and to send a memo for assistance to the Central Consistory.[7]

Alsatian Jews were by and large village dwellers. In the Lower Rhine at mid-century 98 of 129 Jewish communities were located in villages with a population of less than 2,000, as were 38 of 61 communities in the Upper Rhine. According to the conventions of the French census, these Jews were rural

TABLE 3 2
Population of Jewish Communities as Percentage of Communes, 1850s

	<10%	10–25%	>25%	N
Upper Rhine	46	34	20	61
Lower Rhine	50	44	6	129

residents. Another 24 Jewish communities in the Lower Rhine and 17 in the Upper Rhine were in bourgs with populations of 2,000 to 5,000 persons, most in the 2,000 to 3,500 range [8] Although Jews constituted only about 3 percent of the total Alsatian population, in both departments more than half the Jewish communities composed between 10 percent and 66 percent of their communes, with Durmenach and Schirhoffen each having a majority of Jews. (See table 3.2.)

If communities of fewer than fifty persons are excluded, the concentration of Jews in villages and bourgs where they were a notable communal presence is even more marked. In approximately 60 percent of the communes with Jewish inhabitants, at least 10 percent of the population was Jewish.[9] This population pattern resembled that of the shtetl Jews of Poland and Russia. Like those Jews, Alsatian Jews experienced the powerful bonds of communal solidarity and constraint that are linked to this settlement pattern.

Throughout the century Jewish communities in Alsace remained small in absolute size, with the distinction between the Upper Rhine and the Lower Rhine persisting. Fully 70 percent of Jewish communities in the Lower Rhine and 44 percent in the Upper Rhine numbered fewer than 200 Jews at mid-century. (See table 3.3.) The four largest Jewish communities (>500 Jews) in the Lower Rhine, however, accounted for 19 percent of the department's Jewish population, and the seven largest communities in the Upper Rhine constituted 37 percent of the total.

The distribution of Alsatian Jews in the countryside enabled them to pursue the traditional role of commercial middlemen long after emancipation. Gentile observers were disappointed that the Jewish merchant, peddler, and money-lender did not disappear in the wake of the granting of civic equality. As Théophile Hallez wrote bitterly in a volume about the need for the government to mandate the occupational and social improvement of the Jews of France, "The Jews are in 1845 what they were in 1789."[10] In spite of Gentile hopes, Jews did not come to resemble the larger population in occupational profile. As

TABLE 3 3
Size of Alsatian Jewish Communities, 1850s

Percent communities with	<200 Jews	200–500 Jews	>500 Jews
Upper Rhine	44	44	12
Lower Rhine	70	27	3

the French historian Roland Marx has pointed out, only an economic incentive would persuade the Jews to abandon their traditional pursuits in favor of the "productive trades" of artisanry and agriculture. For most Jews, there was no such incentive; commerce offered them greater opportunities for social mobility and profit than either crafts or farming. In the economic sphere, emancipation was followed by continuity rather than change.[11]

From the Restoration on the general economic trend in Alsace was one of expansion. Agriculture, however, was unstable, and food shortages occurred in every decade from the 1810s through the 1850s. Although the *Enquête agricole* of 1866 described Alsace as among "the richest and most populous departments," in many years the yield of wheat, rye, and potatoes, the main Alsatian crops, was sufficient to sustain the dense rural population at only a subsistence level.[12] Commerce and industry fared better The development of canal transportation and later rail links with the interior of France as well as with Switzerland revived Strasbourg's importance as a commercial center.[13] Alsace also experienced considerable industrialization, particularly in the Upper Rhine. Mulhouse, with its cadre of Protestant entrepreneurs, became a center of machine production, chemical engineering, and, especially, textile manufacturing. By 1866, 47 percent of the working population of the Lower Rhine was employed in industry; the nationwide figure was 28.8 percent.[14]

Because of their pre-emancipation role in the region's economy, the Jews of Alsace retained a distinctive profile in the nineteenth century. Although industry recruited increasing numbers of Alsatians, more than half of all Alsatians were employed in agriculture until the second half of the century.[15] Jews, however, chose a different path. Their commercial experience equipped them for survival, and increasing prosperity, in the expanding commercial sector. To be sure, a small number of Alsatian Jews—including Alfred Dreyfus's father and grandfather—became entrepreneurs in the thriving textile industry of the Upper Rhine, but most Jews remained outside the factories.[16]

The occupational distribution of Alsatian Jewry reflected its history as a

TABLE 3 4
Horizontal Occupational Distribution of Jewish Grooms, 1820–1830
(in percentages)

Property	1 5	
Manufacture, artisanry	5 2	
Commerce		
Agricultural produce	19 6	
Metal	0 7	
Money	7 4	
Textiles, clothing	4 4	82.4
Leather goods	1.3	
Food	0 7	
Not specified	48 3	
Nonprofessional services	0 7	
Professions (including schoolteachers)	6.5	
Unskilled labor	1 5	
Public service	0 7	
Other	1.5	
	N = 153	

population long limited to commerce. During the Restoration 82 percent of the Jewish men marrying in Niederroedern, Bischheim, Itterswiller, Colmar, and Strasbourg followed commercial pursuits.[17] (See table 3.4.) Moreover, the smaller the community, the more likely its Jewish residents would be engaged in commerce. (See table 3.5.)

In the villages a considerable number of Jews served as middlemen in marketing agricultural products and especially in selling cattle and horses. For a commission Jews brought together buyer and seller or bought livestock from peasants and sold it elsewhere. Well acquainted with his region, the cattle dealer often dabbled in real estate as well. In 1816 more than 54 percent of the 230 taxpayers in a sample of fifteen villages and towns of the Lower Rhine were cattle and horse dealers, butchers, and hide merchants. In 1826 57 percent of the 306 taxpayers were so employed.[18] Even at mid-century 24 percent of the Jews living in the three Lower Rhine towns I studied intensively—Bischheim, Niederroedern, and Itterswiller—earned their living as traders of agricultural products. "Jews in the countryside," the prefect of the Lower Rhine noted in his 1843 report, "always devote themselves to the commerce of meat marketing, in which they have virtually a monopoly, just as the cattle trade is exclusively in their hands. In Strasbourg, when the weekly market falls on a Jewish holiday, it

TABLE 3 5
Jewish Grooms' Occupations by Size of Domicile, 1820–1862

No. of Inhabitants	Commerce (%)	Industry (%)
<2,000	85	5
2,000–5,000	85	5
5,000–50,000	71	19
>50,000	61	15
	N = 544	

is necessary to change it or see the city deprived of meat for a week."[19] In Strasbourg 9 percent of 118 Jewish taxpayers marketed agricultural products in 1816, and 5 percent did so in 1826. By mid-century this had declined further to 4.2 percent, but even this figure is striking in an urban setting.[20] One historical geographer claimed that rural Jews held Alsatian peasants

> literally in their hands. . . Cattle dealers, usurers, merchants of all sorts, they . . . resided in the bourgs and certain villages   but were strictly excluded from the peasant community . . Their presence exempted the villagers from almost all contact with the outside world They were the almost obligatory intermediaries for the sale of cattle, of grain, of land, for the purchase of fabric, of various utensils, even for the contracting of marriages among the rich.[21]

The life of a rural Jewish trader was not an easy one. In his memoirs Edmond Uhry, born in the town of Ingwiller in 1874, described his grandfather's and father's cattle and real estate trade in the 1850s and 1860s. Basing themselves about twenty-five miles from Ingwiller, they were away from home from Sunday through Thursday and kept a residence, stable, and barns in their trading territory.[22] It was possible to amass sizable wealth as a dealer in cattle and, especially, in horses. Some cattle merchants in the countryside could afford Jewish communal taxes of 140 francs, a considerable sum in 1816. Far more, however, paid only 2 or 3 francs. In 1816 the median tax assessment of traders in agricultural products was just 5.5 francs, below the median of 7 francs for the category of merchants. In 1826 their median tax of 6 francs still did not match the median rate of 7 francs assessed upon merchants.[23]

The Jews' economic profile is distinctive, especially when compared with the occupational distribution of the general Alsatian population. Based upon Emmanuel LeRoy Ladurie's classification system and his findings from his pioneering study of army records from the Restoration, the comparison is striking.[24]

TABLE 3 6
Occupational Distribution of Jewish Men and Male Conscripts in Alsace

	Jewish grooms, 1820–1830	Total army contingent, 1819–1826
Proprietors and rentiers	1	0
Liberal and superior professions	2	0
Commerce	70	20 8*
Employees	11	6 2
Artisans	6	21 4
Unskilled workers	10	47 2
Without profession	0	4.4
	N = 153	N = 6,165

*Liberal and superior professions and commerce were not differentiated by LeRoy Ladurie but were subsumed under "other professions." It is likely that the majority of this figure were in commerce rather than the liberal professions

Source for total army contingent Jean-Paul Aron, Paul Dumont, and Emmanuel Le Roy Ladurie, *Anthropologie du conscrit français* (Paris and The Hague, 1972), pp 94–137

Close to half the Alsatian male population were unskilled agricultural and industrial laborers, but the unskilled workers in the Jewish community—most of them peddlers and hawkers—represented only 10 percent of the sample. (See table 3.6.)

Only in the urban environment of Strasbourg did this economic distribution become somewhat less skewed in the course of the century, although the proportion in commerce remained similar. As the prefect of the Lower Rhine commented in his 1843 report, the different opportunities offered by rural commune and bustling city were crucial in the economic choices of Alsatian Jews.[25] (See table 3.7.)

The wealthiest Jews, living off their investments and property, increasingly concentrated in the city rather than the countryside. The city economy also attracted Jews with the expanded possibilities of artisanry in an urban market compared to the traditional, and marginal, Jewish street trades of peddling and dealing in secondhand goods. More than three times as many heads of household in the city were artisans than in the countryside, and less than half as many were peddlers or hawkers of old clothes. In the city Jews, by mid-century, began to modernize their economic structure in another way—by moving into commercial employment rather than relying on their entrepreneurial skills in mar-

TABLE 3 7
Occupational Distribution—Strasbourg and Rural Communes, 1846 (in percentages)

	Strasbourg	Bischheim, Niederroedern, Itterswiller
Professionals, property owners, rentiers	7	1
Commerce (excluding peddling)	52	49
Commercial employees	7	1
Artisans	16	5
Peddlers, secondhand dealers	11	28
Unskilled workers	4	3
Other	3	13
	N = 424	N = 230

ginal independent commercial enterprises. Commercial employment tapped the skills of a literate population without requiring large amounts of capital. It also offered stability and a sufficient income, two incentives that were often absent in peddling, brokering, and small-scale shopkeeping. Urbanization thus reduced the castelike quality of Jewish economic life, though it did not eliminate it.

The role of Jews in the Alsatian economy emerges most clearly from an analysis of the commercial court records of Strasbourg Jews occupy a prominent place in those records, figuring in approximately one-quarter of the cases between 1826 and 1866.[26] Between 41 percent (in 1826) and 32 percent (in 1866) of the cases involving a Jew record business transactions between Jews alone. For example, a Jewish wholesaler, often in Strasbourg, sued a Jewish shopkeeper or peddler in a village or small town for nonpayment for a shipment of goods or two Jewish dealers disputed the sale of livestock or the commission on a transaction, including military replacement, in which Jewish agents conducted a lively business Most court cases, however, involved at least one non-Jew, as customer or supplier of the Jewish wholesaler, merchant, cattle or horse dealer. Since most of the cases, whether between Jew and Jew or Jew and Gentile, were defaults on letters of exchange or promissory notes, which were passed from hand to hand and were payable only on a specific date in the future, it is likely that a credit component accompanied these transactions. The cases record only the face value of the commercial paper, and so do not permit an analysis of the terms of credit extended.

Because the majority of Jews listed their professions as either *négociant*

TABLE 3 8

Agricultural Commerce as Percentage of Jewish Commercial
Occupations in Court Records

	1826	1836	1846	1856	1866
Horse and cattle dealers	18	5	8	5	18
Marketers of agricultural products	—	5	18	14	12

(businessman) or *commerçant*, it is difficult to assess with any precision the range of commercial pursuits followed by Alsatian Jews. Certain statistics, however, are suggestive Only four Jewish artisans—a shoemaker and three bakers—appear in these records, but Jewish merchants, wholesalers, commercial agents, horse dealers, cattle merchants, butchers, money changers, bankers, cloth dealers, mercers, furniture dealers, grain merchants, wine merchants, dealers in metal and wood, soap manufacturers, agents of military replacement, a soldier, and a rabbi all have their day in court. A significant number of the Jewish litigants were horse and cattle dealers and marketers of agricultural products (grain, wine, hops, animal hides) It is likely that some of the négociants and commerçants also dealt in agricultural goods This sector remained a primary one for Alsatian Jewish businessmen, followed by the supply of cloth, utensils, and clothing to the countryside. (See table 3.8.)

The regional focus of Jewish commerce supports this hypothesis. Transactions limited to Strasbourg accounted for less than one-quarter of the commercial cases involving Jews. Transactions between Strasbourg and the countryside or between two rural villages or towns figured in one-half to two-thirds of the cases. Commercial contacts outside the region, either with the rest of France or with Switzerland or Germany, grew in importance only in the 1850s and 1860s. (See table 3.9.)

The sums disputed in the court cases—averaging 500 to 750 francs— suggest that most commercial and credit transactions were in the middle range of business deals. Only 5 of 248 cases sampled involved sums of 5,000 francs or more, and these 5 exceptionally large cases were excluded from the average. The sums involved and the types of suits remained constant over forty years, reinforcing the picture of economic continuity that emerges from other sources.

Although the Jewish population in the countryside declined after the mid-nineteenth century, it did not develop alternative means of economic support. Petty commerce and marketing agricultural products and animals remained the

TABLE 3 9

Places of Commercial Transactions Involving Alsatian Jews,
1826–1866 (in percentages)

	1826	1836	1846	1856	1866
All in Strasbourg	22	24	23	19	17
Same town or village	2	3	4	—	5
Strasbourg-countryside	37	42	25	26	30
Two or more villages or towns	29	13	39	28	27
Alsace-rest of France	10	18	4	26	12
Alsace-foreign country	—	—	4	2	9

staple of the Jewish economy at least until the 1880s The statistics for the
communities of Bischheim, Itterswiller, and Niederroedern from the patent lists
and name change lists of 1809–13, the censuses of 1846 and 1866, and the
special census of Alsatian Jews taken in 1880 for the purpose of liquidating
communal debts from the ancien régime reflect this continuity.[27] (See table
3.10.) Although the traditional Jewish trades of peddling, brokerage, and old-
clothes dealing declined in the course of the century, they were replaced largely

TABLE 3 10

Occupational Profile of Male Jewish Household Heads in Bischheim,
Niederroedern, and Itterswiller (in percentages)

	1809–1813	1846	1866	1880
Peddling, secondhand dealing	40	44	36	26
Cattle, horse, and grain	28	18	20	19
Leather and textiles	9	5	4	—
Metal dealers	9	1	<1	—
Commerce—unspecified	—	12	22	28
Butchers	9	7	7	8
Innkeepers	2	1	<1	—
Artisans	2	5	6	6
Religious professionals	1	3	<1	6
Money changers	—	1	<1	—
Unskilled day labor	—	3	3	1
Other	—	—	1	6
	N = 141	N = 235	N = 169	N = 99

by shopkeeping. Artisanry never attracted more than 6 percent of the Jewish population in these communities

Occupational classification cannot provide a complete picture of the lifestyle or resources of individuals.[28] Unfortunately, information on the wealth and poverty of Alsatian Jews is fragmentary and only occasionally correlated with occupation It is likely that most Alsatian Jews in the countryside lived at a subsistence level throughout this period. For example, an 1808 census of the Upper Rhine Jewish community of Bergheim, which lists household heads and their financial resources, describes 62 percent of the eighty-four Jewish households of the commune as indigent; 18 percent had resources of 1,000 livres or less; 7 percent were worth up to 5,000 livres; and 13 percent had 10,000 or more livres at their disposal. The six wealthiest Jews, with fortunes of 20,000 (two), 25,000 (two), 35,000, and 60,000 livres respectively, were all members of the Sée family In Horbourg, also in the Upper Rhine, where thirty Jewish families lived in 1808, 80 percent of the Jewish population was described as indigent.[29]

Jewish communal tax records, which were maintained only until 1831 when the state assumed responsibility for paying the salaries of Jewish religious functionaries, provide information only on Jews with taxable resources. A prefect's report of 1828 mentioned that only 865 (25 percent) of 3,500 Jewish household heads in the Upper Rhine had sufficient wealth (a minimum of 1,000 francs) to contribute to the support of religious institutions.[30]

Although there were substantial differences in tax assessments between individuals in the same occupations, it is worthwhile to look at average taxes paid by different occupational categories (See table 3 11.)[31] This evaluation reveals a correlation between occupational categories and wealth. Only in the third category in the villages does the occupational ranking deviate from the ranking by wealth. In the countryside there were few employees and manufacturers, and this group comprised mainly commercial brokers whose only resource was their skill at hustling. It is noteworthy, too, that the traditional Jewish street trades of peddling and dealing in secondhand goods could yield as much income as skilled artisanry (without the investment of time and money in an apprenticeship).

For the 1840s other data—the employment of servants, the selection as a notable (that is, inclusion on a restricted electoral list) and, on the other end of the economic spectrum, receipt of charity—indicate wealth or its absence. The employment of servants declined with each level of the occupational scale. Among merchants and lower professionals in Strasbourg, where almost half of

TABLE 3 11
Mean Taxes by Occupation, 1816–1826 (in francs)

	I	II	III	IV	V	VI
Strasbourg						
1816	35	23	13	7	8	18
1826	26	11	9	5	6	—
Villages						
1816	34	15	4	7	6	—
1826	23	10	6	6	5	—

Note· I = Proprietors, professionals, bankers, and wholesale merchants
II = Merchants and lower professionals
III = Employees, commercial agents, and small manufacturers
IV = Skilled artisans
V = Peddlers and secondhand dealers
VI = Rentiers and without profession

all households employed servants in 1846, merchants were most likely to have servants. Two distinct groups within the third category hired domestic help: commercial and governmental employees, who can be counted among the petite bourgeoisie, and butchers and restaurateurs, whose servants were primarily business employees. Less than 10 percent of peddlers and artisans could afford to keep servants. Members of the lowest socioeconomic groups—artisans, peddlers, and those without profession—also formed the bulk of the relief list of 1856.

In Alsace the notables were chosen from the upper ranks of society From the establishment of the consistorial system in 1808 until the expansion of the suffrage in the mid-1840s membership in the college of notables, which elected members of the consistory, was limited to twenty-five men. The wealthiest male Jews of each consistorial district were eligible for membership if they were at least thirty years old, were not usurers, and had never pleaded bankruptcy. The official correspondence surrounding nominations to this restricted body provides information on the economic elite of the Jewish community.

Until the partial democratization of the college of notables, almost all the notables in both Alsatian departments were listed as property owners and wholesalers (négociants or *marchands en gros*). In 1809, 68 percent of the notables of both the Lower and the Upper Rhine fell into those categories. Merchants, bankers, an innkeeper, and a member of the General Council of

Saverne completed the membership of the college of the Lower Rhine; in the Upper Rhine the college included a money changer, a tanner, merchants, a cloth manufacturer, and a dyer.[32]

In the 1820s and 1830s a similar pattern prevailed. In the Lower Rhine in 1823 two bankers (from the Ratisbonne family), a former captain of the dragoons, a leather manufacturer, and a military guardsman joined the numerous négociants in the college of notables. The prefect suspected that two of the notables were usurers, and a third was denounced as a usurer to the mayor of Strasbourg by one of the city's police commissioners, admittedly without any hard evidence. The fifty wealthiest Jews of the district were recorded for possible inclusion in the college of notables in 1829 The occupations of twenty-nine of these, from that year's tax lists, included nine négociants, four cloth merchants and cattle dealers, two bankers (the Ratisbonnes again), rentiers, merchants, and dealers in metal, as well as a commercial broker, a leather manufacturer, a jeweler, and a grocer. Their direct taxes ranged from an average 103 francs for the merchants to an average of 673 francs for the bankers The négociants paid an average of 318 francs apiece.[33]

Most of the notables in the Upper Rhine at this time were described as property owners, thereby effectively masking the source of their wealth. Those who listed an active profession included four cloth merchants, a hide merchant, a grocer, and a merchant. Unlike the Lower Rhine, where almost half of the notables lived in Strasbourg, only one notable in the Upper Rhine lived in Colmar and two resided in Mulhouse; the others were from a dozen towns in the department. In 1830 the notables in the Upper Rhine paid direct taxes ranging from an average of 35 francs for cloth merchants to an average of 496 francs for property owners. Two of the property owners paid higher taxes (1,301 and 1,429 francs, respectively) than any of the notables in the Lower Rhine. Although the law stipulated that close relatives not serve together in the college of notables, in the Upper Rhine the Jewish oligarchy was linked by ties of marriage. In 1828, for example, eight of the twenty-five notables were related by blood or marriage, as were fifteen of the fifty wealthiest Jews in the department.[34]

The Ordinance of 1844 expanded the college of notables, gave laymen a greater role in the consistories, and strengthened the authority of the Central Consistory. After its passage the range of occupations represented in the college of notables was far wider. In 1845 in the Lower Rhine, for example, eleven officers on active duty, seventeen rabbis, eighteen members of municipal councils, and a mayor automatically earned a place among the notables. The ninety-nine other notables included twenty-four merchants, sixteen cloth merchants, twelve cattle dealers, eight doctors, five manufacturers, five dealers in real estate, and four civil servants as well as property owners (ten) and businessmen and wholesalers (eight), the two occupations that formerly predominated.[35]

Although the Jews' role as moneylenders does not figure directly in the commercial court records, the lists of notables, or the various censuses, it was nevertheless *the* aspect of the Jewish economy that attracted the most public attention. The issue of usury dramatically affected the political and social status of Alsatian Jews as well as the political activity of the consistories There were complaints about Jewish usury at the end of the ancien régime, and these motivated Napoleon's restrictive anti-Jewish legislation of 1808. In 1818, when the Infamous Decree was due to expire and in the years immediately following, the issue of Jewish moneylending was fiercely debated in Alsace. In fact, into the 1820s, the Central Consistory feared the government's imposition of special legislation aimed solely at Jews; instead, as a preventative measure, it urged the departmental consistories to conduct a campaign of their own against usury.[36]

In the absence of competitive banks, individuals with capital lend at interest. In Alsace there were few formal credit institutions, particularly in the countryside; the first rural banks were not introduced until the Second Empire. Even where banks existed, many borrowers who did not want their debt to be notarized, and hence public knowledge, preferred moneylenders. With their commercial networks, Jews in the countryside were well placed to loan money to peasants, though they were by no means the only moneylenders. According to the historian Alfred Wahl's recent investigation of the notarial archives of Truchtersheim (Lower Rhine) from 1849, forty-five of eighty-five transactions involved a Jew. In Wahl's words, "The presence of Jewish intermediaries is striking in its constancy." These Jews did not list their occupation on census documents or marriage records as moneylenders They generally combined moneylending with petty commerce or horse and cattle dealing. Often a loan accompanied a commercial transaction when commercial paper was discounted.[37]

In a book on the rural economy of Alsace published in 1869, the authors, a director of agricultural establishments and a deputy from the Upper Rhine, describe the skills and activity of the Jewish moneylender with a measure of grudging admiration:

Endowed with an uncommon practical sense, singularly active and with a patience that none can rebuff, clever at guessing the most secret dispositions of the

peasant, living on almost nothing, traveling cheaply, going to all the fairs, effect-
ing his transports of cattle and merchandise at very low price, always ready to sell,
to buy, or to exchange, scorning no transaction however small, engaged in every
type of traffic, this trader constitutes a totally characteristic type, and it is self-
explanatory that he comes to cover like a web not only the Alsatian countryside
but also the entire north-east of France . . . His procedures are infinitely
varied . . . It should not be lost from sight that the Jews are almost the only ones
to lend sums of 100, 200, or 300 francs and that the monopoly they exercise
results to a great extent from that; they join to these loans cattle dealing and
mortgages; most of them own, in diverse communes of their choice, several
parcels of land or vineyards, which they are always ready to rent, sell, or exchange
at the first favorable opportunity [38]

A study of notarial records and the estates left by Jews illustrates the
importance of moneylending as a source of capital formation Although such an
analysis does not reveal the percentage of moneylenders in the Jewish population or their proportion among all suppliers of credit, it does suggest the
persistence of moneylending in the Jewish economy The notarial records of
Mutzig from 1855 to 1864 include the estates of 156 Jews. Forty-two (27
percent) of these left loans outstanding, most of them to non-Jews When
estates of less than 1,000 francs are eliminated, the percentage of moneylenders
rises to 38 percent. Sixty percent of the moneylenders were women, suggesting
that it was acceptable for them to engage in this type of commercial activity.
More than two-thirds of the female moneylenders were wives of wholesalers,
merchants, proprietors, cattle merchants, old-clothes dealers, a commercial
agent, and a butcher; the rest were widows Most moneylenders left estates in
the range of the petite and middle bourgeoisie, the majority of nonmoneylenders did not achieve bourgeois status [39] (See table 3 12.)

The account book of Salomon Brunschwig, an active entrepreneur who
apparently lived in Altkirch (Upper Rhine) and conducted his business in the
region in the 1830s and 1840s, gives an example of a moneylender's mode of
operation.[40] The account book, written in Judeo-Alsatian, allotted a page or
two to each town in the moneylender's territory A loan was generally entered in
the format "X owes me Y francs to be paid in Z years (or in installments),"
followed by the date. Between 1834 and 1846 Brunschwig made 524 loans, all
but 10 of them to non-Jews. His Jewish customers included his brother, who
was his occasional business partner, and his two servant girls (who together
borrowed 27 francs). The loans varied in size from 2 francs to more than 4,500
(to his brother); the average amount was 178 francs The terms of the loans

TABLE 3 12
Size of Estates of Moneylenders and Nonmoneylenders

Francs	Moneylenders (%)	N	Nonmoneylenders (%)	N
<2,000	7	3	55	63
2–10,000	52	22	12	14
10–50,000	31	13	22	25
50–100,000	5	2	4	4
>100,000	5	2	7	8

ranged from one or two months to six years, with two years the most common. Only the largest loans were notarized; Jewish clients also signed the account book in Hebrew characters. Brunschwig occasionally assumed loans negotiated by other moneylenders or shared a loan with them Some individuals were regular customers. The most frequent of Brunschwig's clients, M. Froebsch, borrowed money from him fifty-six times between April 1835 and September 1845. Seven others, including another member of the Froebsch family, were involved in at least ten transactions recorded in the account book

It is not possible to calculate the rate of interest charged because the loans were repaid at face value and therefore seem to have been initially discounted. The scope of Brunschwig's business, however, can be gauged from the size of the accounts receivable as well as from the number of transactions. Between 1838 and 1844, with the exception of one year, Brunschwig recorded between fifty-four and seventy-three loans a year By the end of 1838 his outstanding accounts exceeded 20,000 francs and reached a peak of almost 37,000 francs in 1841—this at a time when an estate of 2,000 francs was considered a mark of bourgeois status. That year his loans brought in 8,857 francs With his surplus capital Brunschwig occasionally bought property.

Although Jewish moneylenders became wealthy enough to join the petite and middle bourgeoisie, poverty persisted among Jews in Alsace throughout the first two-thirds of the nineteenth century, though it seems to have declined during the period. A government inquiry of 1856–57 in the Lower Rhine found considerably more poor in the Jewish population than in the Protestant and Catholic populations: 8.8 percent of Catholics were defined as poor, 5.3 percent of Protestants, and 12.8 percent of Jews.[41] This comparison may be misleading for at least two reasons, however. The clergy who assessed the extent of poverty among their constituents may not have followed the same standards. Moreover, as a population without land, the Jewish poor, when deprived of cash income, had no opportunity to support themselves, however minimally, through subsistence agriculture. Still, if Jewish communities in Alsace were not poorer than their Gentile neighbors, but merely more aware of the poor in their midst, the level of Jewish poverty was significant.

The demographics of poverty differed from town to town. In Itterswiller 52 percent of the poor were children under fifteen; in Bischheim only 29 percent were children. On average children accounted for one-third of the poor. Among adults women were only slightly overrepresented. Of eighty-two indigent households in Strasbourg, forty-four were married couples, most with children, fourteen were widows, and three were widowers with children. In nearby Bischheim widows (twelve) and widowers (nine) together constituted 56 percent of the poor households. Although a few indigent families were quite large, in Strasbourg and Bischheim, where information on household structure was complete, poor families averaged 3.5 children per household in Strasbourg and 4.1 in Bischheim, about average for the local Jewish population.[42]

The inquiry classified the poor according to the cause of their unfortunate situation. Some rabbis mentioned the "rigors of the season," the "high cost of living," and the lack of work as the primary reason for "restrained poverty." "Hereditary poverty," though, headed the list of causes in sixty-three communes, followed by infirmity, sickness, vice (one category), age, foreign status, and large families. Only 1.3 percent of the Jewish indigent were unwed mothers and 2 percent illegitimate children. (See table 3.13.) The rabbis assessed the moral level of the poor as generally high. The report of Rabbi J. Baer of Bischheim is typical:

> None of the poor in my parish nor their children, with the exception of the spinster Florette Klein, who has no use of her hands, begs, either in the commune or outside of it. The morals of the poor   are very regular; they support their misfortunes with the resignation that religion commands and that is their consolation in their distress. The children of the poor attend school and take part in religious services. The able-bodied poor find opportunities for work in neighboring communes and especially in Strasbourg.[43]

Begging, a concomitant of rural poverty and landlessness, was often identified as a specifically Jewish problem, although it was not limited to Jews.[44] As early as 1810, the Central Consistory had banned the custom of caring for wandering beggars, especially those of foreign provenance, but begging per-

TABLE 3 13

Causes of Poverty among Jews in the Lower Rhine, 1856–1857

	%	N
Hereditary poverty	34	218
Infirmity, sickness, vice	19	123
Age	17	109
Foreigners	10	63
Large family	7	46
Intellectual incapacity	3	22
Not enough work	2	15
Reversal of fortune	2	10
Illegitimate child	2	12
Unwed mother	1	8
Other (laziness, bad conduct, orphan, abandoned child)	1	8

sisted [45] Alsatian Jews continued to feel a moral responsibility for the indigent, and the commune leadership tried, over the course of forty years, to find a workable solution to the problem. Prompted by a series of thefts by wandering Jewish beggars in 1819, the prefect of the Upper Rhine in 1821 banned both begging and vagabondage by Jews in the department. At that time, the Consistory of the Upper Rhine initiated a program to care for the poor. Fixing the number of "worthy" native indigent to be supported by the community at one hundred, it distributed them throughout the communes, taking into account the local Jewish population and the resources at its disposal. (Foreign beggars were denied assistance.) The poor were to receive their meals at the table of their wealthier coreligionists through a system of meal tickets (*billets d'alimentation* or *d'hospitalité*).[46] The following year the Consistory of the Lower Rhine adopted a similar measure. It would no longer countenance begging; instead, *commissaires surveillants* in each community would denounce Jewish beggars to the authorities. The three hundred meritorious beggars of the department would be settled among the Jewish communities, fed by the well-to-do, and put to work The poor who visited their relatives on holidays for assistance would be permitted to do so twice a year, provided they had a certificate of good conduct. The Consistory explicitly accepted responsibility for Jewish beggars as a religious duty, not a civil one.[47]

This system failed to keep pace with the economic need of the indigent

Jewish population, both native and foreign By 1827 a number of Jewish householders in Durmenach, newly settled in the commune, protested to the government against the system, which imposed a heavy financial burden upon them although they had not consented to its implementation. The number of assisted beggars, they claimed, had swelled to four hundred.[48] The Jewish community of Strasbourg established a Society to Extinguish Begging in 1839. The society reviewed and revised the guidelines for providing aid to beggars. To receive assistance the ever-present beggars would need a certificate of good character from both the mayor and the commissaire surveillant of the Jewish community. Young people capable of working and foreign beggars were excluded, though foreigners in transit, if they had the appropriate legal papers, would be eligible for aid.[49] In spite of these measures, in 1846 a number of donors to the society complained they were still bothered by wandering poor who begged from house to house. The society admitted that even its appeals to the police had not yielded positive results.[50] New regulations introduced in 1847 limited assistance to two francs a trimester for beggars living in the Lower Rhine, one franc to those from other departments, and fifty centimes to those without a fixed domicile and to foreigners with papers. Presumably to prevent promiscuity, women unaccompanied by husbands were denied aid. The economic crisis of 1846–48 was clearly reflected in the repeated discussions of the problem of the wandering poor as well as in prison statistics.[51] Of 124 arrests of Jews between 1847 and 1852, 38 percent were for begging or vagabondage. About 20 percent of the convicted beggars and vagabonds were women, and 20 percent were foreign, primarily of German birth.[52] The Committee for the Amelioration of the Jews, established in 1853 to promote the emigration of the Jewish poor, and the 1862 decisions of the Strasbourg and Colmar consistories to set up another joint commission to eliminate begging were responses, in part, to the problem of public begging.[53]

The Jewish press addressed the issue with some frequency in the 1840s and 1850s.[54] As late as 1858 a debate about begging in the *Lien d'Israël* reported that "schnorrers" (Yiddish for beggars) exhibiting "deplorable, repugnant, and even immoral" traits were still beating their accustomed paths through the province. Traditional Jewish attitudes of concern for the poor coexisted with modern approaches to philanthropy. In contrast to Isaac Levy, the rabbi of Verdun, who described the beggars in the harsh terms cited above and called for putting them to work and placing their families in an institution, Joseph Levy, the rabbi of Saar-Union in the Lower Rhine, bitterly criticized his colleague's approach and referred to Jewish tradition to justify the claim of wandering beggars upon their fellow Jews. He protested against the harsh measures proposed for dealing with the poor and the mean spirit with which the indigent were described [55]

Political emancipation offered Alsatian Jews new economic opportunities, but it did not lead to a radical transformation of livelihood. Their traditional role as mediators between the peasant in the countryside and his markets and suppliers of consumer goods in the town remained attractive to Jews even after all occupations were theoretically open to them. Some Jews purchased property, and a small percentage became artisans, farmers, or even industrialists,[56] but the vast majority chose to support themselves in the trade, along with moneylending, that had been the pursuit of their fathers. Upward mobility occurred by staying within commerce rather than by abandoning it. In this the Jews of Alsace followed the pattern of most Western Jews. The persistence and predominance of village Jews in the province simply retarded the process. The occupational structure and place of residence of Alsatian Jews did not change significantly until the second half of the nineteenth century. The inability of the village economy to sustain the growing Jewish population and the development of banking facilities and peasant marketing cooperatives marked the shift to city living and to new forms of livelihood

FOUR

On the Domestic Scene

The family patterns of the Jews of Alsace, like their economic profile, did not change dramatically as a result of emancipation. The traditional Jewish family was resilient and well adapted to the economic and cultural opportunities of nineteenth-century France. This is not surprising, for the traditional Jewish family displayed many elements of what was later called "bourgeois domesticity" well before most Jews were sufficiently wealthy or acculturated to be full members of the European bourgeoisie. At the end of the eighteenth century, when a lively debate raged in France about the nature of the Jews, even those who criticized their economic practices, religious ritual, and cultural backwardness admired the Jews for the quality of their family lives The Abbé Grégoire, a supporter of Jewish emancipation but a critic of the Jews nonetheless, in a famous essay published in 1789, lavished praise upon the Jews for their domestic virtues: "They placed strong barriers against libertinism. Nothing was more rare among them than adultery; their conjugal union was truly edifying; they are good spouses and good parents. I must also mention . . . [their] profound respect for the authors of their days; they would be desolate to die without receiving the blessing of their fathers, without bestowing one upon their children."[1]

In the absence of a broad collection of letters, memoirs, and diaries, it is difficult to assess the affective quality of family life, but the lack of Gentile criticism suggests that the external signs of family disintegration—such as high rates of illegitimacy, physical abuse of spouses and children, or juvenile delinquency—were not found, or were kept hidden, among Jewish families in Alsace on the eve of emancipation Certainly, bonds of familial and communal solidarity—Grégoire also cited the traditional concern of Jews for their own poor[2]—combined to present a picture of domestic felicity and stability.

Although there were few Jewish reflections on family life until the second half of the nineteenth century, it is significant that Jews then focused on the quality of their families as compelling evidence of the value of Jewish culture and the worthiness of Jews for full equality.[3] After Germany annexed Alsace in 1871, when Alsatian Jews in exile looked with nostalgia to the world they had lost, they often fixed their sentimental gaze on the family. In 1886 Léon Cahun wrote with some exaggeration in *La Vie juive,* his tales of Jewish life in Alsace, "It is neither the rabbis, nor the synagogue, nor the Talmud, nor even the law or persecution which preserved the Jewish religion. It is the love of parents for children, the love of children for parents—it is the family. . One should not mock this quasi-dogma-less religion in which the family is everything, for in giving free rein to the Jew's veneration for his ancestors, it opens the way for his ancient instincts of passionate love for the polity [cité]."[4]

Cahun and others who wrote about life in Alsace described the family as the matrix of traditional Jewish observance and feeling. Daniel Stauben wrote in a volume published in 1860, "In general, the Jews feel the loss of a parent more keenly than other men. . . . Persecuted throughout the centuries, separated from the rest of society by impassable barriers, they constantly had to seek in the unity and joys of the family a consolation in a shelter against the injustices of the world outside."[5] The location of much Jewish ritual within the home lent an aura of religious sentiment to domesticity even for those whose traditional faith had been eroded. The special quality of the Sabbath, for example, was associated with its domestic context. In honor of the Sabbath the home was cleaned, and family members donned festive clothing. The wife rose early on Friday morning to prepare food for the evening meal and Sabbath day dinner. For many Jewish families in the countryside the Sabbath was the only day on which all family members gathered together.[6] In the words of Edouard Coypel, an otherwise hostile Gentile observer of the Jewish scene, "The Friday evening celebration is a sort of festival in each family."[7] After the father recited *qiddush* (the blessing over wine) and the parents blessed their children, the mother served a multicourse meal for which "even the less well-to-do scrimped in order to have meat."[8] On Saturday after morning prayers Jewish women would pick up their *Gesetsi Sup,* the Sabbath dinner dish of split peas or white beans, potatoes, and sausage or other meat, which was most often cooked in the bakery's oven overnight or, if the family had one, in a special oven at home.

Saturday afternoons were spent visiting.[9] The Sabbath, the family, and sociability were thus intertwined

Although there is insufficient memoir literature and literary evidence to substantiate, or qualify, the nostalgic recreations of traditional Jewish family life in the Alsatian countryside, statistical data are useful in plotting the configurations of the Jewish family in Alsace in the two to three generations after emancipation. Such demographic information as age at marriage, age at first parity, age at last parity, and household structure can indicate how Jews organized their private lives in a period of expanding opportunity

Although Grégoire attributed the absence of sexual libertinism among Jews to the practice of early marriage, early marriage was not common among Western and Central European Jews by the late eighteenth century. It was not prevalent in Alsace in the nineteenth century. Extrapolating from census data, it appears that Jewish women in Alsace and Lorraine married at a mean age of about 23 at the turn of the nineteenth century.[10] From the 1820s through the 1840s, civil marriage records reveal that first marriages occurred when brides were 26.7 years old. By the 1850s and 1860s their mean age at marriage had risen to 28.1. Husbands were on average two to three years older than their brides.[11] This pattern of marrying later was also found among Gentiles in Alsace, although during the Second Empire Jews married even later than did Christian Alsatians.[12] In 23 percent of Jewish marriages, the wives were at least a year older than their husbands. In Strasbourg and Colmar, demographic patterns consistent with some embourgeoisement appeared. Jewish brides throughout the period were younger in the cities (24.9 in the 1820s and 1830s; 26.3 in the 1840s; and 26.2 in the 1850s and 1860s) than in the countryside, and by the 1840s their husbands were older (31.3 in the 1840s and 30.6 in the 1850s and 1860s).[13]

The low rates of illegitimacy that Grégoire noted at the end of the eighteenth century continued well into the nineteenth century. Of 2,109 circumcisions performed by two *mohalim* (ritual circumcisers), father and son, between 1819 and 1870, primarily in Strasbourg and Bischheim, 88 (or 4.2 percent) involved illegitimate sons. Until 1860, the rate of illegitimacy varied between 2.0 percent and 4.0 percent of the births, about half the French rate of illegitimate births. Only in the decade 1861–70 did the rate zoom to 6 6 percent, which was 87 percent of the French rate.[14] That increase is substantiated by a report on Jewish births, marriages, and deaths in Colmar in 1860. Of the 284 live births and stillbirths, 5.3 percent were illegitimate.[15] Since the mothers of the illegitimate sons listed in the circumcision records were almost all women who had come to Bischheim and Strasbourg from the countryside to give birth, it is likely that the incidence of illegitimacy is somewhat overstated by the mohalim's records. In the sample of marriage records, only 1.4 percent of the 1,214 brides and grooms were illegitimate (an understated figure, since some children of illegitimate birth were subsequently legitimated and may have escaped notice, and illegitimate stillbirths or childhood deaths would not have been recorded) and 1.9 percent had given birth to illegitimate children [16]

The Jewish marriage market in Alsace was regional and transcended national boundaries. The contours of the marriage market suggest the survival of an Ashkenazi cultural unit linking Alsace, the southwestern German states, and, less important, the neighboring Swiss cantons From 1820 through 1862 more than 60 percent of the grooms marrying in the Lower Rhine were born there, but 11 to 20 percent (depending on the decade) came from the Upper Rhine and 7 to 12 percent from other departments. In the 1820s, 1830s, and 1840s more than 16 percent of the grooms were born abroad, primarily in the German states and Switzerland, but, perhaps because of the influence of nationalism, the international dimensions of the marriage market contracted by the 1860s, when only 4 percent of the grooms were of foreign birth. The brides were more likely than the grooms to be locals, with about three-quarters of them born in the department and 9 to 20 percent born in the Upper Rhine. More than 7 percent of the brides in the 1820s and 1830s, almost 16 percent in the 1840s, and more than 5 percent in the 1860s were of foreign birth. Most telling is the fact that of 368 Jewish marriages that took place in Bischheim, Itterswiller, and Niederroedern between 1820 and 1862 only 26 percent involved a bride and groom born in the same place. In a sample of 176 marriages performed in Strasbourg from 1823 through 1862, only ten brides and grooms shared the same birthplace—Strasbourg. And in 63 Jewish marriages in Colmar from 1822 through 1862 none of the brides and grooms had the same place of birth.[17]

Although Jewish men and women marrying in Alsace cast their nets widely in terms of geography, they were religiously endogamous. In a sample of 607 marriages only 3, all from Strasbourg, were intermarriages reflecting a high degree of social integration. In 1827, a Jewish doctor married the Christian daughter of a colleague. The second marriage, from 1828, was between an illiterate Jewish bride of 34 and a Christian groom of 33, an employee in Customs. And in 1860 a Jewish actor wed a Christian actress who had given birth to his daughter in 1855.[18]

Marriages across class boundaries were almost as infrequent as those between different faiths. Although it is difficult to assess the socioeconomic status of brides and grooms from the available information—primarily the occupations of their fathers—some tentative conclusions can be reached. At the bottom and the top of the social scale, class lines were rigidly drawn. The children of day laborers, commercial agents, and peddlers as a rule married each other, as did the children of wholesalers, bankers, and rentiers. In 26 percent of the marriages the fathers' professions were identical, and in another 34 percent their professions were of equivalent status. In 16 percent of the marriages the bride appears to have moved up, and in 25 percent the groom seems to have made an advantageous match. There were some rare cases of enormous disparity—for example, a barber, son of a day laborer marrying the daughter of a merchant. Without statistics on the wealth of the many Jewish merchants and businessmen, however, the social meaning of different titles is open to question. The middle rank of merchants, commercial agents, and cattle dealers—the majority of the Jews of Alsace—seem to have formed an undifferentiated marriage market.

Jewish marriages were traditionally arranged by a *shadkhn*, a matchmaker, who received a fixed percentage of the dowry. According to literary sources, the shadkhn continued to perform his services at least through mid-century.[19] A book of prayers in French, edited by Rabbi Aron of Strasbourg and published in 1848 by the Consistorial Society of Good Books, also presumed that even in bourgeois Jewish circles marriages were arranged. A prayer for a girl before her engagement reads, "Oh Lord, enlighten the solicitude of my good parents, so that their choice may respond to their wishes and to mine and so that the man to whom they are going to engage me should become a devoted protector for me."[20] *T'naim* (the formal document of engagement, written in Hebrew and stipulating the economic contribution of both parties to the new couple and promising release [*halitza*] to the bride if she were left a childless widow) from 1810 to 1840 have survived in archival collections. Moreover, Alsatian Jews found in the notarized prenuptial contract a modern version of t'naim.[21]

The dowry appears as a regular feature of traditional Jewish marriages, particularly in the villages. In Hegenheim in 1834, for example, Samuel Braunschweig was denied a Jewish burial for his infant son because he had not paid the Jewish community the tax assessed on his dowry.[22] David Schornstein's story "La Dîme," published serially in 1864 but set in an earlier time, tells the story of a greedy man's attempt to win the favor of a poor Alsatian Jewish woman who was betrothed to another after he discovered that her aunt would

provide a substantial dowry.[23] A prenuptial contract of 1867 between a young
man from the small town of Marmoutier in the Lower Rhine and a young
woman from the village of Romanswiller in the same department stipulated a
dowry of 3,500 francs.[24] Hevrot (charitable associations) for providing dowries
to poor young women survived until the end of the nineteenth century. A
modernized hevra, the Society for the Endowerment and the Apprenticing of
Poor Girls, was established in Strasbourg in 1858 and, according to the Lien
d'Israël, met with active sympathy In 1868 Rabbi Aron of Strasbourg announced a public subscription to provide dowries for the orphaned daughters
of the poor Talmudic scholar Rabbi Moïse Bloch.[25] Freddy Raphael, a sociolo-
gist and expert on the folklore of Alsatian Jews, notes that, in the absence of a
dowry from their fathers, Jewish girls in the countryside left school at thirteen
to work as domestics to earn their dowry or called upon their brothers for
assistance. Without a dowry women were attractive primarily to foreign Jews or
to widowers.[26] (Indeed, the marriage documents reveal far more remarriage
among widowers than among widows.) Given the Jewish tradition of the dowry
and the bourgeois concern for the financial stability of families, it is likely that
the dowry persisted among the Jews of Alsace throughout the nineteenth
century, as it did in Germany.[27] Yet, we do not know how marriage customs
changed with time, especially in the cities, and how quickly informal contacts
and supervised socializing replaced the formal recourse to the matchmaker in
both urban and village environments.

The size of Jewish families in Alsace remained about the same during the
first half of the nineteenth century. Census data from 1808 indicate that Jewish
women aged 41 to 45 living in Alsace and Lorraine had an average of 3.78
children living at home at the time of the census. For all Jewish households of
ever-married adults in the two provinces the mean number of children was
3.37. The 1846 manuscript census reveals that completed families in Strasbourg had an average of 3.7 children and in Bischheim, Niederroedern, and
Itterswiller, 4.2 children. This rise in completed family size in the countryside
may reflect lower mortality rates. In Strasbourg Jewish households of the ever-
married (of all ages) had an average of 2.8 children A larger sample from the
same census and covering a broad range of Jewish communities in the provinces of Alsace and Lorraine had a mean of 2.9 children. Age-specific fertility of
married women at mid-century, as calculated from a number of censuses,
demonstrates some postponement of childbearing among Jewish women living
in Strasbourg as opposed to villages in the countryside.[28] (See table 4.1.) Yet,

TABLE 4 1
Age-specific Marital Fertility of Jewish Women

Age	Countryside, 1846–50	N	Strasbourg, 1846	N
16–20	1 0	1	0	6
21–25	2 0	11	1 3	38
26–30	2.1	39	1 8	57
31–35	3 3	38	3.1	60
36–40	3 7	69	3.9	78
41–45	4.2	41	3 1	63
46–50	2.9	34	3 8	52

given the late age of marriage and the relatively high rates of infant mortality, family limitation seems not to have been widespread among Jews in Alsace before the second half of the century.[29]

Alsatian Jewish households were of medium size and varied in both size and structure over the course of the life cycle.[30] In 1846 Jewish households in Strasbourg contained an average of 4.6 persons and those in the town and villages surveyed an average of 4.8. These averages, however, mask the variations in each setting and the differences between them. In both city and countryside almost 40 percent of the total (36 percent in the countryside and 37 percent in Strasbourg) were households of more than six persons. Particularly in Strasbourg, servants, found in 32 percent of the households, and boarders, in 13 percent, swelled the population. (In Bischheim, Niederroedern, and Itterswiller servants were found in 9 percent of the households and boarders in 3 percent.) At the other end of the spectrum, 17 percent of the Jewish households in Strasbourg consisted of a single person, usually a young man who had come to the city to seek his fortune. In the countryside only 3 percent of the households were so constituted. (See table 4.2.)

Local variations were common. In 1850, for example, the Jewish community of 38 households in Uffheim (Upper Rhine) contained an average of 5.8 persons per household; the community of 37 households in Herrlisheim (Lower Rhine) had a mean of only 5.2 individuals. In Herrlisheim 14 percent of the Jewish households housed servants, but in Uffheim fewer than 3 percent did.[31]

Households that were traceable in the 1856 census (240 in Strasbourg and 197 in the countryside) had grown to a mean of 5 1 persons in Strasbourg and 5.3 in the countryside. By 1856 most of the bachelors listed in 1846 had established families or left the city, and the percentage of single-person house-

TABLE 4 2
Jewish Household Sizes, 1846

No. of persons	Strasbourg (%)	Countryside (%)
1	17	3
2–3	22	28
4–5	24	33
6+	37	36
	N = 474	N = 263

holds had fallen to 7 percent. In the countryside the aging of families and resulting rise in widowhood led to an increase in single-person households, to 4 percent. In both settings the proportion of large households (six or more persons) had risen to 41 percent in Strasbourg and 46 percent in the countryside. In 1866, as grown children left home and established their own households, the proportion of large families declined, to 34 percent of the (180 traceable) households in Strasbourg and 39 percent of the (154 traceable) households in the countryside, but the trends in single-person households were confirmed. In Strasbourg 6 percent were single-person households, in the countryside 5 percent. As these settled households in Strasbourg aged, they also prospered, housing more servants and fewer boarders. Thus, the number of households with servants rose to 33 percent in 1856 and to 50 percent in 1866; the number with boarders declined to 9 percent in 1856 and to 4 percent in 1866. The stagnating Jewish economy in the countryside was reflected in the reverse process—the decline in the number of households with servants (to 8 percent in 1856 and 5 percent in 1866) and the rise in the number of households with boarders (to 6 percent in 1856 and 7 percent in 1866).

Most Jewish families in Alsace, like most other western families, were nuclear in structure, composed of a married couple, a married couple with children, or a single parent with children.[32] In 1846, 64 percent of the Jewish families of Strasbourg were nuclear families, as were 84 percent of the families in Bischheim, Niederroedern, and Itterswiller. Within that broad category, almost 10 percent of the Jewish households in Strasbourg consisted of a married couple without children, almost 44 percent of two parents and their children, and 11 percent of a single parent with children. In the towns and villages the proportion of childless and single-parent families was similar. Almost 10 percent of the families were childless couples and 12 percent were single-parent families. The rest of the nuclear families—62 percent—contained two parents and their children

Yet, in both Strasbourg and the countryside, despite the predominance of nuclear families, the bonds of extended kinship are visible in the census data. A significant minority of Jewish households opened their homes, at least temporarily, to relatives. Most common, widowed mothers or fathers lived with a married child. But other relatives—an unmarried sibling or a niece or nephew of one of the parents—appear as well. In Strasbourg these extended families grew from 15 percent of the total number of Jewish families in 1846 and of traceable families in 1856 to 19 percent of the remaining families in 1866. In Bischheim, Niederroedern, and Itterswiller in this period of economic decline, the number of families with resident kin grew from 10 percent in 1846 to 22 percent in 1856 and 26 percent in 1866. In 1850, 21 percent of the families in Uffheim were extended, although in the more prosperous Herrlisheim only 5 percent were In 1860 in Hochfelden (Lower Rhine) only one of the forty-eight Jewish families had a servant and 25 percent of the families were extended.[33]

The percentage of extended families does not do full justice, however, to the importance of kinship networks. Although the majority of Jews in Alsace lived most of their lives in nuclear families, many had kin nearby. From the census data, for example, it appears that at least 29 percent of Jewish households in Bischheim, Niederroedern, and Itterswiller had relatives living in the same or a neighboring dwelling in 1846; in Strasbourg at least 20 percent had relatives in the same quarter, most of them in the same building. The predominance of commerce among Alsatian Jews, often reinforced family ties with economic links. Fathers and sons, or brothers alone, joined in commercial ventures. The family enterprise of Captain Alfred Dreyfus's father and siblings was by no means unique. After working as a peddler and small-scale moneylender, Raphael Dreyfus established a cotton mill in Mulhouse in 1862. As it prospered and became a major textile firm, he brought several of his sons into the business.[34] As noted in chapter 3, the moneylender Brunschwig, loaned the largest single sum to his brother. Henry and Eve Albert Dreyfus of Wissembourg turned in 1817 to Henry's brother Isaac Dreyfus for a loan of 500 francs (at 5 percent interest) to expand their business; their son Israel and his wife, Sara Kossmann, desperately in need of cash to repay a delinquent debt, in 1856 sold their household possessions to one of Sara's relatives.[35]

It is difficult to document the role of Jewish women in the economic life of the family. The professions of all adult males are listed in the censuses; married women appear after their husbands with the simple qualifier "his wife." As

Louise Tilly and Joan Scott have pointed out, married women chose the kinds of work that would necessitate the least separation from their homes.[36] Because few Jewish men in Alsace were engaged in industrial labor, their wives had opportunities to assist in commercial dealings, in stores located in or near their dwellings, or in petty crafts. In the 1846 census data some 50 percent of Jewish men were listed as merchants, and it seems likely that their wives helped them with their stores. David Schornstein's description of the economic role of the wife of a poor *sofer* (scribe) in his story "La Dîme" probably represents a common phenomenon. "The mother was busy with the confection of objects, some belonging to her husband's work, the others necessary for religious practice [*culte*] and whose sale would produce a supplement of income so necessary for the family."[37] After her marriage Alfred Dreyfus's mother, Jeanette, continued to work as a seamstress until her husband's business success enabled her to retire.[38] Such women's work would be ignored by census takers. Similarly, in those families that took in boarders, the housewife, in cleaning and preparing the meals, supplemented the family's income without attracting official recognition A talent for domestic management was recognized as valuable in a prospective bride. Schornstein's greedy bachelor was initially attracted to Perle, the poor daughter of the scribe, not only because of her beauty and charm, but because she was "hard-working, thrifty, . . a mere nothing would be sufficient to adorn her, and . . a husband would find there a true pearl of economy."[39] Married women (see chapter 3) lent money and held mortgages. At least occasionally wives who participated in the commercial affairs of their husbands received legal powers to conduct business. During the First Empire Henry Dreyfus, "businessman from Wissembourg," legally conferred upon his wife, Eve Albert, considerable economic autonomy as his virtual partner. She was to have "the power, for him and in his name, to make, recognize, undertake, consent to, and sign . . . all matters which can concern him and also . . administer his property and affairs, withdraw all packages and registered letters from all postal offices, . . . pursue the recovery of all sums which are or will fall due . . . discuss, close and settle all accounts with all debtors and creditors, . . . make all loans and contract all borrowing whether through private title or through a notarized act."[40]

The census data recognized only the work of independent women with no support—the unmarried and the widowed. Opportunities for women were limited in the French economy of the time, and most women supported themselves as domestics, laundresses, and seamstresses. Similarly, in the marriage records most brides declared themselves to be "without profession." Only forty-two declared a professional status, clearly an understatement of the social reality. The largest group, eighteen, worked as domestics, nine as seamstresses, and seven as merchants (of clothing and notions) The other occupations included a rentière, a butcher, a day laborer, a laundress, a salesgirl, and an ironer. Two widows had assumed their husbands' businesses of cattle dealing and running a cabaret.

Most Jewish families in Alsace did not attain bourgeois status until the second half of the nineteenth century For those that did—almost one-third of Jewish households in Strasbourg in 1846 had at least one servant—women performed the tasks of administering a complex household, of managing the domestic economy with expected thrift and efficiency.

Much as the economic role of women within the family does not find full expression in the census data, so, too, the role of adolescent children and young adult children living with their parents is only partially illuminated by the census takers. The manuscript census of 1846 lists professions for only 129 children among the 200 Jewish families with children living in Strasbourg. Not surprisingly, almost 60 percent of these working youths were commercial employees or artisans. Another 16 percent worked at more menial jobs, as peddlers or as day laborers. There is less information for the countryside, but it is likely, given the nature of the Jewish economy, that most adolescents were recruited into family commercial enterprises after they had completed their primary education And when families were in need, they could call on their grown children for support. Thus, during the First Empire when he was trying to reestablish himself and support his large family, Henry Dreyfus, then 61, shared responsibility for the support of his large household with his son Jonas, then 26 and a shoemaker [41]

As Jews in the West entered the bourgeoisie, acculturated, and abandoned many aspects of traditional religious observance, communal leaders focused on the family and its role in forming Jewish identity.[42] There is some evidence of embourgeoisement in the 1850s and 1860s in the communal activity and public behavior of Jewish women. In Strasbourg in 1858, for example, the Charitable Society of Israelite Women combined modern aspects of female philanthropy with features of traditional women's hevrot. The society distributed food, wood, and money to the sick, to widows, and to poor women with newborns. When there was a death in a poor family, the society arranged for women to "watch" and recite prayers over the body of the deceased, and it placed carriages at the disposition of the "congregation dite Metharet," the women's hevra qadisha (burial society) [43] The society members did not, however, perform the tasks of caring for the dead themselves, as elite women had done in traditional Jewish society. The Jewish press frequently referred to the charitableness of Jewish women, who administered a newly founded orphanage in Strasbourg and were active supporters of the new Jewish hospital in Mulhouse.[44] On occasion it criticized "the unfortunate penchant for luxury, developed especially among the feminine sex, an abuse all the more dangerous in the villages as it forms an odious contrast with rural simplicity."[45]

Both rabbinic and lay leaders in Alsace took note of the contribution of women to Jewish life and recognized their role as transmitters of Jewish culture to their children. Unlike spokesmen in major urban centers of Jewish life, such as Paris, London, and Berlin, where assimilation had made noticeable inroads by the mid-nineteenth century, they did not blame women for the rise in assimilation nor assign to them sole responsibility for cultural transmission. They were aware, however, that contemporary conditions necessitated the expansion of religious education for girls and women. As a rationale for new educational programs aimed at girls, some Jewish spokesmen suggested that educated women made better mothers. A textbook designed specifically for girls, La Fille d'Israël, was published in Haguenau in 1847.[46] Spiritual leaders acknowledged that they were inspired to publish prayerbooks in French because of women's ignorance of the Hebrew prayers and because of the need to replace the tkhines (Yiddish personal prayers for women), which were "written in a corrupt German [Yiddish]."[47] In 1846 the Strasbourg Consistory's newly founded Commission for the Propagation of Books of Morality and Religion, composed of Rabbi Aron and two progressive local notables, argued that the dissemination of religious books, with edifying prayers which met the needs of the day, would be the most effective means to combat the religious indifference of the Jewish elite of Alsace, for "a book insinuates itself into the family." The four-page proposal concluded, "In a word, the pious and well-reared woman, or even the pious man, does not find among us any book that introduces religion into the home, which supports domestic piety. . . In this regard the ancient Jews were more advanced; the rabbis of their time took care to edit in the vernacular books of this type called tkhines [inserted in Hebrew script], and thereby proved that they recognized the needs of their time."[48] Although it mentioned women first, the commission report did not dwell upon their special religious responsibilities within the domestic sphere. The Strasbourg Consistory enthusiastically accepted the commission's report and established the Consistorial Society of Good Books, which published Prières d'un coeur israélite, written and edited by Rabbi Aron, in 1848.[49]

Whether this collection of prayers in French had the desired impact on the religious sensibilities of Alsatian Jews is impossible to tell. That it was a popular volume is beyond dispute, for it went through several editions in the next generation. The personal prayers, which form almost half the volume, revealed an acculturated and moderate rabbi's view of the family considered appropriate for the contemporary Jewish bourgeois and promoted a modern discourse about family life.

The modern Jewish family took its cues from the prevailing notions of bourgeois domesticity. Its members had complementary roles and characteristics. The male head of the household, endowed with strength and rationality, the qualities of a leader, was expected, in a more explicit formula than was found in earlier texts, to protect and provide for his wife. In the prayer designed for him, he recited, "My God, in your goodness you have given me a wife, the inseparable companion of my passage through this life. . . . May I never forget that if strength and reason are the perquisite of my sex, hers is subject to the weakness of body and the feeling of the soul; do not permit me, Lord, to be unjust toward her and to demand of her qualities that are in no way in her nature. . . May her weakness even be her support against my strength; for it would be cruel to take unfair advantage of it toward a weak and delicate being whom love and law have conferred to my protection."[50] This notion of female fragility reflects acculturation to nineteenth-century Western European bourgeois ideals of womanhood. For her part, the wife acknowledged her role as the dependent creator of a domestic haven: "Lord, you have given me a husband as the companion of my life, to guide my steps and to share my destiny. It is from him that I receive my subsistence; make me worthy, Lord, to soften his work by the evenness of my disposition, by the tenderness of my heart, [and see to it that] I not fill with bitterness the nourishment which he earns for me and my children. May I never forget that man's labors overload his soul with cares and pains, and that the duty of a woman, her most sacred mission, is to restore calm and serenity in the heart of her spouse through her obligingness, her submission, her indulgent character."[51]

The prayers also make clear the responsibility of wife and mother for maintaining family harmony. The "unhappy wife" was expected to assume the burden of restoring her husband's affection. Her prayer included the following petition: "Oh my God, enlighten me that I may judge myself with severity; perhaps my husband's conduct is the result of my faults and my defects. . . . Teach me to read his soul, to divine his thoughts, to anticipate his desires, to please him, and to overcome his indifference through my love, his anger through my gentleness. . . . Keep me, my God from every feeling of hatred . . ; and if my husband is inaccessible to pity, . . . make my heart never change in his regard."⁵² There was no prayer for an unhappy husband, who presumably would not countenance the continuation of a difficult marriage

The mother was entrusted with the major burden of rearing children and socializing them as moral beings and as Jews. The father's prayer included, in reference to his children, a general request for wisdom in "direct[ing] them toward the good, distancing them from the bad, cultivating in them goodness and gentleness and forming their intelligence through noble and honest things." The mother, in her prayer, acknowledged specific sacred and God-given duties, and sought assistance in her disciplinary functions: "Preserve me from any weakness that would be harmful to their education, that I may not be blind or indulgent to their defects, so that I may be able to direct them with firmness and perseverance in the path of their duty and inculcate at an early age obedience to your law and faith in your eternal Providence."⁵³

This prescriptive view of Jewish family life did not coincide with social reality for most Jews in Alsace in 1848 Written in French, the prayers would have been unintelligible to the majority of Jews, particularly the women of the countryside. Those Jews, embedded in the traditional Jewish economy, doubtless preserved a style of relations between husband and wife that reflected a more expansive and rigorous economic role for women than was the case in urban bourgeois society. In spite of the pronouncements of radical discontinuity as the hallmark of the first generations of emancipated Jewry, the emancipated Jews of Alsace retained many of the religious and cultural features of traditional Jewish society for two to three generations after the cataclysmic events of the French Revolution

FIVE

The Social Foundations
of Cultural Conservatism

The power of tradition in religious practice is formidable. As long as the social forces, economic patterns, and intellectual climate remain stable, the religious culture they sustain will survive.[1] For the village Jews of Alsace such was the case for generations after the French Revolution decreed a radical change in their political status. Citizenship and its demands, including army service, could be integrated into traditional Jewish culture. Indeed, notions of freedom of conscience could be invoked to defend continuity, rather than to advocate progress. Since emancipation was granted early, the political pressure for change—though articulated by the organs of French public opinion and deeply felt by Jewish elites—was less intense and powerful than that wielded by a polity which still had the power to withhold the gift of political equality. After 1818 the French government used restraint in its political regulation of the Jewish minority, although it repressed dissent from elite norms quite firmly in the Department of the Upper Rhine until 1860. Pressure for cultural and religious change, however, originated primarily from the Jewish consistorial leadership Only after mid-century, when the social structure of Alsatian Jewish life was disturbed, did significant erosion and modification of traditional practices occur.

Because of the continuity of social and economic patterns, change in the Jewish culture of Alsace was slow in coming. Although consistorial leaders proclaimed the need for occupational redistribution and religious reform, the majority of Jews in the countryside retained not only their traditional occupation, but their language and their popular religious customs. This cultural conservatism in the countryside reflected the rootedness of village Jews in their rural milieu and led to conflicts between the rural Jewish population and the mostly urban notables who held consistorial office.

Although Jewish schools taught French with greater enthusiasm and diligence than their non-Jewish counterparts, the Judeo-Alsatian dialect (a version of western Yiddish) persisted throughout much of the nineteenth century.[2] The campaign against its use in the Jewish primary schools met with considerable resistance in the countryside, and it was slow to be eliminated as the language of instruction. In 1837 the progressive Strasbourg Jewish newspaper *La Régénération* noted that "to be a good teacher, one must know the Yiddish-German jargon."[3] Several years later the Alsatian school inspector Chevreuse attacked Jewish schools in the region for teaching in Judeo-Alsatian, "that language we must fight against with all our strength because it is truly the cause of the segregation of the broad Jewish masses from the French milieu."[4]

The use of Judeo-Alsatian was unavoidable in the schools, for many students, and especially girls, had no knowledge of French when they entered the classroom.[5] Until mid-century much of the older rabbinic leadership made its concession to social reality by continuing to speak Judeo-Alsatian in public discourses. Even Salomon Ulmann, who was elected grand rabbi of France in 1853 and who had published a catechism in French, preached mostly in Judeo-Alsatian. Only after 1859, when the Ecole Rabbinique moved from Metz to Paris, was Judeo-Alsatian systematically replaced by French.[6]

In Alsatian villages in the 1850s and 1860s facility with French remained the preserve of the few—the local schoolmaster and the educated young man.[7] In his stories of Jewish life Daniel Stauben described a French-speaking youth and his awkward courtship of a young lady who "as is so frequent among us .. was scarcely at home in the national language."[8] Stauben recounted as well the lament of a bookseller who used to sell Hebrew books at fairs. Now his wares were spurned in favor of French translations of the Bible, prayerbook, and Passover Haggadah, even though "the majority of those who buy them do not understand French any better than you and I."[9] In his 1857 novel *Couronne* Alexandre Weill pointedly noted that the beauteous fifteen-year-old Heva spoke not a word of French, and her mother was able to read only "German written in Hebrew characters."[10]

The civil marriage records of Alsatian Jews also give testimony to the slow diffusion of French in the countryside. In the 368 marriages that took place in Bischheim, Niederroedern, and Itterswiller between 1820 and 1862 signatures frequently appeared in Hebrew characters. (See table 5.1.)[11] Three generations

TABLE 5 1
Hebrew Signatures on Civil Marriage Documents. Bischheim,
Niederroedern, and Itterswiller (in percentages)

	Brides	Grooms	Mothers	Fathers
1820–39	52	26	68	45
1840–59	23	10	38	35
1860–62	16	9	25	31

after emancipation much of this literate population had not begun to master even the rudiments of written French or German Women were more likely than men to be unable to sign their names in Latin characters, or in any language whatsoever.

Judeo-Alsatian persisted in communal documents as well. Although the Strasbourg Consistory corresponded with the Central Consistory only in French, in its dealings with village Jews it was forced to use Judeo-Alsatian. Four certificates attesting to the morality of a candidate for the post of *shohet* (ritual slaughterer), sent to the Consistory of Wintzenheim (Upper Alsace) in 1824 were written in Judeo-Alsatian.[12] In 1833 consistory members signed a contract in Judeo-Alsatian with Maurice Jacob Lowe, who was to serve as cantor in the Strasbourg synagogue.[13] The Bischheim community recorded its deliberations through mid-century in Judeo-Alsatian and conducted most of its correspondence in the same language. When letters were composed in French, they were replete with misspellings and grammatical errors [14] Just as the Jewish community in Bischheim had to conduct its affairs in Judeo-Alsatian, so when a consistorial inquiry into the management of the community was held in the Upper Rhine town of Hattstatt in 1847, the proceedings were held and transcribed in that language, since the local residents knew no French.[15] Finally, the communities of Odratzheim and Bouxwiller kept their *pinkasim* (record books) in Judeo-Alsatian until 1899 and the 1880s respectively. In the Odratzheim *pinkas* only Hebrew dates were used until 1845, when French or German dates began to appear. By the 1860s occasional French words were inserted in the text [16]

As knowledge of written Hebrew declined in the countryside, it was not always replaced by literacy in French, particularly among women Only 9 percent of the mothers of the marrying couple and 12 percent of the brides in village marriage records of the 1820s and 1830s were illiterate, but the percentage of illiterate mothers soared to 37 percent in the 1840s and 1850s and 36 percent in the early 1860s. The number of illiterate brides declined only slightly, to 11 percent in the 1840s and 1850s and 9 percent in the 1860s. The statistics for Strasbourg are similar, though literacy in French was higher there. In Strasbourg, apparently, officials did not permit signatures in Hebrew on civil marriage documents. Hence, in the 1820s, 61 percent of the mothers of the bridal couple and 17 percent of the brides could not affix their signatures to the marriage document, compared to 9 and 12 percent in the countryside, where Hebrew signatures were allowed. Similarly, 11 percent of both the fathers and the grooms could not sign the marriage register in Strasbourg in that period; in the countryside less than 1 percent of the fathers and 2 percent of the grooms could not sign. By the early 1860s literacy was almost universal among males in Strasbourg, Colmar, and in the countryside and among females in Colmar, but 7 percent of brides marrying between 1850 and 1862 in Strasbourg and 9 percent in the Lower Rhine countryside were illiterate, as were 25 and 36 percent of their mothers, respectively. At a slightly later date (1866), by comparison, less than 1 percent of all the men and only 2 percent of all the women in the Department of the Lower Rhine were unable to sign their marriage documents.[17]

The degree of acculturation can also be measured by the adoption of French names among the Jewish population. That, too, was a gradual process, especially in the case of men's names. Because a man's name was used in religious ceremonies, as when he was called to the reading of the Torah in the synagogue, there seems to have been a greater tendency to retain Hebrew names for males. Even before emancipation, however, women's names reflected the fashions of the non-Jewish milieu. Traditional Yiddish names and names of biblical origin are "Jewish names." Thus "Jacob" and "Lipmann" were treated as Jewish names, "Jacques" and "Léopold" as French names, "Rachel" was listed as a Jewish name, "Rachelle" as a French name. Marriage records were the most reliable source of information since persons generally listed their legal names, as well as the names they assumed at marriage, but census data were also helpful

Changes in naming patterns were gradual and late in developing. As with many other indices of social change, there was a disparity in the pace of adoption of French names between the countryside and the city. A high proportion of Jewish men living in villages and small towns retained traditional names. In fact, there was only a slight decline in Jewish names between the cohort born in the 1770s and 1780s (76 percent Jewish names) and that born in the 1830s (69 percent Jewish names). Only in the 1850s and 1860s, as the census data indicate, was there a shift from Jewish to French names.[18] French names for women, however, both in the countryside and in Strasbourg, prevailed well before the Revolution. The use of Jewish names fluctuated during the nineteenth century but did not decline significantly in the countryside until the 1830s. (See table 5.2.)

Some individuals changed their names As early as the 1820s in Niederroedern a Baruch had become Barthelme; his bride, Hindel, had restyled herself Anne Fromet Weill, living in Haguenau, had renamed herself Flore by the time of her marriage in 1834. Though illiterate, Sohrle Klein had adopted the more fashionable Sara. Such name changes, however, are rare in the marriage documents.[19]

The persistence of Judeo-Alsatian and of traditional Jewish names for men reflects a more pervasive pattern of cultural conservatism among Jews in the countryside. Indeed, pre-emancipation attitudes and behavior survived among village Jews into the last third of the nineteenth century, embedded in the continuity of their socioeconomic role in the countryside and in the powerful bonds of Jewish communal life. This cultural conservatism paralleled similar patterns among rural Alsatian Christians.[20]

Popular religious custom flourished throughout this period. In his study of Alsatian Jewish folklore, Freddy Raphael noted the popularity among Alsatian Jewish villagers of a South German "miracle worker," Rabbi Seckel Loeb ben Yehudah Wormser, the Baal Shem of Michelstadt (1768–1847). When faced with illness or other dangerous situations, Alsatian Jews would visit the Baal Shem to solicit protective talismans. They often hung his picture in their houses.[21] Other local rabbis, such as Reb Yohanan of Obernai and Reb Aron Lazarus of Schirhoffen, were well known as cabbalists. For medical complaints, village Jews would consult local faith healers, like Reb Moshe, the wise man of Uttenheim, much as peasants turned to Christian healers [22] The traditional *shul klopfer*, who beat upon the wooden shutters of Jewish homes to summon their inhabitants to services in the synagogue, like the wonder-working rabbi, remained a familiar aspect of popular religious life beyond the middle of the century. Edouard Coypel describes the practice as current in 1876, and Simon Debré traces its decline to the half-century before his book was composed in the 1930s.[23]

Other popular customs were common among Alsatian Jews. Like their Christian compatriots, Alsatian Jews were no strangers to the nuptial charivari, a ritualized melee enacted as part of village wedding festivities. In 1823 the Consistory of Wintzenheim abolished "the established custom . . . by virtue of

TABLE 5.2
Traditional Jewish Names among Jews in Countryside (in percentages)

Date of Birth	Males	N	Females	N
1770–89	76	27	29	49
1790s	73	84	23	64
1800s	74	104	36	100
1810s	70	111	40	101
1820s	78	82	38	82
1830s	69	48	25	67
1840s	69	191	15	165
1850s	64	114	11	132
1860s	52	63	20	41

which young bachelors demanded or rather extorted certain sums of food and drink from the newlyweds."[24] That formal ban was of limited success, for in *Couronne* Alexandre Weill describes at mid-century the persistence of a Jewish nuptial charivari: "It is the custom in Alsace that . . the fiancée offer all the young girls of the village a collation composed of fruit cakes, sweets, and gentle liqueurs while the groom, if he is of the same village, treats all the young men to drink. This custom is so de rigueur that the young persons, without being invited, come on their own to the house of the fiancée to pay their compliments and seat themselves at the table."[25]

There is no indication that the consistories interfered with a less public ritual—a magic ceremony recited in a combination of Judeo-Alsatian and Hebrew for the purpose of drawing a high number in the draft lottery and thereby escaping army service. Here a traditional ritual was adapted to the new circumstances of citizenship. Since there was no effective means of avoiding the military draft, resort to religious magic persisted. At midnight the young man would light a lamp with olive oil and, promising to make a charitable contribution, would recite in a combination of Judeo-Alsatian and Hebrew the prayer for exemption. This prayer invoked the aid of Rabbi Meir Baal Hanes, a second-century rabbinic sage. At the time of the drawing of lots, the candidate would three times call upon the angels Michael, Gabriel, Uriel, and Raphael for their beneficent protection. One extant version of this prayer is signed and dated Strasbourg 1857.[26]

In the nineteenth century patriotic themes appeared in some Alsatian Torah *wimpels,* and some Jews incorporated the French flag and their conscription number in traditional decorative plaques (*shiviti* plaques), which also called upon the four angels for their protection.[27] Although bourgeois Jewish leaders promoted army service as a sign of Jewish patriotism, ordinary Jews, like their Christian countrymen, preferred that their sons do without that particular honor. In Léon Cahun's tales of rural Jewish life, Chmoul, an observant man living in a tiny hamlet, tells his son, "The profession of soldier is the profession of an assassin."[28] Traditional attitudes toward army service are found in the Judeo-Alsatian dialect, which used the term *rek* (empty, or poor one) to refer to a soldier.[29]

Traditional usages may have persisted, in part because village Jews had no higher status group into which they might assimilate. On the level of popular custom they were already acculturated; many of their practices paralleled those of the Gentile peasantry (though Jews did not consciously look to the peasantry for social acceptance). Alsatian Jewish folk art, too, reflected embeddedness in the Alsatian milieu, with local crafts and images adapted for specific Jewish usage. So Jews used painted bouquets of flowers in the Alsatian style for their *mizrahim,* the plaques placed on the eastern wall to indicate the appropriate direction for prayer, and decorated Torah scrolls with the same paper flowers that Alsatians attached to their hats when they wore the regional headcovering, as during the lottery ceremony. Jews also purchased prints of biblical scenes designed by Alsatian Christian lithographers for the local Christian market and adapted for the Jewish customer by substituting a Hebrew caption for the Latin one. When historians speak of assimilation, too often they assume that it is assimilation into the bourgeoisie. When dealing with the social changes that have occurred among most Jews in the past century and a half, it is crucial to qualify the general term "assimilation" by considering such factors as urbanization, secularization, or embourgeoisement as central to the processes of change.[30]

Traditionalism was most pronounced in religious observance. In spite of some references in Jewish newspapers to indifference among the young,[31] Jewish life in the countryside continued to be regulated by the Jewish calendar. Sabbaths and holidays were observed with pomp and extensive preparation. The connection of religious ritual to family life exercised a conservative influence.

Synagogue attendance was widespread and regular. In some towns synagogues were expanded or new ones built to accommodate the number of worshippers.[32] Daniel Stauben wrote of the observance of the penitential services before the New Year: "Whosoever arrived in Wintzenheim at three o'clock in the morning during *selihot* [penitential prayers recited before the

New Year] would already find the population up and on the way to the synagogue."[33] Describing his childhood in Ingwiller in the 1870s and 1880s, Edmond Uhry commented, "In my time, Jewish religious observance in our country was along a line of most rigid orthodoxy."[34] Customs like *capores*, transferring one's sins to a chicken on the eve of the Day of Atonement by swinging the live chicken over one's head, continued in the villages, even as acculturated bourgeois Jews regarded the practice with horror.[35]

The piety of Alsatian Jews was evident from their behavior as well as the decor of their homes. Several sources mention that Alsatian Jews regularly built a *sukkah* (booth) and used a *lulav* (a ritual object composed of a palm frond and myrtle and willow leaves) to celebrate the festival of Tabernacles In a textbook of moral lessons, a story set in the fall includes this passage: "In all the Jewish homes of Bionville, everyone was busy decorating the tents covered with branches under which the Jews take their meals during this . . holiday"[36] Mizraḥim and basins for the ritual washing of hands were fixtures in the home.

Traditional concepts of Jewish solidarity continued to command loyalty in the decades following emancipation. Although nineteenth-century Jews have often been pictured, somewhat polemically, as acquiring a national French or German identity at the expense of a Jewish consciousness which transcended international boundaries,[37] Alsatian Jews continued to express a sense of shared fate with their brethren They regularly collected money for the support of the Jewish community in Palestine. Indeed, an entire network of officials (*gabbaim*) who collected donations flourished in the Alsatian villages. Although these officials often pleaded local poverty as an excuse for disappointing results in their fund-raising efforts, they never discounted the importance of their obligation to their fellow Jews in Palestine.[38] In spite of efforts by consistorial leaders to stem the flow, Alsatian Jews, as we have seen, welcomed the wandering poor on Sabbaths and holidays. When the progressive Jewish press suggested terminating all charity as a means of solving the social problem of itinerant beggars, a village rabbi rejected the proposal with explicit references to traditional Jewish concepts of social responsibility and philanthropy. Rabbi Debré also remembered from the days of his childhood the uninterrupted visits from morning to evening of the "arme leut" (poor people), who knew they would be fed.[39] In 1840 the victims of the Damascus blood libel also found their place in the *Memorbukh* (memorial book) of the Jewish community of the Lower Rhine town of Haguenau, along with European Jewish martyrs dating back to the Crusades. The Jews of Haguenau used a traditional form of commemoration to express their sense of continuity, their identification, with both the martyrs of Damascus and, along with them, the Jewish victims of persecution throughout the ages. The Memorbukh was not just a legacy of the past; it also served a present need and was a gift to the future.[40]

In 1845 Rabbi Samuel Dreyfuss of Mulhouse, recognized as a progressive in the Alsatian rabbinate, acknowledged the importance of a transnational Jewish identity in his discussion of the need for liturgical conservatism: "There exists today as ever a universal synagogue, whose symbols, customs, and prayers are the same in all corners of the world, that makes all the Jews of the world one single family. That unity must be conserved at all costs, it has served us too well in bad times, and certainly it will never be French rabbis who harm it. The prayers must be the same for Jews of all countries."[41] In a pastoral letter of 1856 Salomon Klein, grand rabbi of Colmar, expressed a similar view: "Religion . . . forms the mysterious and providential link of this great family of Jacob dispersed throughout all the corners of the earth. The religious interests of French Jews do not differ from, cannot differ from, those of the other Jews of the world."[42]

The folk customs associated with birth, marriage, and death remained firmly entrenched in the countryside, though they were often modified in the cities. In this preservation of folk tradition rural Jews resembled their Christian neighbors. Alsatian Jews used amulets and hung incantations on the wall of a woman in childbirth to keep away such evil spirits as Lilith, described in one incantation as "the first Eve." They continued to observe the "Wachnacht," the vigil held the night before the circumcision of an infant boy.[43] The "Hollekreisch," the lively birth celebration which took place on the first Sabbath that the mother returned to the synagogue, did not disappear until the eve of World War II.[44]

Popular rituals also accompanied marriage. A circle was drawn around the bridal couple to ward off evil. Brides customarily cut their hair short and tucked it under a bonnet which bore a black velvet bandeau to simulate hair.[45] In 1844 the reformist *Archives israélites* angrily related the story of a young bride from Paris who had married in Mulhouse and had decided to wear her own hair. "Since then, she is no longer received by her husband's family."[46] At a consistorial hearing in 1847 the grand rabbi of Strasbourg accused the rabbi of Haguenau of banning women who showed their hair after marriage. Thirty years later, the custom of the *shterntikhl* (decorated hair covering) had fallen into disuse and was found "only in the depth of the countryside among the elderly." Wigs became popular and replaced the velvet band for those who covered their own hair.[47]

Alsatian Jews also rigorously followed the elaborate mourning ritual. A *hevra kadisha*, a society to care for the dead, washed the body and prepared it for burial, dressing it in the traditional *sarjenes* (white shroud) or, if a woman, in her bridal veil. In the countryside the entire Jewish population of a village turned out for a funeral and marched in disarray behind the coffin, which was borne by porters, just as their Christian neighbors did. Consistorial leaders tried to regulate these "chaotic" outdoor processions as late as 1860, feeling that they lacked the dignity appropriate to the occasion.[48]

The Yiddish will of Yeckel bar (son of) Yitzchak Schwartz of Balbronn in 1871 reflects traditional thought.[49] It began with the phrase "after my death and while I am being lain in the ground" and included seven provisions for the mourning period. Schwartz stipulated that alms in an amount based on the numerical value of the letters in his Hebrew name be distributed to the poor during his burial. He asked that a rabbi teach a chapter of Mishnah in the house of mourning on each of the seven days that followed the burial. The donation for this task and for the funeral eulogy added up to the numerical value of the word *tefilin* (phylacteries). In his will Schwartz requested that a candle burn constantly during the next thirty-day period of mourning, and that prayers be recited and two rabbis teach special lessons in the synagogue in his memory for the rest of the year of mourning. The second rabbi would also deliver a homily when Schwartz's children erected his cemetery monument on the anniversary of his death. Schwartz specifically asked that a *minyan* (quorum necessary for prayer) be present on that occasion. He concluded his will with a request that his children be good and united and say *kaddish* (a memorial prayer) for him whenever possible. (The prayer is traditionally recited in the synagogue at the three daily services) Thus, Schwartz drew upon the traditions of charity and sacred study as he conceptualized ways to memorialize himself and acknowledged at the same time that his children and community had to be reminded of the proper way to observe his death.

Cultural conservatism reigned in other areas as well. The observance of *kashrut*, the dietary rules, appears to have been taken for granted, particularly since Jews dominated the meat trade in the region In 1854 it was noted that the Jewish students at the lycée in Strasbourg, a population that might have broken with tradition, managed to find kosher food.[50] A decade earlier, the *Archives israélites* had reported a bizarre incident. The murderers of a young Jewish couple in Mutzig were apprehended because the victims' observance of kashrut enabled the police to determine the precise time of the crime· Mrs. Levy had last been seen salting her meat at 9·00 P.M., and the meat, which should have been removed after an hour, was still in the salt when the bodies were discovered the next day.[51] And in 1863 an Alsatian Jewish vintner received a certificate in Hebrew attesting to the kashrut of a barrel of white wine, vintage 1861.[52]

Because most of the Jewish population of Alsace followed the Jewish calendar and pursued occupations which did not compel them to change their religious practices, the climate was congenial to continuity. Moreover, as late as 1870 most of the rabbis of the region remained traditional in outlook Some, like Loeb Sarassin, who served for thirty-six years as a respected rabbi in Ingwiller while supporting himself in commerce, were never formally appointed by the consistories. The oldest formally recognized rabbis had been trained before the modern Ecole Rabbinique had been established in 1830. Twenty of the thirty-eight consistorial rabbis and *ministres-officiants* serving Alsace in 1864 had been born before 1812 and had therefore received much or all of their education under the traditional system of private study or in *yeshivot* (schools for higher Talmud study), often in Germany.[53] Even many of the younger rabbis had only a superficial knowledge of secular culture.[54] The low salaries paid rabbis who served in small communities—typically 1,100 francs in 1864—attracted only men with limited social aspirations and those whose education restricted their opportunities in other parts of France.[55]

For the most part, rabbinate and constituency were well matched in their social and religious attitudes at mid-century. Some traditionalist rabbis suspected secular education. Seligmann Goudchaux, grand rabbi of Colmar, declared in a speech in Blotzheim in 1844, that the absence of a modern school in the town was a boon, for it served no useful purpose to have one.[56] The same year the local rabbi in the small Lower Rhine town of Muttersholz forbade the students in the Jewish school from studying secular subjects with their heads uncovered.[57]

Even a relatively progressive rabbi, like Arnaud Aron, refused to accede to each and every request simply because it was made in the name of progress. In 1840 he refused to authorize swimming lessons on the Sabbath for the apprentices of the Society for the Encouragement of Work among Indigent Israelites of the Lower Rhine, though the author of the request was none other than Achille Ratisbonne, scion of the wealthiest Jewish family of Strasbourg and a champion of rabbinic flexibility[58]

The few rabbis in the countryside who saw it as their mission to lead their congregants to what they defined as a more noble and dignified concept of Jewish religious practice met with considerable resistance One of the more militantly progressive Alsatian rabbis, Moïse Nordmann of Hegenheim on the

Swiss border, failed throughout the 1840s to abolish the sale of honors in the synagogue In 1847 he conceded with regret that 95 percent of the Jews of Alsace supported the staunchly traditional views of Rabbi Salomon Klein, then of Durmenach. Klein was the dynamic young leader of the conservatives in the Upper Rhine who viewed with alarm all changes in customary practice, although they did not reject emancipation.[59] Yet, even Nordmann, who served as permanent part-time rabbi in Basel, reacted with displeasure to the introduction in the local synagogue of a stained glass window reminiscent of church decorations. In an 1850 letter to Rabbi Salomon Ulmann, chief rabbi of Nancy, asking for advice about the window, Nordmann claimed that had he been consulted he would not have approved its installation. The traditionalist *Univers israélite* reported in 1850, with reference to Colmar, that even the progressives went "regularly to synagogue, have introduced no changes contrary to our dogmas and traditions, observe[d] the Sabbath . . . [and] raised their children religiously."[60]

The Alsatian situation thus differed substantially from the German scene. There, as Steven Lowenstein has pointed out, young university-trained rabbis took their first pulpits in villages and small towns, where they often introduced reforms in ritual along with new models of behavior.[61] In Alsace, by contrast, the rabbis were a conservative force. This difference between the German and the Alsatian situation derives from two factors: the broader general education of the younger generation of German rabbis and the restrictions the Prussian state, in particular, placed on urban efforts at reform.

In rural communities traditional institutions existed alongside the synagogue and the consistorial administration. The most important communal institution of sociability for Jewish men in the countryside remained the ḥevrot, the associations established for philanthropic and educational purposes, rather than the formal arms of the consistory. Traditional Ashkenazi communities generally supported a number of ḥevrot, ranging from those dedicated to study of rabbinic texts to the *ḥevrat gemilut ḥasadim* that tended the sick and the most prestigious society, the ḥevra kadisha, that cared for the dead There was also a female ḥevra kadisha that sewed shrouds and prepared the female dead for burial.[62]

Within the ḥevrot Jewish men of modest means or youths might enjoy a measure of honor and participate as equals in religious study. Although the consistories seldom mention the ḥevrot, marginal references in consistory records, attacks by the reformist Jewish press, and occasional minute books of ḥevrot that have survived confirm the existence of these organizations A letter from the Central Consistory to the departmental consistories of November 20, 1862, regarding whether members of ḥevrot had the right to vote in consistorial elections, illustrates, though, how the consistories tried to regulate these independent associations. "It goes without saying," the letter declared, "that the associations or Hebrot which have a purely religious or philanthropic purpose and *which are approved by the consistories* confer electoral rights on their members."[63]

Ḥevrot were an important communal resource for village Jews. In 1828 a ḥevra in Belfort, composed mostly of young men and the newly married, complained to the Central Consistory that its members, who were donating a Torah scroll to the synagogue on Pentecost, were denied their request to read the Torah on that day because on such occasions the young were denied all religious honors. To ensure peace and stability and because of the religious motivation of the petitioners, the Central Consistory advised the Colmar Consistory to accede to the wishes of the members of the ḥevra.[64] In describing the civic consciousness of the Jews of Bischheim, who came to the aid of their Gentile neighbors when a fire broke out on a Saturday morning in 1845, the *Univers israélite* mentioned in passing that almost all the Jews "were then meeting in various *confréries* (ḥevrot) to hear, as the ancient custom would have it, words of morality and religion."[65]

In 1847 *L'Ami des israélites* printed a letter from the village of Duttlenheim in the Lower Rhine, which offered mocking criticism of the ḥevrot The correspondent admitted that these associations were quite common in Jewish communities and were frequented not only by fathers of families but also by young men, meeting together to discuss the interpretation of a passage of the Bible or Talmud. What offended the correspondent was the lively gossip that engaged the attention of the participants more than the Torah study as well as the warm welcome accorded to wandering preachers with their "subtle dialectic," their "useless knowledge," and their "sterile mind games." The writer, a member of the Consistory of the Lower Rhine, suggested banning wandering *maggidim* (preachers) and the consistory's taking over the ḥevrot in order to teach the Jews of the countryside the moral and religious truths of Judaism.[66] The rabbi of Mutzig (Lower Rhine) supported these suggestions, noting with reference to the maggidim that "the saddest thing is that this trivial charlatanism amuses the majority of the people, who applaud these 'masterpieces' and become accustomed to listening only to those preachers who . can make them laugh."[67]

The statutes and account book of the Chevras Shocharei Hatov (Association of the Seekers of the Good), founded in Riedseltz in 1837, illustrate the functions of a hevra.[68] Established by married men and unmarried youth who bound themselves to its regulations, the society fulfilled needs of religious piety, philanthropy, and sociability. The members of this hevra promised to have a Torah scroll written and to meet weekly for Torah study, which was to be conducted without disturbance. They agreed to pay monthly dues, to appear appropriately dressed in the synagogue, to stay in their seats until the end of the service (through the Aleinu prayer), and to fast on the eve of the new month. They would spend the nights of Shavuot (Pentecost) and Hoshana Rabba (the seventh day of Tabernacles) in study, as custom dictated. Representatives of the association would attend all local funerals and would stand watch at the bed of a sick member If a member or one of his relatives died, at least two members of the society would be present at the ritual purification of the corpse and would follow the body to the cemetery. On happy occasions, such as their marriage or the circumcision of a son, members were required to make specified contributions to the society's treasury. Finally, members were forbidden to go to any dance of Gentiles or to dance at all during traditional mourning periods of the Jewish year.

Each infraction of these regulations incurred a fine. Indeed, the account book of the society, which extended through the 1840s, is replete with fines.[69] Members were fined most frequently for failing to fast monthly, for skipping religious services or study sessions, for falling asleep or laughing during either, and for dancing with a Gentile woman ("getantz mit eine shikze"). (Village Jews were clearly sufficiently integrated into their local milieu to attend dances organized by non-Jews, the society's stipulations notwithstanding.) One member incurred the attention of the fine assessor for having danced in too lively a fashion. The fines enabled the society to raise money for its charitable endeavors and permitted members to indulge in harmless violation of acceptable norms, knowing they could atone for their infractions by paying a fine. Those fined for dancing with Gentile women, for example, were generally "repeat offenders." The account book gives a glimpse of the behavior and social norms of Jews in one Alsatian village in the 1830s and 1840s.

The local institutions and social structure reinforced traditional practice and shaped the identity of Alsatian Jews. It is not surprising, then, that there was popular resistance to the efforts of the urban elites, who wielded power in the consistories, to reform the governance of local synagogues. The post of commissaire surveillant was the source of conflict The consistory's delegate to the local community, the commissaire surveillant headed the consistory-appointed commission that chose local religious functionaries and supervised the communal budget and the collection of taxes. As the historian Phyllis Cohen Albert has pointed out, "The relationship between the communities and the consistories was based on necessity and characterized by hostility."[70] Hundreds of letters and petitions of protest against commissaires surveillants were submitted to departmental consistories and the Central Consistory, and some were even published in the press.[71] The Strasbourg Consistory, whose progressive lay leadership closely monitored its member communities, was the target of numerous protests, at least in part because of the cultural gap between the consistorial leadership and village Jews

The consistorial leadership saw in the commissaire surveillant a potentially progressive influence on populations that seemed backward to them. An 1830 letter from the Administrative Commission of the Strasbourg Consistory to its parent body, the departmental consistory, about replacing a commissaire surveillant asserts that the post must be filled "to maintain order within the Temple. But," continues the letter, "we must not deceive you as to how delicate the choice is and how it demands discernment. By virtue of being the head of our administration, his opinions and his approach must be as close to our own views as possible. . . . It seems to us that your choice must fall on a man of moderate character, endowed with some education and zeal for the general welfare and whose religious sentiments are in no way exaggerated."[72]

With these qualifications and the fact that the commissaire surveillant was often imposed from above, it is no wonder that protests erupted. In 1820 the residents of Wissembourg had complained to the Strasbourg Consistory about the "arbitrary conduct" of the commissaire surveillant and asked that a new administrator be chosen "from the bosom of the community."[73] In 1844 the popular opposition of the Jews of Rosheim to a tax imposed by the commissaire surveillant led that functionary to deny both synagogue honors and the use of the *mikveh*, the ritual bath, to his opponents.[74] That year members of the community of Sélestat railed against the "despotic power" of the commissaire surveillant, who had dismissed the beloved local cantor, had regulated hours of prayer, and had controlled the distribution of honors in the synagogue. Two years later the same commissaire surveillant was denounced for denying one local matron access to the ritual bath, thus depriving her and her husband of their conjugal rights. The consistory supported the commissaire's right to refuse synagogue honors and the use of the mikveh and accused the petitioners of ingratitude to its official, "who has introduced dignity in the divine service." Denied satisfaction, the recalcitrant Jews forwarded their petition directly to the

Ministry of Justice and Cults.[75] Similar incidents occurred in the 1850s and 1860s, and the consistorial leadership did not always emerge victorious In the towns of Bischwiller and Wissembourg local elites retained the upper hand, as the consistory acknowledged with some regret.[76] As late as 1867 the Ministry of Justice and Cults reported to the Central Consistory that it had received a petition from the Jews of the Lower Rhine town of Reichshoffen, threatening that the commissaire surveillant, an outsider imposed upon them, "would be rejected by the immense majority of the members of the community." When the matter reached the Senate, the Strasbourg Consistory yielded to the complainants by appointing seven of them to the local administrative commission.[77]

Traditionalist Jews registered their protests in other ways as well. In June 1846 a petition signed by 123 Jews from the Department of the Lower Rhine and by other Jews from individual communities in both Alsatian departments was sent to the Central Consistory. The petition expressed opposition to the circular of that March, which had solicited from candidates for the post of grand rabbi of France their attitude to nine proposed articles of religious reform. The petition stated:

> The undersigned . . basing themselves upon the authority of more than three hundred of the most distinguished rabbis of Europe, among whom are a large number of French rabbis, declare their formal opposition to all the reforms sought to be introduced in Judaism. They hope that the Central Consistory will not desire to produce a schism in our religion; and will not seek to deprive us of that precious liberty of conscience that we obtained only after long centuries of persecution That which our ancestors were able to maintain despite their persecutors throughout centuries of intolerance and barbarism, we will not allow to be removed by our coreligionists in an era of liberty and emancipation [78]

In 1858 an observant Strasbourg Jew protested the ruling of the Strasbourg Consistory that his son could not read Torah in the synagogue because he had not participated in the new ceremony of religious initiation, which was limited to boys and girls who had received a modern religious education.[79]

Under the vigorous leadership of Salomon Klein, who became the grand rabbi of Colmar in 1850, the Consistory of the Upper Rhine became the center of organized resistance to consistorial reform. The Consistory of the Lower Rhine, which had a progressive rabbi as its steward from 1834 on and a number of enlightened urban notables in its lay leadership, promoted social change By contrast, the Colmar Consistory, especially after the expansion of the franchise in consistorial elections in 1844 and the introduction of universal male suffrage in 1848, stood firm against concessions to the "spirit of the age." The Upper Rhine became the setting for conflict between traditionalists and progressives.

Even the more moderate rabbis of the Upper Rhine opposed the cavalier spirit of reform emanating from Paris, which they felt was accompanied by disdain for the sensibility of local congregations. Led by Rabbi Samuel Dreyfuss of Mulhouse, in 1840 they publicly declared themselves in opposition to the continued naming of commissaires surveillants by the departmental consistory. They believed that this policy was responsible for the regular conflicts in the communities, because the consistory was not familiar with the needs of the towns and villages. Moreover, espousing freedom of religious belief in support of tradition, these rabbis spoke out for local congregants who feared the consistory and its rabbis and the power they had to regulate the length of religious services and to modify both ritual and liturgy. "The signatories believe," declared the rabbis firmly, "that even with the consent of the grand rabbis, these modifications cannot be accomplished without causing injury anew to the conscience of the majority of the faithful in France."[80] Although they favored "amelioration of the cult," including abolishing the sale of honors, these moderate rabbis expressed concern for retaining the respect for tradition and for the legitimate fears of the Alsatian population.[81] Breaking with the Archives israélites of Paris, the first French Jewish newspaper and one that described itself as the promoter of "progress in matters of religion," Dreyfuss and his colleagues established a journal for the dissemination of their policy of "moderate progress," the Lien d'Israël, which was published from 1855 to 1861.

More powerful than these moderate forces were the conservative Rabbi Salomon Klein and his followers. They organized the electorate of the Upper Rhine and dominated, particularly after 1848, the departmental consistory until Klein's death in 1867, in spite of the government's evident preference for their progressive opponents. During consistorial electoral campaigns the traditionalists attacked both moderates and progressives in pamphlets published in Hebrew and Yiddish.[82] Since the departmental notables were, for the most part, wealthy men whose fortunes were derived from commercial pursuits in the countryside rather than new industrial ventures, they were susceptible to the arguments of the traditionalist party. They saw the reforms of the consistory as an attack on hallowed religious practice.[83] The traditionalists of the Upper Rhine were suspicious of all the projects of the progressive camp. For example, when under the control of the traditionalists the Consistory of the Upper Rhine refused to lend its support to the Ecole Israélite d'Arts et Métiers in Mulhouse, founded by Léon Werth, a wealthy progressive textile industrialist from

Ste. Marie-aux-Mines, who championed vocational education and agricultural training for Jews.[84]

In 1846 traditionalist rabbis in Alsace and Lorraine organized a petition campaign protesting the Central Consistory's polling of candidates for grand rabbi. Although Grand Rabbis Seligmann Goudchaux of Colmar and Lion-Mayer Lambert of Metz were the formal leaders of the campaign, the petition may have been drafted by Salomon Klein, for its rhetoric was similar to that of his sermons.

The petition campaign expanded on a pastoral letter, circulated by Rabbis Goudchaux and Mayer in response to the Central Consistory's questionnaire of March 31, 1846, designed to ascertain the position of candidates for the grand rabbinate on issues of religious reform. The four propositions of the pastoral letter asserted the immutability of both the written and oral law and of all regulations introduced into Judaism to safeguard the law.[85] Large numbers of privately trained rabbis, who were not recognized by the consistory and whose status was threatened by the strengthening of consistorial authority under the Ordinance of 1844, served as the troops of the petition campaign, traveling from village to village to arouse opposition to the Central Consistory's latest assault on the Jewish tradition and to collect money and signatures. On April 23, 1846, the traditionalist party convoked a meeting in Colmar to which Jewish communities from both departments sent representatives. A commission of the two departments, headed by Grand Rabbi Goudchaux of Colmar, was established to carry on the campaign against the Central Consistory. A deputation was sent to the grand rabbi of Strasbourg to urge him to convoke a rabbinical conference. He had, however, already sent to Paris a message, signed by all the rabbis and notables of the department, which expressed disapproval of the Central Consistory's questionnaire and advocated the selection of a traditionally minded grand rabbi. The traditionalists continued to collect signatures on their petition, ensuring the defeat of the progressive candidate for grand rabbi. The voice of the Jewish masses of Alsace spoke for too great a proportion of French Jewry to be ignored.[86]

The following year Rabbi Klein, then only thirty-three years old and serving in Durmenach, emerged as the most articulate spokesman of the traditionalist cause. In the *Univers israélite,* the organ of the conservative forces of French Judaism, established in Paris in 1844 in opposition to the *Archives israélites,* he published a sharp critique of the speech delivered by the president of the Central Consistory at the inauguration of the new grand rabbi, Marchand Ennery, former grand rabbi of Paris and a moderate traditionalist. In particular, he took exception to the president's statement that the belief in monotheism was the fundamental aspect of Judaism. This doctrine, Klein observed, was shared by many faiths. Rather, the essential element of Judaism was the immutability of the law, the omission of which "could compromise the entire practical religion of the Jews."[87]

In a guest sermon delivered in Paris and later published, Klein eloquently defended traditional Judaism, a faith that imposed upon its followers the great responsibility of serving as a priesthood for all of humanity. Powerful nations had disappeared from the earth, but Judaism had survived because it emanated from God, the divine legislator. It was, therefore, "the only example of stability in the midst of so many vicissitudes." Because of its divine origin and because it was the first to teach fraternal love and justice and concern for the poor and the weak, Judaism merited the continued respect of its adherents: "No, Israel," Klein declared, "your religion has nothing to envy in philosophy or other religions." In this sermon Klein, who had mastered classical philosophy as well as rabbinics, responded to popular criticism of Judaism by claiming that Judaism did not teach scorn and hatred of humankind and that Israel's separation from all other peoples had been necessary to preserve for humanity the truths of Judaism. Now, in an era of tolerance and prosperity, Klein concluded, Jews must not destroy that "which time and misfortune have respected and [must not] remove with a bold hand a stone from the imposing edifice of Judaism."[88]

In 1850 Klein succeeded Goudchaux as grand rabbi of Colmar, easily defeating Rabbi Dreyfuss of Mulhouse. At the same time traditionalists swept the elections for lay members of the Colmar Consistory.[89] The *Archives israélites* commented on these elections by noting that it had fewer subscribers in the entire Department of the Upper Rhine than in any city with a major Jewish settlement in the rest of France.[90] As an activist Klein continued to promote traditional conceptions of Judaism through pastoral letters and sermons, occasionally addressing not only his own jurisdiction but also all the grand rabbis of France.[91]

In 1856, when three progressives were elected to the departmental consistory, Klein publicly opposed their administration and traveled throughout the department speaking and raising funds for his own special project, an Ecole Talmudique in Colmar. Upon the arrest of one of his elderly followers for insulting the local rabbi in Wintzenheim, who had eliminated a number of prayers from the penitential selihot services, Klein appeared in court on behalf of the defendant and chastised the rabbi for not having followed his instructions As we shall see, the conflict between Klein and the progressive laymen on the consistory became so heated that both the Central Consistory and the Ministry of Public Instruction and Cults became involved in restoring order in the district.

Klein also emerged as a staunch defender of traditional Judaism on the larger European scene. Addressing himself to an audience steeped in traditional Jewish learning, throughout his life he engaged in polemical attacks upon proponents of reform and of the critical study of Jewish sacred literature. His first Hebrew pamphlet, *Ma 'aneh Rakh* (A Gentle Reply), written in 1846 when he was the rabbi of Durmenach, defended the efforts of his colleagues Goudchaux and Lambert to organize the Jewish populace against reformist tendencies. To Klein the reformers were men who "struck with the sword of their tongue all the words of the Torah, our legacy from Sinai. . . And the affliction has spread, for many of the poor of the land believed their words."[92] Citing traditional sources to prove the immutability of the Torah, Klein argued that human capabilities are fallible: "I have brought proof that we cannot make changes in religion, for we cannot know when we have been put to the test . . . for we are human and we have eyes of flesh while the ways of God are higher than ours and of his secret wisdom we can know only what He will let us know, and He will teach us from His Torah."[93] In response to the claims of Reform ideologues that change had been a permanent feature of Jewish life, Klein devoted the bulk of his pamphlet to refuting apparent contradictions in both biblical and rabbinic literature. As for the argument that no one form of Torah, written and oral, was ever accepted by all Jews, he could only respond. "Clearly, there is no need to reply to these words. . . . The defender of his soul will stay far away from them."[94]

In 1861 Klein again picked up pen to alert the Jewish world to the dangerous implications of a major work of German Wissenschaft des Judentums scholarship, Rabbi Zacharias Frankel's *Darkhei HaMishnah*, the first critical analysis of the sources of the oral tradition. Klein knew that modern critical scholarship was one of the tools of German Jewish reformers, and he no doubt feared that French Jewish reformers, who followed German events closely, would draw upon Frankel's work to legitimate their own efforts. In a pamphlet that was designed as an open letter to the scholar S. Y. Rapoport, Klein defended Samson Raphael Hirsch's criticism of Frankel. Hirsch had attracted Rapoport's ire particularly because Hirsch had written in German and hence had aimed at a popular rather than scholarly audience. Like Hirsch, Klein believed that Frankel's work undermined belief in the sanctity of the oral law. Justifying his initiative in writing to one of the internationally recognized scholars of his time, Klein fell back, with feigned humility, upon the rationale of the need to serve God and his truth· "Now let us debate together, your eyes see that I speak to you in the holy tongue and if I am small and you are great did not [God] . . . speak His words to Jacob. to the small and the great shall you listen."[95]

Later that year Klein published *Mipne Koshet,* a larger work that offered a full-scale critique of Frankel's work [96] In it he noted that he wrote at the request of "some men, learned in Torah and lovers of faith, anxious for God's word [who sought] my insignificant opinion about the trumpet sound of war heard in the Hebrew camp in the land of Germany."[97] Klein's response was a fervent restatement of traditional Jewish concepts of the revelation of the written and oral law, in their entirety, at Sinai.[98] Frankel's deviance from tradition, in Klein's eyes, emerged in his conflicts with earlier authorities, and particularly in the fact that "he did not open his mouth to declare at the beginning of his work that the oral law derived its holiness from Sinai "[99] For Klein "the faith interpreted in *Darkhei HaMishnah* is far from the received faith And just as Karaites could not take a teacher from the Rabbanite congregation and the Rabbanites from the Karaites, because they were different faiths, so those who believe in the tradition received from our fathers cannot take as a guide to the way of God anyone who . . . accepts the Oral Law as interpreted in *Darkhei HaMishnah,* for their religions are different."[100] In this argument Klein followed the separatist path of his colleague Samson Raphael Hirsch and revealed the lack of conciliatory spirit, which ultimately prevented him from becoming the grand rabbi of France

Klein forcefully rejected the reformers' concepts of intellectual progress, to wit, that "only in our day did the sun of wisdom spread her wings over all the land . . . ; we are as wise men and the Talmudic sages as infants who have not seen the light."[101] Rather, Klein saw around him a decline in Jewish learning and in the search for truth: "Now the ignorant are many and those who desire to know God and thirst for His words are few . . . , for the houses of study have ceased in Israel, wherein could be heard the whistling of the flocks, the holy flocks who were diligent at the doors of the Torah. Secular learning has become essential and our holy Torah secondary and relegated to a corner."[102] For Klein the progress of enlightenment and emancipation was as potentially dangerous from a religious point of view as it was beneficial from an economic or social perspective.

Although Klein's death at age fifty-three removed the most articulate defender of resistance to religious reform from the Alsatian stage, the Alsatian rabbinate, like most of the Jewish population, remained deeply committed to tradition. Even those who championed the cause of dignity and beautification of religious practices—the first step in reform and a sign of the adoption of prevailing bourgeois aesthetic standards—did so with the caveat that such changes must not violate Jewish law.[103] Traditional religious observance in 1870 remained widespread in the countryside, where the majority of Alsatian Jews still resided. Indeed, Klein's strength had derived from his ability to speak for the masses and to mobilize them, through petition campaigns and, after 1848, through their electoral clout.

In spite of these traditionalist tendencies, some innovation in religious practice and in social customs had occurred. Klein's comments about the substitution of secular learning for Torah study are very much to the point. The dominant theme of Alsatian Jewish culture in the nineteenth century was continuity and stability, but forces were set in motion that stimulated change, and particular segments of the Jewish population were most susceptible to those forces. Emancipation was not directly responsible for significant socioeconomic and cultural adaptation on the part of Alsace's Jewish population, but political emancipation made it possible for Alsatian Jews to take advantage of those economic and social trends that ultimately led to the modernization of Alsatian Jewry.

SIX

Migration

Although many factors contributed to the persistence of pre-emancipation socioeconomic and cultural patterns among the Jews of Alsace, powerful countervailing forces promoted acculturation, social mobility, and the reshaping of Jewish identity and practice. The cultural conservatism of rural Jewish communities was initially reinforced, and ultimately disrupted, by one important consequence of political emancipation—migration. Migration occurred in stages. The elite and ambitious were the first to leave the villages and small towns of their birth By 1870, however, migration appeared attractive even to the less adventuresome. To the Jews of Alsace, who in the past had been restricted in their rights of residence, geographic mobility was the most significant benefit of emancipation. They could now move wherever they chose in pursuit of prosperity.

And move they did, within the province as well as to other parts of France and abroad. The 1872 census revealed that at least 34 percent of the Jews living in Paris had been born in Alsace and Lorraine.[1] Still, as a result of high fertility and the immigration of Jews from German states, the Jewish population of Alsace increased until mid-century. By 1863, however, the effect of outmigration became visible; the Jewish population of the Department of the Lower Rhine declined 8 percent in one decade from 22,806 to 20,861, and the Jewish population of the Upper Rhine increased by only 1 percent, from 16,547 to 16,719 (in 1861). The Jews became more urbanized as well: half of the Jews in Alsace lived in communes of more than 2,000 inhabitants and more than 13 percent of them lived in Strasbourg.[2]

The geographic mobility of Alsatian Jews was a regional phenomenon Migration and emigration were spurred by the enormous population growth, the inability of a newly industrializing region to keep pace with the demographic explosion, and the parcellization of rural lands. By 1861 the Alsatian population, which had numbered between 600,000 and 700,000 on the eve of the Revolution, had expanded to about 1,093,000 The Jewish population had also grown, though at a slower rate, from an estimated 22,500 to 37,655. This growth led to urbanization and emigration. Thus, from 1854 to 1863, 80 percent of Alsatian Jewish communities located in villages and small towns (with populations under 5,000) declined in population, paralleling a similar decline in communes of that size.[3]

In the half century after Jews were granted mobility by Napoleon, Alsatian Jews, like other Alsatians, participated in three streams of migration. The smallest contingent left France to seek their fortunes abroad. Five percent of the children of Alsatian Jews who left estates in the 1850s and 1860s had settled in foreign countries, with the United States the most favored, though by no means the sole, destination.[4] Alsatian Jews helped to establish California's Jewish community during the Gold Rush, became merchants in the American Midwest, and populated the emerging Jewish settlements of South America. Aron Dreyfus, born in Wissembourg in 1791, made his fortune as a businessman in Rio de Janeiro before returning to France to settle in Metz, where he purchased a house for 12,500 francs in 1855.[5] Jews from all social classes emigrated from France. Aron Dreyfus, for example, was the son of a merchant and sometime butcher. An 1837 government list of emigrants from the Lower Rhine explicitly revealed, however, that the rural poor predominated. The list included twenty-six Jewish household heads (with twenty-four dependents), who were for the most part peddlers, brokers, and artisans. They took with them an average of 273 francs per person, as compared with 571 francs per person for all the emigrants from the department in that decade. Sixteen of the twenty-six were emigrating alone. Although there are no systematic studies of general Alsatian migration in this period, the information available suggests that poverty and rapid population growth also spurred the migration of Christian Alsatians out of the province in considerable numbers. Between 1828 and 1837, for example, 14,000 emigrants departed from the Lower Rhine for America. Other emigrants headed for Algeria or for the city, whether Mulhouse or Paris.[6]

It even became explicit Jewish communal policy to encourage the poor to emigrate. The Committee for the Amelioration of the Jews established by the Strasbourg Consistory in 1853 offered financial assistance to emigrants. It abandoned this approach after several years, however, because of the lack of sufficient resources.[7]

The majority of Alsatian Jewish migrants remained within France, indeed within Alsace Marriage records and notarial documents suggest that between 1820 and 1870 one-third to one-half of the Jews of Alsace relocated at least once.[8] Migration was a phenomenon of youth; it was most likely to occur before marriage or for the purpose of marriage. Women were more likely to migrate (at least regionally) than men, since they tended to settle in their husbands' domicile. Although 35 percent of the male heirs at mid-century had left their parents' domicile, 53 percent of their sisters had done so.[9] All of the Alsatian members of Jewish mutual aid societies in Paris in the 1860s, except for one, had arrived in the capital when they were under the age of forty.[10]

The experiences of the Uhry family of Ingwiller in the Lower Rhine demonstrate the migration patterns of Alsatian Jews in the second half of the nineteenth century. Edmond Uhry's paternal aunt, Leah, married the local schoolteacher and relocated with him to Obernai, a Lower Rhine town of more than 5,000 persons, before settling in Strasbourg, where two of her sons opened a large wholesale business in cotton and linen goods and upholsterers' supplies. His paternal uncle, Isaac, left Alsace to become a lycée teacher in Bordeaux On his mother's side, his aunt Sara married a man from Wintzenheim (Upper Rhine) and emigrated with him to the United States. Another maternal aunt, Rosalie, moved to the village of Romanswiller (Lower Rhine) to marry a prosperous cattle dealer. Both of his maternal uncles, whom Uhry describes as failures, remained in Ingwiller, although one emigrated to Brooklyn after the German conquest of Alsace.[11]

Alfred Dreyfus's family history, too, illustrates how migration opened new opportunities to ambitious Jews. A dealer in secondhand goods and a small-scale moneylender, Dreyfus's grandfather Jacob had amassed sufficient capital by the mid-1830s to move from his native town of Rixheim (Upper Rhine) to the city of Mulhouse, where he and his only son Raphael became merchants. In 1841, three years after Jacob's death, the twenty-three-year-old Raphael married another young Jewish migrant, Jeanette Libmann, a seamstress and the daughter of a butcher from the town of Ribeauvillé. Working as a traveling commission agent, in this case a broker for textile manufacturers, and lending money at interest, Raphael Dreyfus shared in the prosperity of the Protestant textile industry of the city and, after two decades of saving, succeeded in establishing his own thriving textile firm. As the major center of Alsatian industry, Mulhouse offered three generations of the Dreyfus family a bustling market for the entrepreneurial skills they had honed in the countryside.[12]

In their origins, if not the magnitude and speed of their socioeconomic

TABLE 6 1
Geographical Origin of Grooms by Size of Birthplace, 1820–1862

Population	Groom Migrated (%)	Total Sample (%)
Less than 2,000	34	37
2,000–5,000	31	45
5,000–50,000	11	5
More than 50,000	4	8
Foreign-born	21	6
	N = 105	N = 463

mobility, Alfred Dreyfus's forbears were typical. Since most Alsatian Jews were village and small-town dwellers, it is not surprising that more than two-thirds of the migrants came from villages and towns of less than 5,000 persons. Migrants, however, were disproportionately recruited from towns and cities of 5,000 to 50,000 residents, where urban skills were more likely to be sharpened and communal ties were more relaxed than in the villages. (See table 6.1.)

There were fewer migrants from Jewish communities with the highest concentration of Jews (more than 25 percent of the total population). In those communities, one might posit, the bonds of communal feeling and constraint were so strong that migration was discouraged. (See table 6.2.)

Most striking, though, is the difference in socioeconomic status between the migrants and their stationary brethren. Both the migrating grooms and their parents were two to three times as likely as the nonmigrants to come from the highest economic strata; conversely, they were far less likely to be at the bottom of the Jewish socioeconomic scale, plying their wares in the traditional Jewish street trades of peddling and dealing in secondhand goods. In this the migrants differed from those who emigrated abroad. (See table 6 3)

TABLE 6 2
Jewish Population Density of Groom's Place of Birth, 1820–1862

	Groom Migrated (%)	Total Sample (%)
Less than 3% population	10	9
3–10%	33	18
10–25%	43	50
More than 25%	15	23
	N = 105	N = 463

TABLE 6 3
Socioeconomic Status of Migrants vs. Nonmigrants, 1820–1862

Groom's Occupation	Groom Migrated (%)	Groom Stationary (%)
Bankers, professionals, wholesalers	18	6
Merchants	36	41
Commercial agents, employees	18	21
Artisans	18	11
Peddlers, street traders	9	19
Unskilled laborers	2	2
Rentiers, students, unemployed	1	1
	N = 148	N = 454

The migrant grooms were almost twice as likely to be artisans or to enter commercial employment as the nonmigrants. (The migrant grooms of category 3 were mostly settled employees; the nonmigrants in that category were mostly petty brokers) Part of this disparity can be attributed to the economic differential between city and village, but even migrants who settled in towns no larger than those they left were more likely than their stay-at-home brethren to assume new economic positions. Moreover, a disproportionate number of the parents of the geographically mobile grooms were from the highest status rankings and surprisingly low numbers were peddlers and street hawkers. (See table 6 4.)

Furthermore, although Alsatian Jews as a whole had a high rate of literacy, the migrants tended to be even more literate, especially in French, than the stationary Jews. They also married later, at a median age of 32.4 years, compared with 28.8 years for the stationary grooms.[13]

These differences between the mobile and the stationary suggest that a combination of success in the village economy and high aspirations stimulated migration. Or, to put it another way, upward social mobility preceded migration for the majority of those on the move. Although there were some poor regional migrants, in the countryside migrants were often recruited from the elite who were attuned to new economic possibilities (which they sought to maximize whenever possible). In this pattern of upward social mobility preceding migration, the Jews of Alsace were similar to the Jews of Germany in the nineteenth century. As Steven Lowenstein has shown, the ambitious vanguard of German Dorfjuden (village Jews), already exponents of urban culture, took the lead in the mass urbanization of German Jewry.[14]

TABLE 6 4
Migration and Socioeconomic Status of Groom's Fathers, 1820–1862

Father's Occupation	Groom Migrated (%)	Groom Stationary (%)
Bankers, professionals, wholesalers	11	6
Merchants	51	42
Commercial agents, employees	12	24
Artisans	10	6
Peddlers, street traders	9	18
Unskilled laborers	4	2
Rentiers, students, unemployed	4	1
	N = 107	N = 432

The lists of members of the college of notables from both the Lower and Upper Rhine demonstrate the phenomenon of elite migration. In 1828 only seven of the twenty-five notables of the Lower Rhine and eleven of the twenty-two notables of the Upper Rhine were living in their place of birth.[15] It is also significant that those who followed the most traditional Jewish economic patterns, that is, peddlers and their children, were underrepresented among the migrants. People who chose this traditional Jewish occupation seem to have been less likely to break with the customary and confront the changes necessitated by migration.

This phenomenon of elite migration from the villages is confirmed by a letter from the Administrative Committee of the Jewish community of Bischheim in response to a request for a donation from the Society for the Encouragement of Work. The community could not support such a charge, the letter stated, because its "most heavily taxable [members] have just left our community to fix their domiciles in Strasbourg."[16]

Although these conclusions are derived primarily from data on mobility within Alsace itself, Doris Ben Simon-Donath's analysis of the Parisian Jewish population in 1872 reveals that Alsatian-born Jews living in Paris were remarkably similar in socioeconomic profile to the migrants who remained in the eastern provinces.[17] (See table 6.5.)

Like them, the migrants in Paris had broken with traditional patterns of Jewish economic activity and entered artisanry and commercial employment. The larger number of proprietors and rentiers among the Parisians can be attributed to the difference in age structure between the two populations. The sample of Alsatian grooms, with a median age of 32, would necessarily contain

TABLE 6 5

Socioeconomic Profile of Jewish Migrants: Alsace and Paris

Occupation	Regional Migrants (%)	Migrants to Paris (%)
Proprietors and Rentiers	3	8
Liberal and superior professions	6	7
Independent commerce	48	35
Employees	20	19
Artisans, skilled labor	12	20
Street trades, unskilled labor	11	11
	N = 107	N = 1,825

Source for Migrants to Paris: Doris Ben Simon-Donath, *Sociodémographie des juifs de France et d'Algérie* (Paris, 1976), p. 150

fewer elderly heads of household living on investments and pensions Alsatian Jewish migrants in Paris were, however, more likely to engage in artisanal trades and less likely to be independent merchants, in part because of the opportunity structure of the Parisian economy.

Alsatian Jews not only contributed to the rapid growth of Paris's Jewish community; they also spurred the development of new communities in the provinces. In 1861 twenty-five of the fifty-five male Jews in Lille eligible to vote in consistorial elections were originally from Alsace.[18] By 1868 the descendants of Jews who lived in Alsace during the ancien régime were dispersed in forty-two departments.[19]

In their socioeconomic profile Alsatian Jewish migrants, both those who remained in the region and those who relocated in Paris and other French cities, differed substantially from non-Jewish migrants in France. Although the general overpopulation of Alsatian villages spurred the migration of Jews, they were not peasants who had been forced from the land as were most of the Gentile migrants. Many were recruited from towns of substantial size. Moreover, even those who lived in rural communes had some experience with the workings of a commercial economy. When they reached their destination, Jewish migrants joined the commercial sectors of the urban economy. By contrast Gentile migrants swelled the ranks of the urban working classes. Jews were similar to other regional migrants, though, in their tendency to migrate in family groups; women were equally represented among the migrants, even in long-distance internal migration Siblings, too, often migrated together. Thus, in Strasbourg, at least 20 percent of the Jews had close relatives within the

neighborhood. This element of solidarity of kin and *landsmen* (persons originating from the same place), which was a feature of French regional migrants
in general, enabled Jewish migrants to flourish in their new locations.[20]

The consequences of elite migration were considerable for Alsatian Jewry
Although migration spurred social change and acculturation in the cities, it
removed potential agents of change from the countryside and hence retarded
economic, religious, and cultural innovation. The patterns of cultural conservatism described in chapter 5 are thus related to the structure of migration.

Voluntarily uprooted from small traditional communities, the Jews who
moved to towns or cities were freed from the constraints of social disapproval
that prevailed in village society. The city permitted a measure of social ano-
nymity to its new inhabitants. Often more adventuresome than those who
stayed put, migrants may also have been predisposed to experiment in social,
cultural, and religious behavior. The Alsatian Jewish storytellers Daniel Stauben
and Léon Cahun both write of the deleterious impact upon traditional ways of
life of migration to the large city. Cahun's hero Anselme, the village schoolteacher, stops attending the synagogue regularly when he settles with his family
in Paris, though he continues to celebrate Jewish festivals and the anniversary of
his parents' death. In Cahun's words, "Now . . . the bonhomme Anselme feels
that he has left the narrow circle of the Jewish community to enter in the great
French family."[21] Moving into a new environment in the city, migrants could be
tempted to create themselves anew. Cahun writes mockingly of the successful
scion of a simple Alsatian Jewish family, an employee in a large commercial
house, who returns home to Alsace for a visit. "The monsieur from Paris," notes
Cahun, "has even changed his name: he no longer responds when he is called
Isaac; at present his name is Gaston. . . . When he is addressed in Alsatian, he
answers in French."[22] Stauben expresses his longing to immerse himself once
more "in this simple life, the last vestige of a civilization which is disappearing.
In Paris . . . for us transplanted Alsatian Jews, the customs of our ancestors, alas,
are too quickly reduced to memories."[23] Such rapid adaptation to a new locale
suggests that the oft-noted traditional piety of Jews in Alsace can best be
characterized as "milieu piety," a type of cultural behavior that is not based
upon ideological conviction but is intimately linked with the entire social fabric
that sustains a culture.[24]

Although both Stauben and Cahun describe migrating to Paris, and are
writing in a nostalgic vein, the effect of moving to such cities as Strasbourg and
Mulhouse, though less pronounced, was similar. Indeed, a non-Jewish and not
particularly sympathetic observer of Jewish practices in Alsace in the 1860s and

1870s, Edouard Coypel, noted that in the cities Jews were more sensitive to Gentile opinion and introduced changes in their funerals, for example, "so as not to present too great a contrast to Gentile customs "[25] Similarly, in his study of Judeo-Alsatian humor, Rabbi Simon Debré, writing of his childhood in the 1860s, commented that the Jews in the villages remained observant while those in the cities had not.[26] Although the distinctions between city and countryside cannot be entirely explained by migration, the newness of the urban settlements contributed to the undermining of traditional custom. The phenomenon is more striking in new urban communities composed of immigrants from abroad, such as London in the Georgian period and American cities in the years of mass immigration,[27] but the nonideological assimilation that accompanies migration was visible in the urban Jewish centers of Alsace as well.

Generalizing from the example of Alfred Dreyfus's grandfather, who migrated from Rixheim to Mulhouse in the 1830s, and from the evidence of pervasive hostility and sporadic violence against Jews in the Alsatian countryside, Michael Burns has argued that Jews flocked to the cities as a response to the anti-Semitism of the years 1819 through the early 1830s.[28] Yet the data drawn from a broader sample of the Alsatian Jewish population do not confirm such an hypothesis. A significant proportion of the migrants relocated from one village or town to another of approximately the same size in the countryside; in doing so they would not have escaped from the animosity of the peasantry. More important, with the exception of 1848, there appears to be little correlation between periods of anti-Semitic tension and violence and Jewish migration

Although popular anti-Jewish sentiment in Alsace was high from 1819 through 1832, migration did not begin in any significant way until the 1830s. It continued through the Second Empire, accelerating in the late 1850s, a period of social calm. Membership lists of two Jewish mutual aid societies of Paris, dating from 1866, which include the place of birth of their members as well as the date of their arrival in Paris, indicate that most of the Alsatian members had arrived in the 1840s and 1850s, though a few migrants from the 1820s and 1830s were also represented [29] The pogroms that accompanied the Revolution of 1848 did lead to an influx of Jews from the countryside into Strasbourg. The Strasbourg community wrote the departmental consistory in the summer of 1848 that it planned to deny religious honors during the high holidays in the fall to all male Jews whose dues were in arrears. That, it declared, was the only way to "constrain . . Jews from the countryside who have come to establish themselves here . . . so as not to be obliged to contribute to the fees of worship."[30] This movement appears to have been temporary, however, as the size of Jewish communities in the countryside did not decrease appreciably until a decade later. Of seventeen sites of anti-Jewish riots in 1848 in the two Alsatian departments (where population figures were available for 1840 and 1851), only three Jewish communities decreased in size during that decade and six grew by more than 10 percent. The generation that suffered the greatest measure of post-emancipation popular anti-Semitism did not flee the countryside; most Alsatian Jewish communities continued to grow into the 1850s. Whatever their disappointment that emancipation did not confer full social equality, village Jews seem to have found the local hostility tolerable

Only in 1864 did the *Archives israélites* take notice, favorably, of "the movement that is pushing the Jews to quit the countryside of Alsace." According to the newspaper, this should be encouraged because "in the countryside alone, our coreligionists, fatally pushed toward peddling, dealing in old clothes, and petty trade, form a population apart in the midst of farmers. In the city, in contrast, they find all the facilities for devoting themselves to the manual, industrial, and liberal professions "[31] Contemporary observers seem to be accurate in attributing the urbanization of the Jews of Alsace to economic factors; insofar as we can evaluate the motives of the migrants, anti-Semitism seems not to have played a central role. In the absence of a body of memoir literature, the demographic evidence suggests that the search for broader economic opportunities stimulated the migration of Alsatian Jews. The sample of grooms who married in the Lower Rhine between 1820 and 1862 confirms these contemporary impressions; the greatest percentage of migrants was found among the marriages after 1850, in spite of the fact that violence against village Jews seems largely to have spent itself in the revolutionary unrest of 1848. Although migrants were also slightly overrepresented in the 1820s, they were distinctly underrepresented during the July Monarchy. The lure of the city clearly grew after mid-century.

Although Alsace is renowned in the history of modern French Jewry as an exporting province, it also received Jewish immigrants during the nineteenth century. Of the 112 migrating grooms in my sample from the Lower Rhine, 20 percent had been born abroad and were now domiciled in the department. Germany accounted for more than two-thirds of the foreign immigrants with others originating in equal proportions from Switzerland, Bohemia, Austria, and Poland. Of 41 migrating grooms marrying in Colmar, only 3 were from abroad, from Baden, Latvia, and Holland, respectively. In both departments a small proportion of the migrants (11 percent in the Lower Rhine marriages and

5 percent in Colmar) had been born in French provinces other than Alsace and had settled in the east.[32]

Strasbourg and Mulhouse in particular were communities of migrants. Although never the seat of the Consistory of the Upper Rhine, by mid-century Mulhouse had the largest Jewish community in the department. Its Jewish population had grown from 163 in 1808 to 1,224 in 1851 and 1,527 in 1853, when it constituted more than 5 percent of the energetic industrial city of 30,000. By 1866, 1,939 Jews made their home in Mulhouse. As early as 1838 the Central Consistory sought a raise for the rabbi there on the grounds that the cost of living was very high because Mulhouse was "a city of industry . . . which incessantly draws a considerable number of foreign businessmen." Mulhouse's Protestant elite, nonsectarian public elementary school, and Jewish artisan trade school attracted young Jews eager to make their fortune in congenial surroundings. An 1844 report in the Archives israélites pointed to the unique qualities that attracted Jews to the city. It described Mulhouse as "the city where Jews devote themselves with the greatest ardor to honest industry and where religious tolerance is truly striking . . . Only there . . where an invasive clergy does not seek to dominate those of other cults is a [religiously] mixed school without danger." The statistics provided in 1851 by the departmental consistory also included the observation that Mulhouse had "a newly constructed magnificent synagogue."[33]

The largest city in Alsace, Strasbourg was the seat of the Consistory of the Lower Rhine and site of the largest Jewish community in the province. As a regional commercial hub and a center of French bourgeois culture, Strasbourg, like Mulhouse, was attractive to Jewish merchants and commercial agents. The Ecole de Travail, a Jewish vocational training school, and a first-rate lycée drew young Jewish men to the city. Strasbourg's Jewish population grew from 1,476 in 1808 to 1,628 in 1833. In the next two decades it increased by more than 30 percent, to 2,387 in 1854. The Jewish population mushroomed to 2,820 in 1863, making it the second largest Jewish community in France, after Paris; Jews constituted 3.4 percent of Strasbourg's total population. At mid-century more than 72 percent of the adult Jewish males and almost 75 percent of the females living in the city had been born elsewhere. Of the non-natives, about 70 percent of both sexes originated in the department, and another 10 percent in the neighboring department of the Upper Rhine. Almost 14 percent of the immigrant men and 11 percent of the immigrant women hailed from Germany and Switzerland.[34]

In 1858 the Lien d'Israël offered a sharp analysis of the complex of "push-

and-pull" factors that led to the extraordinary growth of Strasbourg's Jewish population in the 1850s In addition to what it called "ordinary causes," it listed a number of other specific stimuli of migration. "The troubles that burst forth in 1848 in several communities of Alsace occasioned, at that time, the emigration of a rather large number of families who came to establish themselves in Strasbourg, where the excesses to which they had fallen victim are happily not to be feared." To this political factor it added economic and cultural considerations. "The abolition of military replacement left many of our coreligionists out of work and compelled them to come to the big city to seek new means of existence. Finally foreigners tired of the worries to which Jews are still subject in some parts of Germany and in some cantons of Switzerland, heads of family, desirous of attending to and supervising the education of their children who are taking courses either in the Faculty [of the university] or in our excellent lycée, have also come to settle among us."[35]

The regional migration, and particularly the urbanization, of Alsatian Jews in the middle of the nineteenth century enabled Jews to apply their skills in commerce where opportunities were greatest. By migrating to urban centers they also established contact with bourgeois society and its institutions, in their general and specifically Jewish manifestations. In particular, their children had greater access to new educational institutions that were designed to foster adoption of French culture and to instill the norms of citizenship Patterns of migration thus promoted the acculturation and social mobility of those Alsatian Jews who were on the move during the nineteenth century.

SEVEN

Education and
the Modernization
of Alsatian Jews

The emancipationist ideology promoted by bourgeois Jewish leaders of the consistories as well as by progressive French civil servants emphasized inculcating the values of productive citizenship into a new generation of Jews. They believed that education would shape a new Jewish identity, in which French national consciousness would be harmonized with Jewish religious sensibility. Following the doctrine of Napoleon's Sanhedrin, Jewish citizens would abandon their ethnocentrism and see their Gentile compatriots as brethren. Secular culture would become central to their lives, with traditional Jewish learning relegated to an ancillary position. Primary education, properly conceived and made available to the masses, would help young Jews realize the moral degradation inherent in the traditional Jewish occupations of petty commerce and would lead to their "regeneration." Finally, the establishment of modern Jewish schools would persuade Gentiles that a "new Jew" was in the making. Through education, then, the consistorial leadership believed that it would remake the consciousness, moral vision, cultural preferences, and occupational profile of Alsatian Jewry.

The attitudes of Alsatian Jewish elites toward education reflected the presumptions of their bourgeois Christian counterparts as well as late eighteenth- and early nineteenth-century Jewish debates, centered in the German Haskalah (Jewish Enlightenment movement), about the proper curriculum for the modern Jew. The Jewish notables of Strasbourg saw primary education as a moral and civic task, which would teach "the love of work, the habit of order and cleanliness. . . . [The graduates of Jewish schools would] struggle successfully one day against the degradation that awaited them." The consistorial leaders accepted the prevalent views of the nineteenth-century French bourgeoisie that moral instruction was crucial to creating self-disciplined citizens loyal to national rather than local popular culture [1]

Disciples of the Enlightenment, urban Jewish leaders saw the child as tabula rasa, to be molded in the proper direction. They touted education as the source of well-being. "Everything is flexible, is supple in the child," proclaimed one speaker, a physician, at the Jewish primary school in Strasbourg in 1824.[2] Jewish bourgeois leaders defined their task as particularly daunting because their clientele was culturally deprived and entered school speaking "that Hebraic-German jargon which offends the ears of every well-reared person."[3] They looked forward to the day when "the Jews of Lower Alsace can say to their fellow citizens: 'And we, too, have finally reached the standard of European civilization.'"[4] Like the leaders of the German Haskalah, they believed that secular education was essential to transform the Jew into a cultured human being

This far-reaching and ambitious program of social change through primary instruction ultimately attained many of its objectives, but it required a generation of efforts, initiated in the period of the Restoration and expanded during the July Monarchy. Only by bringing to bear the power of the state did consistorial leaders eradicate the popular resistance in the countryside, by both Jews and Gentiles, to their educational institutions.

In the villages of Alsace local Jewish schools and private tutors had traditionally taught Jewish children. Each Jewish community hired a teacher, a *melamed,* to provide its sons with a basic Jewish education. reading and writing in Hebrew, the study of the Bible, and, for the able, an introduction to Talmud and rabbinic literature. The language of instruction was Yiddish. The melamed's modest salary was paid by parents, supplemented by a communal subsidy for the children of the indigent. As a form of social segregation and as a badge of status, wealthier parents often hired private tutors for their offspring.[5]

This long-standing educational system had weathered both the Revolution and the Napoleonic period of reaction. Indeed, Napoleon's 1808 inquiry into the educational practices of Jewish communities had found that only 10 percent of Jewish children in Alsace were attending public primary schools.[6] Given the high degree of literacy of the male Alsatian Jewish populace,[7] the other 80 to 85 percent of Jewish males, it may be assumed, were educated under Jewish auspices, whether communal or private. Such was to be expected, for the public schools were, in essence, Christian schools, and Jewish parents suspected that their children, although exempted from religious instruction, would be indoctrinated with Christian dogma and perhaps lured away from the Jewish community.

In 1819, amid the public debate about extending Napoleon's restrictive anti-Jewish legislation, the Consistory of the Lower Rhine had voted to establish a model school in Strasbourg. Following the popular model of mutual education, in which more advanced pupils assisted the less able, the school was "destined for the instruction of everything connected with the knowledge of Religion, Morality, and the Holy Scriptures; of reading and writing in Hebrew, French, and German, and of a segment of arithmetic."[8] The children of the poor were to be admitted free of charge.

In 1820 the Strasbourg Consistory established a Cantonal Committee of Schools of the Hebrew Faith Although the Strasbourg school remained the center of the consistory's educational ventures, the Cantonal Committee followed the advice of the rector of the Academy of Strasbourg "to bring the Jews of this department to establish schools for their children"[9] and embarked upon a project of introducing modern Jewish primary schools in every commune with a Jewish population of at least 200 persons. It sought to shut down the old schools, the *ḥadarim,* and to organize new ones with a curriculum appropriate to the needs of emancipated Jews. To do so, it employed the power of state licensing combined with the power of the consistorial purse.

The Cantonal Committee's first goal was to replace the melamed with a qualified modern *instituteur.* Local melamdim, who had long administered their own schools, often held in their homes, faced two alternatives. A melamed who wished to receive a *brevet* (license) had to pass an examination testing his proficiency in French or German. Or he could declare his school to be limited to the study of Talmud and hence inappropriate for primary instruction. In practice most melamdim did neither. Lacking in secular education, they had no chance to pass a licensing exam. Yet they continued to run their schools not as specialized Talmudic institutions for those seeking a rabbinical career but as popular schools open to all Jewish children.

The Consistory of the Upper Rhine, which lacked a cadre of progressive notables such as existed in Strasbourg, had to be urged to address the issue of modern education. In December 1821 the Central Consistory wrote to Wintzenheim that it was pained to see that its earlier exhortations to establish primary schools had had no effect. The Central Consistory pointed out the civic and political benefits of such schools, "one of whose salutary effects would be to prove to the authorities and to your fellow citizens that you are making the greatest efforts to tear away the Jewish youth of your district from idleness and ignorance and to inspire them at an early age with the sentiment of their duty toward God, toward the fatherland, and toward society."[10] The last consistory to assume responsibility for modern primary schools, the Upper Rhine administration was still seeking advice on how to accomplish the task in 1826. The experience of Strasbourg served as its model.[11]

The survival of traditional Jewish schools, called "clandestine schools" by the Cantonal Committee, was a form of passive resistance to consistorial-imposed education. During the 1820s and 1830s complaints were repeatedly leveled against clandestine schools in such Lower Rhine communities as Zellwiller, Marmoutier, Dettlenheim, Bouxwiller, Bischheim, and Haguenau. Even after these schools were discovered, the committee found them difficult to close, for many parents preferred them to the authorized educational institutions. In 1823 the Consistory of the Lower Rhine remarked that "all clandestine schools [had] been closed."[12] Yet that conclusion was clearly premature. As the Cantonal Committee wrote in an 1826 letter to the rector of the Academy of Strasbourg, "Most communes have only 'rabbinical schools' [sic] that are not recognized and are led by ignorant masters who perpetuate their gross ignorance upon the generation which is coming to maturity. It is to these schools that poor Jews are constrained to send their children, while the more comfortable ones send them to Christian schools."[13] Indeed, Alexandre Weill attended a clandestine school in the early 1820s [14]

In Strasbourg the committee succeeded in prohibiting teachers of Talmud from accepting students who could neither read nor write—that is, primary students. It also stipulated that Talmud students must provide certificates attesting to their completion of their primary education in an authorized school. The committee recognized, however, that it was not possible to impose such a condition in the countryside, where there were "very few authorized schools."[15] Occasionally village Jews objected so strenuously to the imposition of a new schoolmaster that they physically abused him.[16] Even in Strasbourg enthusiasm for modern education was limited. In an 1831 letter to the Administrative Commission of the Strasbourg Jewish community, the Cantonal Committee lamented that only sixty children attended the Strasbourg school and attributed this to "the antipathy of our poor coreligionists for moral and religious instruction."[17] The elderly and traditional grand rabbi of Strasbourg, Seligmann Goudchaux, refused to oppose clandestine schools—a factor that led in 1834 to his forced resignation and relocation to Colmar.[18]

In 1831 the Cantonal Committee found a useful stick to supplement the carrot of free modern education. It proposed that charitable assistance be denied to parents whose children did not attend an authorized school.[19] Such rulings eventually became widespread in both Alsatian departments. For example, the 1861 regulations of the Israelite Charitable Society of Colmar included a provision disqualifying for assistance parents of school-age children who did not send their children to approved primary schools.[20]

In 1832 the Committee of Primary Instruction for the Schools of the Lower Rhine wrote to the minister of public instruction that only 17 of 110 Jewish communities in that department contained authorized primary schools. Of these, only 4 received municipal allocations. "To bring about the complete regeneration of the Jews of this department," added the committee, "it is urgent that youth who are for the most part delivered to the ignorance of Talmudic teachers receive a liberal education appropriate to our civilization And if local biases, ancient prejudices deny the Jews the necessary support for this patriotic task, a paternal government should accord it to them."[21] The following year it was estimated that the 17,568 Jews of the department included a (primary) school-age population of approximately 4,000 children. Of those, 365 were receiving a modern education. Twenty-six communes with more than 200 Jews were eligible for the establishment of municipally assisted Jewish communal schools.[22]

The Guizot Law of 1833 established universal—though neither compulsory nor free—primary education, with religious minorities entitled to their own schools. An 1833 government inquiry on its implementation found eight clandestine Jewish schools operating in Alsatian communes and four others of dubious status. Other clandestine schools probably escaped the inspectors' attention. There were authorized schools in twenty-three communes in both departments, with a total student population of approximately 800.[23]

The physical conditions of even the authorized schools left much to be desired. One inspector reported on the ten schools he visited in the Lower Rhine: "In most cases, there is no schoolroom, school is often held in the house where the teacher is lodged. The children are enclosed there in an unsanitary hole, lacking in furniture and horribly dark. Often they are even obliged to remain standing for the duration of the school The uncleanliness which reigns in these schools is extreme and often revolting."[24]

Although the better schools taught French, German, and Hebrew, arithmetic, religion, and geography, many had a limited curriculum, in part because of the modest educational accomplishments of their instructors, many of whom served their communities as *ministres-officiants*. In 1833 only two Jewish teachers in Alsace (in Strasbourg and Haguenau) had a first-degree license and none was a normal school graduate.[25] One inspector wrote of the curriculum of Jewish schools in his district: "Except for the schools of Wissembourg and Niederbronn, one can say that the others do not deserve the name of schools. Only Hebrew reading and writing are ordinarily taught there, and even in that language little progress is made. [Students] read poorly, without knowing the rules of grammar." Another inspector commented of one school in his district, "The children . . . learn nothing of what a French citizen should know." Still, the Jewish schools in Bischheim, Hegenheim, Durmenach, Quatzenheim, and Strasbourg earned the inspectors' praise, particularly for their success in teaching French.[26] In spite of their defects, the Jewish schools compared favorably, especially in the teaching of French, with Christian elementary schools, which were also of mediocre quality.[27]

The Guizot Law of 1833 in theory facilitated the establishment of Jewish primary schools by mandating local governmental subsidies for salaries and school buildings for primary schools of each religious denomination. To Jewish leaders seeking the acculturation of the Jews of Alsace, the law was a turning point. Simon Bloch, the editor of the short-lived Strasbourg newspaper *La Régénération,* wrote in 1836, "The law of June 28, 1833 was for us the dawn of a new life; one sees Jewish schools rising up in many places."[28] Yet, the law's implementation in Alsace was fragmentary. The Strasbourg Municipal Council had granted a subvention to the local Jewish school as early as 1826 and Louis Cottard, the rector of the Academy of Strasbourg from 1829 to 1847, was a strong supporter of Jewish primary schools.[29] Many village and town councils, however, were reluctant to support what they viewed as a pernicious form of Jewish separatism.[30] As the mayor of Sélestat wrote to Cottard in 1834, "The interest of the villages is decidedly opposed to the creation of special Jewish schools for Jewish children. The opening [of such schools] will only encourage the prejudice of their parents against the Catholic and Protestant population."[31] In 1843 the General Council of the Upper Rhine responded to calls for increased assistance to Jewish schools by criticizing the unwillingness of Jews to send their children to Christian schools.[32] Local councils, particularly in the Upper Rhine, regularly denied Jewish schoolteachers the subsidy allotted as a matter of course to their Christian colleagues.[33] Because of this local governmental footdragging, the Strasbourg Consistory in 1842 still deplored the conditions within many Jewish primary schools of the district.[34]

If elementary education in general was of mediocre quality, primary education for girls received little more than verbal support until the 1840s The

Jewish girls' school in Strasbourg, established in 1824, limped along for several years, unable to secure the necessary funding from the Jewish community. After its demise a new school for girls was created in 1844.[35]

During the 1840s Jewish primary education in Alsace became more established. Although town councils were still reluctant to grant subventions to Jewish schools, the government in Paris responded favorably to Jewish requests for assistance. Thus, in 1841 the minister of justice and cults strongly urged the minister of public instruction to provide the village of Odratzheim in the Lower Rhine with the communal teacher of their religion that the Jews had requested. Although sharing the popular image of Alsatian Jews as backward, uncultured, and unproductive, the minister used this stereotype to justify public expenditure of funds:

> This request seems worthy of your attention, and I cannot recommend it too highly to your benevolent interest; the information that I had the opportunity to collect on the moral and religious situation of the Jews of Upper and Lower Rhine is far from satisfactory; the state of degradation into which this part of the population has fallen seems to me to be attributable principally to their ignorance, to the vices which are the consequence, and to the resulting prejudices against them on the part of the rest of the population You know better than any .. the great influence which the benefits of instruction can exercise in similar circumstances, and you will agree with me that the best means to make the Jewish population leave its state of abasement and to quiet the unfortunate prejudices [against them] is to organize good schools in their midst where the children will acquire, along with the solid principles of a sane moral and religious education, the knowledge necessary for the exercise of useful professions [36]

The Central Consistory also used this approach in a letter to the minister of public instruction of December 8, 1841. In asking for equal fiscal treatment for Jewish schools in Alsace, the Consistory concluded: "The Jews of Alsace have been reproached for the slowness of their progress in moral emancipation. . . . In admitting that this reproach may be well founded in some respects, it must be recognized   that more than elsewhere the Jews [of Alsace] have been the object of scorn and almost of the hatred of their fellow citizens of other faiths. . . It did not suffice that the law proclaim equal rights for the bad habits which our Alsatian coreligionists had naturally contracted in the[ir] state of social inferiority to disappear."[37]

Sharing the French elite's view of the ultimate success of education in forming good citizens, the confidential report of 1843 by the prefect of the

Lower Rhine expressed a similar confidence that education would ultimately promote the acculturation of Jews and improve Christian perceptions of their Jewish neighbors. Among the Jewish urban middle classes the prefect found that "the liberal education that they generally give their children will activate [social] fusion: already a sizable number of young Jews who follow . . . a career in science and the arts are absolutely ignorant of the harassment of which, just a short time ago, they would have been the object on the part of their colleagues." Even in the countryside, where prejudices remained stronger, the prefect reported that "in many rural communes Jewish children attend Christian schools, and their rapprochement with Christian children brings about in the latter a more benevolent disposition."[38]

Rabbi Arnaud Aron's 1843 report on Jewish primary education in the Lower Rhine reveals the impact of government policy. He visited thirty communes, all seats of consistorial rabbis or possessing public communal schools (that is, the more important communes), and cited only four where the Jewish school had been refused assistance from the local municipal council and another three where government contributions were minimal. He singled out several municipal councils—Bouxwiller, Wissembourg, and Haguenau—for their generosity. Although there were considerable variations in the quality of the schools, Aron noted with some satisfaction that "the difference between the intellectual state of the Jews of the Lower Rhine ten years ago and now is immense." He pointed to the growing acceptance of the public school by Jews in the countryside and praised the many small, and poor, Jewish communities that had made enormous sacrifices for primary education.[39] That approximately 35 percent of the pupils in the Jewish schools were female also attests to acculturation, since girls had traditionally been accorded little formal instruction within the Jewish community.[40]

Great strides were made during the Second Empire. In 1846 there were only eighteen Jewish public communal schools in the 108 Jewish communities of the Lower Rhine. Several of the larger communities complained that the mayor, in refusing a communal subsidy, insisted that the Jews could attend Christian schools. In 9 small communities the children did attend the Christian *école communale* and studied Hebrew and religion in private lessons with the local cantor.[41] By 1854, 35 of 39 communes in the Lower Rhine with a Jewish population of more than 200, and hence eligible for a public school, had some type of primary school. Twenty-eight of these were écoles communales (public schools) and seven were private. In addition, 23 smaller Jewish communities boasted their own schools, of which four were communal and nineteen were private.[42] In 1847 these schools had 2,230 pupils, with an additional 450 Jewish children in the department studying in Christian schools.[43]

The Department of the Upper Rhine had a less meritorious record In 1851, 29 of 34 communities with a Jewish population greater than 200 had some form of Jewish school, and Colmar had two such schools. However, only 4 communes—Horbourg, Ribeauvillé, Biesheim, and Durmenach—had Jewish écoles communales.[44] Not until November 1853 did the Municipal Council of Colmar grant the status of école communale to at least one Jewish primary school. In 1857–58, 1,862 Jewish children were studying in recognized schools.[45]

With its self-consciously progressive bourgeois population, the industrial city of Mulhouse was unique in having a multiconfessional primary school (école publique mixte), founded in 1831. At the encouragement of their rabbi, Samuel Dreyfuss, the local Jews sent their children there. Indeed, Dreyfuss claimed in 1847 that "despite the passionate opposition of the hyperorthodox, the good sense of the majority of this commune has provided such a sanction to this new system that the creation of a special Jewish school would be considered a calamity." Not a single Jewish child in Mulhouse, he added, rich or poor, received less than five consecutive years of primary education. Moreover, Dreyfuss asserted that a mixed school conferred civic benefits not found in a Jewish school: "Children of different religions, placed from the most tender age side by side on the school bench, easily become accustomed to see themselves as comrades and equals and lose . . . those feelings of hatred and scorn to which our children have previously been exposed because they were set apart in a Jewish school."[46]

Mulhouse's example, however, remained unique in Alsace, where religious feelings ran strong. Secular culture was acquired through the Jewish primary school network, in an environment that cushioned the cultural shock of a traditional Jewish youngster confronting the glories of French civilization. In the 1840s the first Jewish graduates of the Ecole Normale of Strasbourg, the oldest in the country, and of the Ecole Normale of Colmar, took their places in the province's schools. The physical facilities of the schools also improved, particularly as public funds became more available. As early as 1847 Le Progrès, a Colmar newspaper, noted with satisfaction the growing interest of poor Jews in "social amelioration" and the consequent proliferation of Jewish primary schools. These schools were now flourishing, especially in Colmar, Mulhouse, and Sierentz, and were attended by "perfectly behaved children of extreme cleanliness and of enormously lively intelligence."[47]

The local Jewish schoolmaster, by the 1840s and 1850s often a graduate of a departmental normal school, had become a model of acculturation for Jewish youth. As Daniel Stauben described him at a social gathering, "He alone affected to speak French; he alone, amidst all this conversation, so confused, boisterous, and so unliterary, hazarded several observations about the sciences and letters. . . . He betrayed his social position through a prodigious emission of imperfect subjunctives. No doubt was left to me: I had before me the communal schoolmaster of the Jewish school of Wintzenheim."[48] Although Stauben's tone mocked the pretentiousness of the local schoolteacher, Salomon Klein, grand rabbi of the Department of the Upper Rhine, took seriously the obligations that were incumbent upon schoolteachers in his district. In a letter of 1858 to M. Vurmser, the Jewish schoolteacher in the village of Hagenbach, he chastised the unfortunate Vurmser for violating the norms of his profession. "You have now told me that you danced only with Madame Vurmser. You agree nonetheless that dance halls are not the sort of place that a schoolteacher should frequent, and even less a ministre-officiant [which Vurmser sought to become], especially if the ministre-officiant must dispel from his conduct everything that could give him the appearance of a spirit of frivolity."[49]

By the 1860s Alsatian Jews congratulated themselves on their progress Thanks to the joint efforts of the Strasbourg Consistory and the prefect of the Lower Rhine, the department had thirty-seven Jewish écoles communales in 1860. It sponsored special pedagogical conferences for Jewish teachers to promote professional development much as it did for Catholic and Protestant teachers.[50] Jewish students were welcomed in departmentally subsidized Christian public schools and in private Catholic schools, where they were said to constitute 20 percent of the student population.[51] Wealthier parents were most likely to enroll their children in private schools.[52] Mere prejudice contradicted by the facts, wrote one Strasbourg correspondent to the *Archives israélites,* led persons ignorant of the real situation to treat Alsace's Jews as backward.[53]

Simon Bloch, then editor of the traditionalist *Univers israélite,* waxed enthusiastic as he compared the desolate state of his Lower Rhine home village of Reichshoffen in 1835, when he left it, with its evident prosperity and culture in 1868, when he returned for a visit. In 1835 "there was no school, but a *heder* in a small and hideous room, without air and light, where boys and girls were piled up pell-mell and received a poor education from an old and impoverished *rebbe*." In 1868, in sharp contrast, the Jewish school in Reichshoffen was known as one of the best in the department. Its director was "a learned and enthusiastic professor." Its building was "vast and well laid out, the classroom magnificent and full of light." Furthermore, the local municipal council supported it generously Bloch expected much from the generation educated in that school.[54] The changes that Bloch celebrated reflected both the Jewish communal concern with education and the high degree of education achieved in general in the departments of eastern France [55]

As with all educational institutions it is difficult to assess precisely what the Jewish primary schools accomplished. Minimal literacy (signing their names in Latin script) among the Jews of Alsace did increase, as it had among all Alsatians. Except for women in the countryside, there was virtual universal literacy among the generation of Jews that attended primary school in the late 1830s and the 1840s. (See table 7 1.)[56]

Indeed, the consistorial inspectors of Jewish schools insisted upon serious attention to French. As the Cantonal Committee wrote to the director of the Jewish school in Haguenau in 1831:

> The French language, from what we saw, is somewhat neglected [in your school], it is considered only a secondary subject while it should be the basis of all elementary instruction Only the language of our country can make commerce with our fellow citizens easy and pleasant Therefore, apply yourself to inspire your pupils with a passionate love of this beautiful language, recommending its use both in school, where it must be spoken exclusively, and out of school. . . Pronunciation must also be carefully supervised; it is painful for us to see that the majority of pupils pronounce French with a Germanic accent [57]

Reflecting on the impact of secular education on the Jews of Alsace, Maurice Bloch wrote, "Do you know what infraction of discipline was considered the most serious at Strasbourg's Ecole de Travail? It was not speaking French. All the rigors of the regulations fell upon the unfortunate youth overheard expressing himself in the jargon of his fathers." In this approach consistorial leaders embraced an emancipationist ideology, identifying themselves not with the local population, most of whom spoke the Alsatian dialect, but with the urban bourgeoisie and with the central government in Paris, the source of pure French and the guarantor of Jewish emancipation. Jewish leaders seem to have been far more concerned with the Jewish masses' acquisition of facility in French than were contemporary Protestant or Catholic religious leaders in Alsace with regards to their constituents. No one among the Alsatian Jewish elites promoted German, rather than French, as the language of culture. Such was not the case among Alsatian Christian elites.[58]

TABLE 7 1
Ability to Sign Marriage Register in Latin Script

	Lower Rhine Villages		Strasbourg		Colmar	
	Groom (%)	Bride (%)	Groom (%)	Bride (%)	Groom (%)	Bride (%)
1820–39	73	42	89	83	96	44
1840s	90	63	100	86	95	90
1850–62	95	77	100	93	100	100

In addition to French, the Jewish schools taught moral and religious educa-tion. So important was religion in primary education that the Local Inspection Committee chastised Jonas Ennery, the director of the Strasbourg primary school, for failing to attend synagogue at least twice a week.[59] Although Hebrew was taught and prayers were recited in that language and translated into French, most religious instruction in the primary grades was conducted in French with consistorial-approved catechisms, books of moral lessons, and Bible stories. Indeed, an 1854 regulation promulgated by the rector of the Academy of Strasbourg, reinforcing a practice that derived from the earliest days of Jewish education in France, declared that only books approved by the consistory could be used for Jewish religious instruction.[60] There is no evi-dence that students were taught from traditional Jewish sources other than to read selections from the Hebrew Bible and painfully translate some passages into French. Students were not ordinarily introduced to rabbinic literature in the original, for Jewish educators of Haskalah bent had long considered the Talmud irrelevant to a modern Jewish primary education Unlike the Hebrew Bible, it was not a legacy shared with Christians.

The goal of religious education was to provide students with an outline of their obligations as Jews and as citizens. Although the catechisms and books of religious instruction were traditional in their acceptance of the immutability of Jewish law and in demanding adherence to that law,[61] they promoted an abstract philosophy of religion and did not succeed in demonstrating the links between observance of the law and the general goals of religion. In presenting Maimonides' Thirteen Articles of Faith, Rabbi Salomon Ulmann, later grand rabbi of France, defined the duties of a Jew as "the beliefs and practices that constitute Jewish life, the rules according to which God wishes to be adored by us."[62] The Jewish mission he promoted, however, was general in the extreme:

"God has charged Israel with the mission of preserving and teaching, in all its purity, the knowledge of God, one and unique, eternal, infinite, Creator of all that exists, exercising his justice and goodness toward all his creatures."[63] This statement, which could have been signed by any Reform rabbi, mandated no particular form of religious observance. Similarly, Rabbi Lazare Wogue of Paris, in his extremely free translation of a book of religious instruction written in Hebrew by the elderly Paris teacher L. Sauphar, defined his goals for youth in the following terms: "I wish to open [before youth] the vast field of faith and morality, the cultivation of which leads us to God, *that is, to truth and happiness* [words not included in the Hebrew original]."[64] Only the Alsatian school-teacher S. Hallel, in his annotated prayerbook *L'Encens du coeur* (Incense of the Heart), published in 1867 and endorsed by the Central Consistory for use in Jewish schools, explicitly addressed such ritual observances as phylacteries, and provided an explanation drawn primarily from Moses Mendelssohn, the eighteenth-century German Jewish philosopher and promoter of Haskalah (Jewish Enlightenment). "The ceremonial acts," he commented, "become a safety anchor for the Jewish religion. . . . [They] are a powerful means to support faith and to perpetuate in the nation the truths, virtues, and beliefs of which they are the symbol."[65]

As for the relations of Jews with the larger society, the approved catechisms promoted patriotism and civic rectitude and called upon young Jews "to unite our interests and our destiny to the common destiny and the general interests of the land in which we live."[66] Students were encouraged to display kindness, honesty, and charity toward their neighbors.[67] Ulmann also pointed out that during their army service Jewish youths could dispense with religious practices that conflicted with their military obligations. Jews were defined as forming a "religious society" in contrast to the civic and political society that had existed before the destruction of the Second Temple.[68] Hallel pointed out apologetically that the several daily prayers calling for the restoration of Jewish sovereignty in the land of Israel did not conflict with loyalty to France "as long as the celestial banner announcing this miraculous deliverance was not raised" and "in no way expressed contempt for French legislation or the virtuous judiciary in which we have had the good fortune to find equality of rights."[69] By reminding his readers that these prayers were, in any case, directed toward "that reign of universal justice which the prophets foretold," Hallel offered a universalist legitimation of traditional Jewish particularist sentiment.[70] The lessons of the catechisms found expression in the schoolmaster, who served as a model of dedication to Judaism and loyalty to France and its culture, a living example of the compatibility of acculturation and Jewish tradition. Although the Jewish normal school graduates sought to define their profession as distinct from the religious professionals in the community, the fact that in Alsace so many ministres-officiants continued to serve as teachers in Jewish primary schools blurred the distinction.[71]

The doctrine of integration and universal religious morality coexisted, however, with a different message, that of Jewish uniqueness and distinctiveness. As Wogue put it in *Gan Raveh,* "I wish [Jewish youth] to understand that a holy task is imposed upon it, to continue the traditions of our fathers, so that Israel may always be the great people, the protégé of God."[72] Hallel defined this holy task in terms of Jewish chosenness articulated in its modern nineteenth-century version, the mission concept: "This chosen nation must serve as a model for humanity; its mission is to shine with all the virtues exemplary for humanity and for social life, as well as with beliefs conforming to sound reason. . . . This distinction which is called the election of Israel, far from inspiring in us a foolish pride or pretensions of superiority with regard to [other] nations, on the contrary has imposed upon us the great and eternal obligation to serve as a perfect model for humanity."[73] To achieve that goal, the readers adopted by Jewish schools, in addition to teaching general moral lessons drawn from Jewish and French sources, contained brief biographies of exemplary Jewish personages, from Maimonides to Moses Mendelssohn, in whom young Jews might find a model.[74]

The teaching of a modernized version of the concept of chosenness seems to have stimulated ethnic pride. Auguste Widal [Daniel Stauben] remarked of the impact of one popular reader, *Les Matinées du samedi:* "From it . . . there crept into the minds of its young readers a double sentiment—for which the author must be thanked—a proper pride in race and a great love of the fatherland."[75] Even the *Archives israélites,* which sought both moderate reform and acculturation, recognized the retention of Jewish distinctiveness as a legitimate concern. In 1855 it printed an article calling for the intensification of Hebrew-language instruction in Alsace with the argument that "the preservation of the Hebrew language is the sole connection between Jews of all lands."[76]

For traditional Jews the religious instruction in primary schools was sorely inadequate It used few Jewish sources and by the 1840s was limited to two hours a day. This was compounded by the lack of advanced religious training for Jewish teachers available at the écoles normales of both Strasbourg and Colmar. Moreover, progressives were not committed to serious Judaic study for primary school students As one observer commented, "To instruct children

destined for the most part to devote themselves to labor or commerce, we do
not see the necessity for the teacher to be a master of Hebrew [un grand
hébraïsant]."[77] Licensed normal school graduates gained little knowledge of
Hebrew or Judaism in their three-year program. Not until 1857 was a professor
of religion and Hebrew appointed to the Ecole Normale of Colmar.[78] Even that
measure was found wanting, and in 1862 the Central Consistory petitioned the
minister of public instruction and cults, unsuccessfully, for the concentration of
all Jewish normal school students in one school to assure that they received
adequate religious instruction.[79]

The success of modern Jewish primary schools in changing educational
priorities may be measured in part by the reactions of traditionalists. By the
1840s traditionalists did not deny the value of secular education, but they
lamented the sorry state of religious education and began to organize a bet
midrash (institution for traditional Jewish learning). In 1845 the Univers israélite
reported that a "beth hamedrash" was established in Ingwiller, at the initiative
of the local rabbi and with the support of Jewish notables, "to raise religious and
theological studies from the deplorable decadence into which they have fallen,
due to lack of encouragement and support." The journal commented pointedly
that the Strasbourg Consistory was not involved although the consistory ener-
getically supported the Jewish vocational school (l'école de travail), where
young Jews could learn the trade of tailor or locksmith.[80] The Ingwiller
institution seems to have had little success. In 1856 the Univers israélite
reported that in Strasbourg "a great number of heads of families have turned to
the consistory to complain about the insufficiency of the religious instruction
which exists in our community and to ask the administration to remedy the
situation."[81]

In 1853, three years after announcing the project, Grand Rabbi Salomon
Klein opened L'Ecole Talmudique de Colmar, designed not only to prepare
youth for study in the Ecole Rabbinique in Metz but also to offer poor boys an
education and an opportunity to become teachers of religion.[82] The school was
all the more necessary since the traditional Talmud school in Sierentz had
closed with the death of Rabbi Jehoschuah Wahl in 1847.[83] Although Klein's
Ecole Talmudique was officially a preprofessional school, its founding was
intended as a statement about the importance of "talmud Torah" (traditional
Torah study) as a curriculum for Jewish youth and an appropriate focus of
consistorial educational activity. Since the school included some secular studies, it appeared to compete directly with other Jewish schools. Thus, the
Central Consistory argued in 1857 that Klein raised funds for "an Ecole

Talmudique which does not even have legal standing" while he refused to support the Ecole d'Arts et Métiers in Mulhouse, designed to "regenerate" impoverished Jewish youth by providing vocational training. In spite of the opposition of the Colmar Consistory, Klein also hung fund-raising appeals for his Ecole Talmudique within the Colmar synagogue.[84] Klein publicly argued that his school was particularly useful for poor youths, who would "find an opportunity to enrich themselves with the scientific treasures of our holy Torah and at the same time receive the necessary instruction in other fields which is demanded today."[85] Through the force of his personality Klein was able to keep the school afloat, despite consistorial opposition, for several years; ultimately, however, financial problems forced it to close.[86] Perhaps more effective were Klein's efforts to establish supplementary evening courses of religious instruction for youth in local synagogues in recognition, as one rabbi put it, of the threat posed by "la vie civile" to "la vie religieuse."[87]

In spite of these criticisms, most Jewish leaders were pleased with the results of Jewish primary instruction in teaching French, basic secular studies, and the fundamentals of religion and morality to Jewish children. Nevertheless, they believed that a radical regeneration of the Jewish poor depended not only on primary education but on a restructuring of their economic way of life. There had been a lively debate about the need to "productivize" Jews through introducing "useful professions"—that is, agriculture and industry—since the end of the ancien régime.[88] Consistorial leaders essentially agreed with Gentile public opinion that transformation of the Jewish economic profile was a fundamental aspect of the moral and civic education of the Jews. They did not apply the tenets of productivization to themselves, despite their overwhelming concentration in commerce, but they were eager to remake the Jewish lower classes to correspond with regnant social beliefs. Although a few called for agricultural training for the Jewish poor, the obvious impracticability of this approach led Jewish notables to select vocational education as their means to channel Jewish youth who would otherwise swell the ranks of peddlers, commercial brokers, or wandering beggars into useful professions.[89] Jewish vocational schools thus had a philanthropic and political aim and recruited students from the lowest classes, unlike the French *arts et métiers* schools, which trained an elite of skilled workers and foremen.[90]

Although industry was far more developed in the Upper Rhine than in the Lower Rhine, it was the more acculturated notables of Strasbourg who established the first Jewish vocational school in Alsace in 1824.[91] Founded as a charitable society, entitled the Israelite Society for Encouragement of Work, the

institution's initial mandate was to propagate love of work by arranging appren-
ticeships for Jewish boys, supervising the young apprentices, and helping them
establish themselves after they completed their training. The demands of
religious observance and the need for Jewish religious instruction necessitated a
separate Jewish institution. To be accepted into the program, a candidate had to
be a graduate of an authorized primary school. The society quickly earned the
support of Jewish notables like the Ratisbonnes and Worms de Romilly, as well
as the General Council of the Lower Rhine and Gentile officials and philanthro-
pists. By June 1826 twenty-eight apprentices had been placed in workshops in
the city [92] After acquiring property to house the apprentices and receiving a
municipal subsidy, the society expanded into an école de travail, which provided a full program of general primary studies, moral and religious education,
and technical training for boarders and externs.

A similar school, the Ecole d'Arts et Métiers, was founded in Mulhouse in
1842, under the presidency of Léon Werth, a prosperous, progressive, and
religiously observant owner of a cotton-spinning factory in Ste. Marie-aux-
Mines [93] The school encountered significant opposition from traditional Jews
in its early years. Traditionalists were particularly angered by the consistorial
decision to exact a mandatory contribution from all synagogues in the department in support of the school.[94] By the 1850s, however, traditionalists had become, for the most part, reconciled to the institution. Its location in Mulhouse
made available support from Protestant industrialists and the local municipal
council as well as numerous possibilities for placement of its graduates.[95]

These two vocational schools did succeed in providing artisanal training,
mostly to indigent young male Jews, though paying pupils were also accepted.
In 1864 Jean Macé, the pedagogue and founder of the Ligue de l'enseignement,
a civic association that promoted compulsory primary education, commented
that "in all of France the Jewish schools of Strasbourg and Mulhouse had best
solved the question of professional education."[96] Even at their peak, however,
their facilities could accommodate only 50 to 60 students apiece, with 10
graduating a year, and applicants were turned away for lack of space Students
were recruited primarily from the countryside. In 1862, for example, the
Strasbourg Ecole de Travail had 58 Jewish boarders and 4 Jewish externs, the
latter all from Strasbourg. The 58 boarders came from thirty towns and villages
as well as from Strasbourg. They were apprenticed in no fewer than twenty-two
artisanal trades, the most popular being lithographer, tailor, locksmith, and
upholsterer. Three-quarters of the students were apprenticed to Gentile masters, the rest to Jewish artisans. (In addition, 12 Christian externs from Stras-

bourg were affiliated with the school.)[97] By 1870 the school in Strasbourg had trained more than 500 skilled artisans, and the Mulhouse establishment had about 250 graduates.[98] Clearly, these two institutions alone could not solve the economic problems of the Jewish masses in the countryside.

The elan and public relations capital that the vocational schools generated was at least as important as the number of skilled artisans they produced. The Strasbourg graduates established an active alumni association, with a strong Paris branch, to provide mutual assistance to its membership.[99] More important, the leadership of both schools used annual exercises to hail their establishments as significant institutions of regeneration and of defense against anti-Semitic charges. In 1845 the Israelite Society of Encouragement for Work stated that its educational program "made [its poor students] worthy of equality"—a claim regretted by the newly established *Univers israélite,* which argued that civic and political equality adhered to all French citizens who obeyed the law, be they locksmiths or peddlers of old clothes.[100] The *Archives israélites,* in contrast, found vocational education "the only means to regenerate Jewish Alsace," as did Adolphe Franck, scholar and member of the Central Consistory.[101] The Mulhouse school was described in its annual exercise in 1858 as "an arm against all attacks, a consecration of our rights and our liberties in society" and in 1859 as an institution that "had silenced many prejudices."[102] Thus, some of the bourgeois leaders of French Jewry, even three generations after emancipation, still articulated the notion that Jews must prove themselves worthy of the title "citizen."

Although the diffusion of primary education provided Alsatian Jews with the rudiments of French culture and civic consciousness, and the écoles de travail secured respectable skilled trades for a few sons of the Jewish poor, the entry of significant numbers of male Jews into Alsace's lycées and collèges ensured that the province's growing Jewish bourgeoisie would share the same cultural formation as its Gentile counterpart. Sharing a common education was ultimately more significant to Jewish acculturation than the possible social or professional mobility afforded to fortunate lycée graduates. Most Jewish graduates, like their Gentile counterparts, did not scale the social or professional heights, even though secondary education was designed for a relatively small group. Rather, they secured modest positions in the lower bourgeoisie, within which most of them had been reared.[103] Nevertheless, in his 1868 annual report the inspector of the Academy of the Lower Rhine noted, with reference to Haguenau, "Many Jews who intend to put their sons into trade want them to take the classical course."[104]

There is no series of statistics on Jewish attendance in lycées and collèges during the nineteenth century Impressionistic evidence, however, indicates that a growing number of Jews entered the secondary track beginning in the 1840s.[105] Earlier, higher education had been reserved for the sons of the truly wealthy. The consequences of that education were mixed. The most notorious cases of apostasy occurred among the well-educated sons of the elite, who had few social peers within the Jewish community. Theodore and Alphonse Ratisbonne, for example, two sons of the wealthiest Jewish family in Strasbourg whose members served prominently on the Strasbourg Consistory, converted to Catholicism and found a vocation in the church in 1827 and 1842, respectively, providing a telling illustration of the potential dangers of higher secular education.[106] Moreover, Jewish students in secondary schools were sometimes exposed to verbal and physical abuse.[107]

The Jewish press celebrated the increasing acceptance of Jewish students in the lycées and collèges of Alsace and promoted higher education among its readers. By 1847 Rabbi Samuel Dreyfuss of Mulhouse commented that thirty-one Jewish students attended the collège in Mulhouse, bringing home their share of prizes. In the same year the Strasbourg Consistory rejected a plan for a separate kitchen for Jewish students in the local lycée. Such a step, argued the consistory, could "give rise to serious and numerous inconveniences, by disturbing the good relations which should exist among boarding students irrespective of their religion. Religious needs could be satisfied by authorizing Jewish [students] to take their meals outside."[108] In a similar fashion Jewish students were taught religious education by rabbis offering a class within the lycée.

In the 1850s and 1860s reports on Jewish successes in the lycées of Strasbourg and Colmar proliferated.[109] The Strasbourg lycée had 25 Jewish boarders and a larger number of externs in 1856, and 60 Jews (out of a total school population of 600) attended the Colmar lycée in 1860.[110]

The Univers israélite, the organ of the traditionalist party within French Judaism, highly recommended the Imperial Lycée of Colmar, which integrated Jewish students yet enabled them to observe their faith:

> All provisions have been made so that our young coreligionists can frequent this establishment and observe all religious prescriptions. A rabbi   has just been appointed as Jewish chaplain In that role he is present each day at the lycée to ensure that the students of our religion recite their three daily prayers, in a special chapel where there is a Torah scroll; he takes part in their meals, furnished by a Jewish restaurateur He gives them religious instruction   ., he supervises the

accomplishment of all duties prescribed by our religion. This is a great benefit for our coreligionists of Alsace, where the fear of irreligion has prevented so many Jewish families from sending their sons to university establishments, from having them participate in a national education which sooner or later must vanquish the prejudices which can still exist against us.[111]

The Imperial Lycée of Strasbourg provided similar facilities for its Jewish students. As the *Archives israélites* put it, "For us, as Jews, this lycée has a special merit: there our children enjoy all the advantages of boarders, without any religious scruple being able to impede parents, even the most orthodox."[112] There were no Jewish traditionalists in France who rejected higher education as ultimately corrosive of Jewish faith and practice, in contrast to the situation in Hungary and Poland. As long as there was a framework for Jewish observance, traditionalist spokesmen accepted the civic, moral, cultural, and economic benefits of advanced secular education. Symbolic of this acceptance was the presence in the Colmar lycée of at least one of the sons of Rabbi Salomon Klein, the leading figure among the traditionalists.[113] In France, acculturation was indeed consonant with traditionalism.

Some information on Jewish students in lycées and collèges in Alsace can be gleaned from the government survey of secondary schools of 1864, which listed names, desired professions, and father's occupation of current students and names and actual careers of recent graduates.[114] Public secondary schools were not socially exclusive in the Second Empire, and it is not surprising that most Jewish students came from lower-middle-class families. There were, however, notable differences between the class origins of Gentile and Jewish students, which reflected the occupational distinctiveness of the Jews in Alsace even in the 1860s By far the largest group of Jewish students were the sons of shopkeepers and commercial employees, a sector only one-third as large proportionally among their Gentile classmates. The most prominent occupation among the fathers of Gentile secondary students in Alsace was the civil service (21 percent), but only 5 percent of Jewish fathers were so employed. This discrepancy suggests that Jews did not yet see—or experience—equal opportunity in government positions and may therefore not have aspired to civil service positions. Jewish fathers of secondary school students, however, were more than twice as likely as Gentile fathers to be independently wealthy (rentiers and proprietors) and were represented in a somewhat greater proportion among the industrial and commercial bourgeoisie. Surprisingly, however, there were no professionals among the Jewish fathers—perhaps due to the small size of the sample—although 8 percent of the Gentile fathers were

TABLE 7 2
Professions of Fathers of Secondary School Students in Alsace, 1864

	Jews (%)	Gentiles (%)
Rentiers and proprietors	20	8
High professions	—	8
Industrial and commercial bourgeoisie	15	11
Civil Service	5	21
Low professions (clergy, teachers, veterinarians, pharmacists, military doctors)	5	8
Shopkeepers and white collar employees	45	14
Artisans	10	15
Peasants	—	11
Workers	—	3
	N = 40	N = 534

professionals. Finally, the lower classes—of peasants and workers—which together accounted for 14 percent of the Gentile fathers, were missing entirely from the Jewish parent body. (See table 7.2.)

As was appropriate to their commercial background, 65 percent of the Jewish students were in the special course, a track designed for those planning a career in commerce or industry rather than in the professions. Fifty-two percent of Gentile students in Alsace were also enrolled in the special course. At the Collège of Obernai the director commented that peasants, artisans, and especially Jewish merchants sent their children to the special courses.[115] Although the 1864 inquiry found that "very few pupils . . . expressed a positive preference for commerce or industry," with the exception of special course students, Jewish students in Alsace expected to follow their fathers into commerce and white-collar employment. Even those who aspired to one of the *grandes écoles* were more likely to select the Ecole Centrale, the Ecole Polytechnique, or Ponts et Chaussées, all of which prepared for technical and industrial careers, rather than the prestigious Ecole Normale Supérieure, which led to a professional career in the high civil service.

The actual careers of Jewish secondary school graduates did not differ substantially from their aspirations. Like their Gentile fellow students, they were less likely to be accepted in the grandes écoles than they anticipated.[116] That discrepancy seems to have been compensated for, however, by those who found positions in the commercial and industrial bourgeoisie. (See table 7.3.)

TABLE 7 3

Aspirations and Early Careers of Secondary School Students

	Jews		Gentiles	
	Aspirations (%)	Careers (%)	Aspirations (%)	Careers (%)
Ecole Normale Supérieure	8	2	2.4	0.4
Ecole Centrale	11	2	3 1	1.3
Polytech/Ponts et Chaussées	5	3	7 1	5 0
Chalons/Arts et Métiers	3	2	3.8	3 1
St. Cyr/Naval College	—	—	8 6	4.6
Ecole Forestière	—	—	1.9	0 6
Rentiers and Proprietors	—	—	—	0.4
High prof	8	7	9.0	9 9
Commercial and industrial bourgeoisie	—	7	9.3	12 6
Shopkeep/white-collar employee	56	56	14.5	17.6
Low professional	6	10	23.1	13 9
Civil service	—	4	6 4	7 8
Artisans	3	4	6 2	8.8
Military Service	—	—	0 7	8 4
Agriculture	—	1	3 1	3 9
Worker	—	2	0 7	1.8
	N = 36	N = 57	N = 420	N = 921

The similarity between the occupational profile of recent Jewish secondary school graduates and that of their fathers is striking, although there are no rentiers and proprietors among the younger generation and the proportion in artisanry had declined. In comparison with their Gentile classmates Jewish secondary school students were far more likely to seek (and establish) careers in commerce and white-collar employment. Approximately the same percentage of Jews and Gentiles attended the prestigious government schools, with the exception of St Cyr, the school for military officers. Relative to their classmates the Jewish students avoided the lower professions, artisanry, the civil service, the industrial bourgeoisie, agriculture, and especially military service. Thus, studying side by side with Gentile members of the lower middle and middle classes did not erode the economic and cultural legacy of the past for Jewish lycée and collège graduates. Although French secondary education was de-signed to reward merit and offer a career based upon talent—and to a large extent it met these goals—it had not, by 1864, transformed the value system of its Jewish participants.

The governmental survey of lycées and collèges also provided fragmentary evidence of the social experience of Jewish students. Many school directors remarked on the tolerance found in their institutions, but others admitted that there was prejudice against Jewish students. In the collèges of Obernai, Sélestat, and Saverne, Jewish students, and especially the externs, who were singled out by their residency at home, encountered discrimination from their classmates, or, as the director of the Collège of Obernai delicately put it, the Jewish students "are not always treated with perfect fraternity"[117]

After 1830 education promoted the acculturation and, to a lesser extent, the integration of Alsatian Jews, but within a framework that supported the retention of Jewish identity and religious observance The religious denominationalism and mandatory religious instruction of French primary and secondary education from the Restoration through the Second Empire meant that most Alsatian Jews acquired secular culture and civic consciousness within a specifically Jewish context. Even in the lycées and collèges, separate dining facilities and classes of religious instruction reinforced Jewish identity. Although some wealthy Jews sought a non-Jewish educational environment for their children, they remained a minority. The bonds of community in Alsace were transferred to the school setting Yet even with the confessional division of French education, the level of Jewish religious instruction was low and could not compete with the rigorous classical and technical education provided by French secondary, and even vocational, schools.

Traditional Jews, who recognized that Jewish learning had eroded in modern schools, attempted to restore the primacy of Jewish study by establishing competing institutions or supplementary classes, but they were unsuccessful. The financial and governmental power of the consistories, committed to modern education, prevailed. Moreover, parents doubtless came to realize that modern education offered possibilities for economic and social advancement that could not be matched by traditional schools, which, after all, prepared students only for the modest positions of schoolteacher and rabbi. Knowledge of Hebrew declined among Alsatian Jews in the nineteenth century, as did the proportion of lay leadership who were learned according to the norms of traditional Judaism. Many lay leaders in Alsace, educated before the reforms of the Restoration, could, for example, correspond in Hebrew with the Amsterdam committee collecting funds for the Jews of Palestine.[118] Although the general level of traditional Jewish scholarship was not high in Alsace as it emerged from the ancien régime, in the course of the nineteenth century the traditionally educated elite became increasingly limited to the professional rabbinate

Educational institutions provided a new definition of culture for Alsatian Jews, albeit two to three generations after emancipation. Just as historians have pointed to the survival of the economic ancien régime at least until the 1840s,[119] so the cultural ancien régime survived among Alsatian Jews at least until that decade. It is important to recognize, too, that even after traditional Jewish culture was eroded, the acquisition of secular and professional skills did not forestall the assertion of fierce ethnic pride and sense of religious distinctiveness. Jewish primary school personnel certainly saw no conflict between French patriotism and Jewish identity, and they taught the consonance of French and Jewish values. Jewish leaders put great stock in education as the seal of social acceptance. The success of their educational efforts was to be measured, then, not in the prizes brought home by Jewish students, or in the diffusion of French among the Jews in Alsace, but in changing public opinion about Jews in the workplace, political life, and society.

EIGHT

Acculturation and
Social Mobility

The development of a modern Jewish primary education that emphasized
secular culture and harnessed religious instruction to instill civic responsibility
both promoted the acculturation of Alsace's Jewish population and reflected the
values of its leadership. Although the Jews of Alsace did not fulfill the expecta-
tions of France's political and cultural elite—who had assumed that after
emancipation the Jews would be easily assimilated into the larger French
population—they did gradually acculturate to the norms of French bourgeois
culture. Moreover, their long experience as commercial middlemen in the
countryside gave them the skill and capital for economic mobility. Not surprisingly, the first signs of social change occurred among the Jews who had
migrated to the cities, where they came in contact with the local bourgeoisie.
Although social critics and government officials lamented the slow progress of
Jews in the countryside well into the second half of the nineteenth century,
small town and village Jews were hardly more backward than their Gentile
neighbors, as Jewish spokesmen did not hesitate to point out [1] They were
simply a conspicuous minority. And, as the Jewish role in the rural economy
eroded, as modern education penetrated the region, as contact with successful
urban relatives became more extensive, the Jews living in the smaller communities began to adopt the cultural patterns of the urban Jewish elite. Because the
social contexts of city and countryside influenced both the pace and the style of
assimilation, it is important to situate the cultural adaptation of Alsatian Jews
within local frameworks.

TABLE 8 1
French and German Names among Jews in Strasbourg (by percentage)

Date of Birth	Males (%)	N	Females (%)	N
1760–89	33	82	70	81
1790–99	41	92	78	73
1800–1809	33	120	87	143
1810–19	48	147	91	180
1820–29	46	188	88	274
1830–39	59	232	91	222
1840–49	73	208	92	208
1850–59	82	78	93	86
1860–69	80	50	88	50

In the new urban communities of Strasbourg, Mulhouse, and to a lesser extent Colmar, there emerged a wealthy Jewish elite whose cultural values and style were shaped by the surrounding bourgeois population, which was, in the words of one Alsatian historian, "resolutely bilingual "[2] Because Strasbourg and Colmar were the seats of the departmental consistories of the Lower and Upper Rhine, respectively, wealthy elites who served as lay members of the consistories were able to extend their influence beyond the boundaries of their cities. Furthermore, Strasbourg and Mulhouse were served by energetic and progressive rabbis who supported and encouraged the Jewish elite to embrace the cultural opportunities available to French citizens.

A change in naming patterns is one of the first steps of acculturation. Traditional Jewish names persisted among males in the countryside until the second half of the nineteenth century, but in Strasbourg, where French cultural influence was strongest and the traditions of the village no longer prevailed, the pace of change was more rapid. Although 67 percent of Jewish males born in the 1770s and 1780s living in Strasbourg between 1846 and 1866 bore Jewish names, that percentage declined precipitously after 1810 and reached a low of 20 percent by the 1860s Women's names, which were less constrained by religious practice and hence always more sensitive to fashion, reflected French taste even earlier In Strasbourg Jewish names virtually disappeared for girls as early as 1810. (See table 8.1.)

It is more difficult to ascertain changes in cultural patterns. Yet some indications of new self-perceptions vis-à-vis the larger society emerge in scattered references. Alsatian Jewish leaders saw the state as the source of their civic equality and protector of their rights and recognized the importance of teaching French to Jewish youth and promoting patriotic symbols. This identification with state symbols can be seen in some Jewish ritual objects. The tricolor appears on a few Torah binders, and a tricolor vase graces at least one Seder show towel (*Sederzwehl*), the decorative cloth used to cover soiled linen during the Passover festivities.[3]

In religious practice, in particular, the process of modifying traditional modes of behavior reflects not only the decline of the authority of custom but also the adoption of new definitions of spirituality and new criteria of propriety. Undoubtedly aware of contemporary reforms initiated by acculturated German Jews,[4] the wealthy and educated lay leaders of the Consistory of the Lower Rhine and the commissaires surveillants whom they appointed took the lead in promoting a form of Jewish practice consonant with bourgeois aesthetics and norms of decorum. Beginning with the Strasbourg community, they instituted a number of nondoctrinal changes in synagogue worship to meet the needs of a population concerned with its social acceptability.

In 1831 the Strasbourg Consistory set up a commission composed of five imposing members of the communal elite, including Louis Ratisbonne, to "investigate the obstacles which are still opposed to the complete regeneration of the Jews of Alsace and to indicate the most appropriate means to make such obstacles disappear."[5] The commission report of September 6, 1831, declared as the goal of regeneration that Jews should "have the same manners, the same customs, the same occupations" as the rest of the Alsatian population and recommended a series of measures to strip away outmoded practices which left "too little space for the accomplishment of . . . political and social obligations." Most of the recommendations, however, were not measures for civic improvement. Instead, they were proposals to eliminate aspects of traditional Jewish practice that were embarrassing to those who considered themselves enlightened or that had no direct counterparts in Christian culture. The commission suggested, for example, suppressing the auction in the temple of synagogue honors and banning the special robes worn by laypeople on the high holidays, setting up the temple in such a manner that girls could enter; regulating ceremonies in the temple in a "more seemly" manner; enforcing a twenty-four-hour waiting period before burial; abolishing the custom of wearing a beard; banning the practice of capores (in which sins are transferred to a chicken on the eve of the Day of Atonement); administering the mikveh so as not to compromise the health of women; and introducing weekly sermons by rabbis and laymen to inculcate morality and social responsibility.

The overarching goal of the commission was to reconcile Judaism with French law and custom and to symbolically affirm the fraternity of Jews and their Christian fellow citizens. The commission called for the suppression of prayers in the traditional liturgy that expressed hostility toward other religions and proposed suspending the law banning the use of Gentile wine. It also urged that all references suggesting that Jews do not have a fatherland to call their own be removed from the ceremonies commemorating the Ninth of Ab, the day of mourning for the destruction of the Temple in Jerusalem and for the sufferings of exile.

To ensure that Jews would soon bridge the social distance separating them from their Gentile neighbors, the commission stressed the importance of educating rabbis to have a broad secular culture and of providing modern religious instruction to youths of both sexes Indeed, their concern for integrating girls within the synagogue, both through religious instruction and through introducing a confirmation ceremony for them, reflected their own high level of acculturation. Jewish leaders steeped in Enlightenment values were particularly concerned with the role of women in the synagogue because the difference from Christianity was so visible. They were sensitive to charges that the segregation of women in public Jewish ritual reflected the Oriental origins of Jews as well as Judaism and hence their foreignness.

Most of the recommendations of the commission for modifying distinctive customs, not to mention its more radical proposals for abridging the liturgy and abolishing the second day of festivals, found no receptive audience even in Strasbourg, where in spite of a progressive urban culture much of the Jewish population retained a sentimental attachment to traditional custom. Within the decade, however, the Strasbourg Consistory introduced reforms that touched upon the aesthetics of public worship. Its major success was to abolish the public auction of the honor of being called to the Torah and to insist on quiet worship following the lead of the cantor rather than the spirited anarchy that characterized traditional Jewish communal prayer. In opposition to Jewish custom (but in consonance with Enlightenment views) it also mandated a delay of at least twenty-four hours before burial.[6] In the 1840s the pace of change accelerated In response to a petition, evidently from the most acculturated members of the community, the Consistory of the Lower Rhine in 1842 decreed that a ceremony of religious initiation for both boys and girls, preceded by a public examination of religious knowledge, be instituted in all the temples of the circumscription. The consistory declared that it was motivated by recognition of the "supreme importance that girls . . . be admitted in to the temple of the Lord and that the accent of their voices blend in public prayer." Rabbi Aron helpfully added that Jewish tradition did not prevent the admission of girls into the part of the temple reserved for men.[7] The following spring the consistory responded to a petition requesting significant changes in the observance of the Ninth of Ab by stating that, although most of the modifications could not be instituted without convening a rabbinic synod, the sanctuary could be draped in black—the Western color of mourning in place of the traditional Jewish color, white—and worshipers could be refused admission into the synagogue if they were not decently attired. (In traditional Judaism grief over the destruction of the Temple took precedence over the state of one's clothing; indeed, one sign of mourning was torn attire) The tactic of a petition failed, however, in 1845, when the consistory refused to consider the demand for the introduction of an organ, ostensibly because the petition was initiated improperly by a member of the Administrative Commission.[8]

This reluctance to introduce an organ into the synagogue and the failure to adopt the proposals of the 1831 commission reflected the fact that most of the consistorial leadership, not to mention the Jewish masses, were closer to Jewish tradition than one segment of the Jewish elite of Strasbourg The absence of a critical mass of enlightened and educated Jews in Alsace led some progressive Jewish leaders, like the Ratisbonne brothers, to convert to Catholicism, it led others to withdraw from Jewish communal life. Thus, in 1853 the secretary of the Strasbourg Consistory chose dismissal from his post rather than have his son circumcised Another lay member of the consistory, a physician, resigned in frustration when his proposals to initiate religious reforms and to increase the pastoral function of the rabbis were met with disdain by Grand Rabbi Aron, who saw in them a desire to Christianize Judaism.[9]

The reforms that were initially introduced in Strasbourg during the July Monarchy were diffused over the next two decades to the towns and villages of the countryside Information provided by the departmental consistory, occasional regional meetings of rabbis, and the gradual acceptance of urban mores appear to have been the crucial factors in the adoption of new types of ritual behavior. In spite of initial opposition, the abolition of the auction of synagogue honors, the practice of praying quietly, and the introduction of ceremonies of religious initiation became widely accepted in scores of Jewish communities in Alsace. By 1866, even in the more traditional Department of the Upper Rhine, the auction of synagogue honors had virtually disappeared. Other innovations were limited in scope. The organ, played for the first time in the Strasbourg temple in 1857 at the marriage of a daughter of the Ratisbonne family, was the cause of heated dispute in that community in 1865 when it was played on the holidays. Yet in 1868 the new community of the industrial town of Bischwiller, comprising many immigrants from Strasbourg, introduced the organ into its relatively new and elegant synagogue apparently without discord And in Colmar the installation of the new grand rabbi, Isaac Levy, in 1869 was accompanied by the playing of a Mozart sonata as well as music from Wagner's *Tannhaüser*.[10]

By the 1860s bourgeois standards of decorum had penetrated deeply into the countryside. As the traditionalist *Univers israélite* commented in 1861 in an article on the religious state of French Jewry, "The least hamlet sees one or several of its children betake themselves to a large city where they are initiated to a superior civilization and from which, returning transformed, they bring back to their home what they have seen. They are so many missionaries of civilization; after having experienced [its] irresistible influence, they become the agents to propagate it around them."[11] One example of this diffusion of bourgeois standards, influenced perhaps both by Alsatian urban Jewish practices and by measures introduced in southwest German Jewish communities, emerges in the pinkas (minute book) of the Jewish community of Bouxwiller, a small town northwest of Strasbourg, which in 1863 had a population of 3,825, of whom 312 were Jews On December 31, 1863, a new set of regulations for proper behavior in the synagogue were recorded in Yiddish in the pinkas. "Entry into the temple," noted Article I, "should take place without noise, without wandering from one place to another. Each person should go directly to his own seat " Article III added that it was "strictly forbidden" to switch seats. Adults and children were banned from the courtyard of the synagogue during services. Worshipers in the synagogue were enjoined not to sing along with the cantor; violators were subject to fines Although the traditional synagogue had welcomed children of all ages, the new sense of propriety dictated that children under four could not enter the synagogue except under the close supervision of their fathers. When they became adolescents, girls were not permitted in the men's section of the synagogue nor boys in the women's section. Dress regulations were also promulgated. On the Sabbath and holidays, at morning and evening prayers, each male worshiper was expected to attend synagogue services wearing "a high black hat " The wearing of a smock or round camisole— work clothes—was forbidden. Finally, the regulations confirmed a custom that appeared sporadically in traditional Jewish communities, that menstruants were strictly forbidden to enter the synagogue before they had undergone the requisite ritual immersion [12]

The introduction of bourgeois standards of religious practice was only one response to the new social context created by emancipation. For an increasing number of Jews in Alsace, although clearly a minority in the nineteenth century, acculturation was accompanied by what critics labeled religious indifference and lack of respect for rabbinic authority. Indeed, progressive rabbis buttressed their call for moderate religious reform with arguments that reform was the sole means to stem defection from Judaism, particularly among youth.[13]

In the 1840s neither the lay elite nor the progressive rabbis, not to mention the masses, were so distant from tradition as to mount a serious challenge to the authority of rabbinic law. Those rabbis, like Aron of Strasbourg and Dreyfuss of Mulhouse, who favored the accommodation of Judaism to the social demands of the age, insisted that change must be regulated by halakhic (Jewish legal) considerations. They supported the convocation of a rabbinic synod to introduce systematic changes supported by rabbinic authority.[14] Even wealthy lay leaders did not dare to make policy for a Jewish communal institution without securing rabbinic approval. In 1840 Achille Ratisbonne, for example, had asked for rabbinic authorization for an innovation (permission to allow swimming on the Sabbath for students of the Ecole de Travail). When his request was denied, he suggested in the Jewish press that the decision was too rigorous an interpretation of the law, although he accepted the rabbi's authority to issue such a decision This was not the case in 1862 when Rabbi Raphael Wurmser of Soultz ordered the secular date removed from a Jewish tombstone. By then a change had occurred The family had applied the secular date to the tombstone without consulting a rabbi. When the local rabbi declared his opposition, rather than acceding to his authority, the family brought him before a French court.[15] As the Napoleonic Sanhedrin had suggested more than fifty years before, civil law offered an alternative to religious law, and by the second half of the nineteenth century it took precedence over halakha for most French Jews, even in Alsace. Moreover, the consistorial system, which placed increasing power in the hands of laymen in the consistories, had gradually eroded the authority of French rabbis.

Although Gentile observers continued to criticize the Jews of Alsace, particularly for their economic role in the countryside, Jewish spokesmen pointed to the enormous strides the Jews had taken. Writing in an apologetic tone in 1836, Rabbi Samuel Dreyfuss queried rhetorically:

If Alsace still contains some Jewish usurers, if one still sees there so many Israelites who . . . continue to devote themselves to an ignoble commerce or to beg for their bread at the doors of their coreligionists, if, in short, all have not yet abandoned the [peddler's] sack for the plow, cattle dealing for agriculture or the liberal professions, is it just to conclude that the Alsatian Jews are unworthy of their emancipation?   Are you so blind as to be unable to see the rapid progress that the Jews of Alsace have made since they have been permitted to walk with their head raised? . . . Among the Alsatian Israelites at least three-fifths can read and write in the two languages, more than half of them can even speak the two languages, and isn't it true progress, when we remember that some thirty years ago they felt qualms about reading a book not written in Hebrew![16]

By the 1840s some government officials recognized that the Jews had made great progress toward assimilation. The prefect of the Lower Rhine, for example, was enthusiastic in his 1843 report:

A new era has begun for the Jews. . . In Strasbourg   . peddlers open stores, secondhand dealers become peddlers. They have begun to frequent shows, the public promenade For that, they had to rid themselves of uncleanliness and of negligence in appearance, and they have done so well in that regard that now the Jews of the middle class flaunt a luxury that threatens to lead to the other extreme. Finally, their new position, in tearing them away from their stay-at-home habits and in exposing them more to notice, has led in their private lives to a host of improvements [17]

The improved social conditions of the Jews, especially in the cities but also in towns and villages, led to increased social integration, at least in the civic sphere. In the 1830s a wealthy Jewish proprietor, Joseph-Daniel Sée, one of the notables of the Consistory of the Upper Rhine, served on the municipal council of Ribeauvillé, and he was followed by Jewish municipal councillors in such communes as Bischwiller and Thann [18] In 1852 a Jew was elected mayor of the Lower Rhine town of Rosheim, even though Jews comprised only 6 percent of the total population.[19] And in Strasbourg in the 1850s and 1860s several prominent Jews sat on the municipal council. Rabbi Aron had prepared the way by promoting civic consciousness in his constituents. In 1846, for example, he issued a pastoral circular to the rabbis of the department urging them to impress upon the Jews their duty to vote even though the elections fell on the fast day of the Ninth of Ab. Aron asked the rabbis to release their congregants from the obligation to recite dirges (kinot) after morning prayers.[20]

Jewish relations with their neighbors seem to have improved in other ways as well. Town councils in the 1850s and 1860s contributed public funds for the construction of new synagogues and the expansion of old ones. Pictorial representations of the dedications of new or restored synagogues show a mixed crowd of Jews and Gentiles, mingling among the flying tricolors.[21] The Jewish press described with pride such incidents as the mayor of Lingolsheim heading the list of subscribers for the local temple and non-Jewish citizens contributing almost 800 francs. It also highlighted the participation of local notables and the general population in the ceremonies inaugurating Jewish houses of worship and occasionally at religious services. The presence of "a crowd of spectators, belonging to all religions" testified, to Jews at least, to their harmonious integration in the Alsatian milieu. Even more impressive was the attendance, in this case in Belfort, "in the beautiful and large courtyard of the synagogue . . . [of] the mayor and his assistants, the members of the municipal council and of the judiciary, of several superior officers as well as all the Christian notability." So moved was the reporter that he confessed, "We were seized involuntarily by an electric thrill which reminded us of what Israel must have experienced during a differently powerful revelation: the Sinaitic proclamation of the decalogue."[22]

The very elegance of the new synagogues was a mark of Jewish civic virtue. Thus, in its report of the well-attended inauguration of the new synagogue of Thann, the *Univers israélite* pointed out that the new building "constituted a work of architecture to which neither the state nor the town could regret their contribution."[23]

The Jewish press paid much attention to other signs of the social acceptance of Jews. When the mayor of Reichshoffen (Lower Rhine) sponsored a successful fund-raising campaign in 1862 on behalf of two poor Jewish households that had suffered severe losses in a fire, the *Univers israélite* saw the incident as a mark of a new social climate in Alsace. "The Catholic inhabitants who were formerly very intolerant demonstrated the most charitable readiness to take part in this act of philanthropy and fraternity. Such an act does honor to the French spirit and to the religious progress of one of the most fervent Catholic populations of Alsace."[24] Jewish students and teachers who won prizes figured regularly in newspaper columns. The career successes of Jewish professionals, including their nomination as members of the Legion of Honor, were also duly noted. To give but one of many examples, the *Archives israélites* announced in 1866 that M. Auscher of Lauterbourg received a silver medal for his hops in an agricultural competition held in Strasbourg.[25]

Reports on the 1857 funeral of a prominent Strasbourg physician, Maurice Ruef, provides examples of the discourse of Jewish opinion makers on the subject of social integration. Dr. Ruef was a model of Jewish accomplishment. A respected and popular physician, he served heroically, especially among the poor, during the cholera epidemics of 1849 and 1854. For his service he was awarded both a gold medal and the cross of the Legion of Honor. In 1848 he was pressed to stand as a candidate for the Constituent Assembly but declined. He was elected that year, however, to the Strasbourg municipal council, where he served until his death. In addition to his professional and civic duties, he was active in the Jewish community. A lay member of the local consistory, in the words of the editor of the *Lien d'Israël,* "he did not cease for an instant to belong entirely to the synagogue." The editor noted with pride, "He was accompanied to his last abode by an immense cortege formed by the most eminent men of our city, at whose head we noticed with true happiness the chief magistrate of the department, our honorable and excellent prefect." Ruef's combination of civic devotion, political popularity, and Jewish loyalty testified to the benefits that Jewish emancipation had brought, not only to individual Jews but also to the Alsatian population at large. The *Archives israélites* reflected the Jewish community's pride in this illustrious citizen in its report of his death and funeral: "Such an existence does honor to our cult. . . . We place [his life] also, above the warmest writings, [as a statement] in favor of our equality."[26]

The patterns of acculturation and the growing formal integration of Jews were linked to the economic mobility of the Jewish population, particularly beginning in the 1840s. Although the occupational distribution of the Jews of Alsace displayed a marked continuity throughout the first two-thirds of the century, the general trend for individual males and their sons was one of steady improvement, largely within the ranks of commerce.[27]

Nineteenth-century economies have often been described as providing little stability for individuals. Not only was status difficult to transmit from father to son; even those who found a niche in the middle class could easily be dislodged by economic crisis or the vagaries of personal fortune. In Alsace, however, despite increasingly common migration due to restricted economic opportunities, only a moderate-sized Jewish underclass failed to share in the larger Jewish economic success story. This group formed 12.8 percent of the total Jewish population of the Lower Rhine as recorded in the 1856 governmental questionnaire on poverty in that department.[28]

During the July Monarchy and the Empire, when Alsatian Jews experienced the greatest measure of social integration, their pattern of individual mobility was by and large upward. This upward mobility was especially apparent in Strasbourg where the opportunities of urban life led to social and economic advancement for many Jews. (See table 8.2.)

TABLE 8 2
Jewish Social Mobility, Strasbourg (1846–1866)

Occupation, 1846		Occupation, 1856 (%)							Occupation, 1866 (%)					
	N	I	II	III	IV	V	VI	N	I	II	III	IV	V	VI
I	33	73	15	12	0	0	0	27	70	19	7	4	0	0
II	44	14	64	16	0	6	0	30	10	60	20	4	3	3
III	47	16	8	63	2	6	4	29	11	21	62	3	3	0
IV	28	0	14	14	72	0	0	13	8	15	23	46	8	0
V	33	0	12	12	3	70	3	22	0	22	22	0	56	0
VI	4	—	—	—	—	—	—	4	—	—	—	—	—	—

Note: I = Proprietors, professionals, bankers, and wholesale merchants
       II = Merchants and lower professionals
       III = Employees, commercial agents, and small manufacturers
       IV = Skilled artisans
       V = Peddlers and secondhand dealers
       VI = Without profession

Between 1846 and 1856 the majority of household heads in the two highest socioeconomic classes maintained or improved their positions; fewer than 20 percent declined in status, and then usually to the ranks of commercial agents or clerks. Twenty-four percent of commercial employees and agents moved up to independent status, and only 12 percent declined in rank. Of the artisans more than one-quarter changed their occupations in the direction of higher level commercial pursuits, as did 20 percent of the peddlers and semi-skilled laborers. As the population aged, the percentage supporting themselves from investments and pensions increased As noted in chapter 3, the percentage of Jewish households with servants rose from 32 percent in 1846 to 50 percent of those who remained in Strasbourg in 1866

The insignificant proportion of unskilled day laborers in the Jewish population and the relatively unattractive position of artisanry is particularly striking. Although Jewish leaders had established the Ecole de Travail and promoted arts and crafts, manual work never acquired the status within the Jewish community that it was accorded in the larger society Only the poorest Jews apprenticed their children as craftsmen. Among Jews in Western Europe there was no tradition of corporate artisanal solidarity, which played such a central role, as William Sewell found, in keeping artisans and their children within the ranks of the working class by choice.[29] Moreover, the social problems—and resistance on both sides—that arose from apprenticing Jews to Gentile master artisans also diminished interest in artisanal training, even though Christian masters made allowance for the observance of the Jewish Sabbath and holidays.[30] Cultural resistance to artisanry among the Jewish population remained strong; and the artisan trades that attracted Jews were those most congenial to commercial expansion.

By 1866 the trends of the earlier decade were confirmed. Indeed, fully 46 percent of the artisans of 1846 had moved up the socioeconomic ladder. Clearly, nineteenth-century artisanry was considered a way station toward independent commerce. Similarly, more than 40 percent of the peddlers of 1846 had parlayed their stakes into settled commerce or commercial employment. Between 1846 and 1866 only 16 percent of the veteran Jewish population of Strasbourg (those who had been residents in 1846) declined in socioeconomic rank.

Although there were fewer economic opportunities within the towns and villages than in the city, similar, though less dramatic, patterns emerge in the twenty-year period. Artisanry, however, was even less attractive to village Jews than to their urban coreligionists, and the very highest status occupations were largely absent. As in the city, there was some regressive mobility in the countryside, with village Jews slipping from independent commercial pursuits into peddling. Fifteen percent of village Jews declined in rank between 1846 and 1866. (See table 8.3.)

The Jewish leaders and government observers who noted at mid-century that the economic situation of the younger generation of Jews was improving appear to have been accurate in their assessments. Although they were particularly struck by those who achieved prominence in business and the professions, census data reveal that most within the younger generation built upon the success of their fathers. True, straitened economic circumstances are reflected in the inability of some higher status Jewish fathers to pass on their rank to their sons. In the years 1820 to 1862 there was as much downward slippage as upward mobility among Jewish grooms, particularly in the top two occupational categories. A substantial minority of proprietors and merchants owned just enough to support themselves but not to assure their sons a career as independent businessmen. Even leaving aside the sons in category III with fathers who were businessmen (assuming that most were employees and hence potential heirs of their fathers), still, nearly a quarter of the children of the highest status fathers (categories I and II) could not maintain the position achieved by the older generation. Moreover, although almost one-fourth of the

TABLE 8 3

Jewish Social Mobility· Bischheim, Niederroedern, Itterswiller (1846–1866)

Occupation, 1846	N	Occupation, 1856 (%)						N	Occupation, 1866 (%)					
		I	II	III	IV	V	VI		I	II	III	IV	V	VI
I	0	—	—	—	—	—	—	0	—	—	—	—	—	—
II	50	4	88	8	0	0	0	48	6	67	17	2	8	0
III	43	3	22	51	0	21	3	32	0	9	69	0	19	0
IV	4	—	—	—	—	—	—	4	—	—	—	—	—	—
V	55	4	22	5	7	62	0	40	0	25	13	2	60	0
VI	4	—	—	—	—	—	—	0	—	—	—	—	—	—

Note. I = Proprietors, professionals, bankers, and wholesale merchants

 II = Merchants and lower professionals

 III = Employees, commercial agents, and small manufacturers

 IV = Skilled artisans

 V = Peddlers and secondhand dealers

 VI = Without profession

children of commercial agents and employees acquired commercial enterprises of their own, more than 30 percent became artisans, peddlers, or unskilled laborers. Artisanry, in particular, was far more attractive to the grooms than to their fathers. Of course, part of this downward mobility was a factor of age; unlike their fathers, the grooms were not at the peak of their careers. In the lowest status categories, upward mobility was not impossible. More than a quarter of the children of artisans and peddlers moved into the top two status categories. And the majority of Jews did assure their sons a position comparable to their own. (See table 8.4)

It is of particular interest to examine the sons of peddlers because there has been some debate as to the role of peddling in the upward mobility of the Jewish population. Thomas Kessner and Stephen Thernstrom have argued in the American context that peddlers, as petty entrepreneurs, acquired mobile capital and acquainted their children with business skills and commercial aspirations that enabled them to succeed in the business world.[31] Others, including Doris Ben Simon-Donath, have placed peddlers in the same category as unskilled laborers [32] The data from Alsace suggest that the former view is more accurate, especially since peddlers made petty loans to their customers when the opportunity arose. Ten percent of the highest level proprietors and businessmen were the children of peddlers; and more than half of the peddlers'

TABLE 8 4
Intergenerational Occupational Mobility, 1820–1862

	N	I	II	III	IV	V	VI	VII
Father's		*Groom's*						
Occupation		*Occupation (%)*						
I	37	57	19	19	3	3	0	0
II	229	4	58	17	8	11	2	0
III	112	0	23	46	14	14	2	1
IV	37	3	24	13	38	19	3	0
V	85	5	22	9	15	44	5	0
VI	11	0	27	27	0	46	0	0
VII	10	30	20	30	0	0	0	20
Groom's		*Father's*						
Occupation		*Occupation (%)*						
I	39	54	26	0	2	10	0	8
II	229	4	67	13	4	10	1	1
III	115	6	33	44	4	7	3	3
IV	62	2	29	26	23	21	0	0
V and a few VI	101	1	27	18	9	40	5	0

Note· I = Proprietors, professionals, bankers, and wholesale merchants
 II = Merchants and lower professionals
 III = Employees, commercial agents, and small manufacturers
 IV = Skilled artisans
 V = Peddlers and secondhand dealers
 VI = Without profession
 VII = Rentiers

offspring moved up the status scale, 36 percent into independent commerce or commercial employment. Although Jewish peddling was often attacked as an economic scourge, as "the source . . . of so many vices,"[33] even in the first six decades of the nineteenth century peddling was a stepping stone to more stable commercial enterprises.

The patterns of mobility of Alsatian Jews differed substantially from those of their non-Jewish compatriots. In fact, the experience of Alsatian Jews suggests that Jews and non-Jews responded differently to the capitalist developments of the nineteenth century, in large part because Jews had never been peasants. A combination of Jewish cultural values, learned skills, and economic networks on the one hand, and persistent socioeconomic discrimination on the other, convinced Jews that opportunities for economic success lay with continuity rather than radical change The vast majority of Jews thus rejected the exhortations of both Gentile critics of Jewish society and Jewish communal spokesmen. Although the sponsors of emancipation urged Jews to become farmers and craftsmen, only a small percentage heeded that call. Jews ambitious for economic success did not regard moneylending as an evil. For Alsatian Jews the direction of economic change lay within commerce, though their fellow Alsatians were concentrated in agricultural or industrial labor. Occupational diversification occurred, but within traditional channels.

The distinctive patterns of Jewish social mobility were largely determined by the initial skills of the Jewish population. As the few previous studies that touch upon Jewish social mobility have indicated, Jews entered the city with economic skills easily adaptable to urban living.[34] Furthermore, they had more ready access to fluid capital than the children of peasants. It was easier and more sensible for Alsatian Jews to exploit the known in the post-emancipation period; indeed, it would have been economically irrational for them to turn to agriculture or crafts in a period when economic expansion lay in other sectors Although the Alsatian population as a whole was among the best educated in France, virtual universal literacy by mid-century among Alsatian Jewish males gave Jews additional advantages in the world of commerce. It was primarily the children of the economically disadvantaged who abandoned commerce, at least temporarily, in favor of artisanry.

Not only did Alsatian Jews have special skills and predilections, they also maintained their own economic networks, partly to counter discrimination. In spite of their emancipation, Jews were subjected to a considerable amount of popular anti-Semitism in nineteenth-century Alsace. In the liberal professions and the civil service, in particular, Jews often found their way blocked by concessions to popular prejudice. Upwardly mobile Jews correctly assessed that their prospects were better in the business world than in either the professions or government service.

Despite lingering discrimination, the Jews of Alsace recognized that France offered them opportunities for economic advancement and for civic participation that were unavailable in other countries of Europe. As a community they had experienced considerable improvement in their fortunes, and their efforts at acculturation had been rewarded with signs of civic integration. By the 1860s the Jews of Alsace were also aware that their traditional mode of life in the countryside was vanishing. The sense that they had transcended their country origins enabled such Jewish writers as Alexandre Weill, Daniel Stauben, Léon

Cahun, and Georges Stenne (David Schornstein) to write nostalgic tales of traditional Alsatian Jewish communities and allowed many Jews of Alsatian origin to read them with pleasure. The successful marketing of nostalgia, in the form of genre tales or cultural artifacts, such as the decorative cloth commemorating the Jewish pilgrimage festivals that hung on the walls of Alfred and Lucie Dreyfus's Paris apartment, suggests that by the last third of the nineteenth century French Jews of Alsatian origin felt reasonably sure of their place in the French bourgeoisie. They could take pride in their humble and quaint origins, now merely a memory, as well as in the distance their families had traveled in the generations since the Revolution.[35]

NINE

Political Power and
Social Engineering

Given the predominance of economic and demographic factors in the transformation of Alsatian Jewry, how does one assess the role of elites—both within the French government and in the Jewish community—in influencing the processes of change? Certainly the highly centralized nature of the postrevolutionary French state as well as of the consistorial system initiated by Napoleon presented opportunities for intervention. Moreover, both the representatives of the state and the Jewish consistorial elite shared a vision of the desirable end product of emancipation—the fully acculturated, economically assimilated, patriotic, and socially integrated French Jew. As early as 1819 Isaac Goudchaux of Saverne, one of the newly elected lay members of the Strasbourg Consistory, stated in a public speech that the task of the consistorial leaders was: "the encouragement among their brethren of the exercise of the arts and the cultivation of the sciences, teaching . . . youth that one of the fundamental bases of religion lies in respect of the laws of the State and devotion without limit to the fatherland."[1] Consistorial and governmental leaders could mandate certain forms of behavior and constrain others, although popular resistance set limits to the exercise of their power.

Before emancipation traditional Jewish communities had the power of taxation, supported by the state, and could enforce their rulings through sanctions ranging from fines to the social ostracism of the *ḥerem* (excommunication declared by a rabbinical court). Respect for rabbinic authority, combined with compulsory membership in the local Jewish community, reinforced social compliance. Although the post-emancipation community was voluntary and the nineteenth-century French Jew could seek redress from the government for perceived inequities of consistorial rulings, the consistories maintained traditional forms of suasion, except for the use of the ḥerem, which depended upon a closed community for its effectiveness.

Local consistories in Alsace levied dues on Jews within their jurisdictions and informed newcomers, after assessing their wealth, of the fees expected of them as potential members of the community. Thus, in 1853 the Administrative Commission of Strasbourg informed Israel Dreyfus that "in conformity with the statutes that govern our community it is the duty of each Jew who fixes his domicile in Strasbourg to contribute to the common expenses, both for the maintenance of religious ritual [culte] and for assistance to the poor . . Toward that end we have the honor of informing you, doubtless anticipating your desire, that we have set your part at twelve francs per year." A cemetery plot for himself, his spouse, and any unmarried children would cost seventy-five francs, the sum to be paid in full within seven months Although Dreyfus had the right to spurn this call to membership, the letter spelled out the penalties of such a refusal. he would be ineligible for religious honors in the synagogue and would have no right to burial in the Jewish cemetery Indeed, in 1847 the commissaire of Rosheim announced to the Strasbourg Consistory that David and Samuel Netter had been excluded from all synagogue honors because they were not paying their dues.[2] Only an urban migrant with no social or business connections with other Jews could escape such a solicitation; only those unconcerned with religious rites de passage would feel free to ignore it.

Jewish communities could deny access to religious ritual to meet the financial needs of their institutions. In Hegenheim (Upper Rhine) in 1834, for example, an infant boy was brought to the community for burial. When it was ascertained that the boy's father, Jacob Braunschweig, had not fully paid the communal tax due on his dowry, though he had been married five or six years, the community refused to bury the baby Community leaders then demanded that Jacob's father, Samuel—who had accepted responsibility for acquitting his son's tax arrears and paying for the burial of his grandson (a total of eight francs)—deposit an additional ten francs with the community until the matter of a fine could be determined at the next meeting of the community's cemetery commission. Samuel was unwilling to pay the additional deposit and turned to government authorities, the adjunct mayor and a justice of the peace, to compel the burial of his grandson. In response the community declared him a recalcitrant (obstiné) and vowed to punish him after his death by burying him alone and separated from the rest of the community[3] In 1838, after Braunschweig had taken his complaints, without success, to the prefect and the *procureur du roi,* the Colmar Consistory intervened with the Jewish community of Hegenheim to prevent further conflict and the latter suggested that Braunschweig pay the community forty francs in legal costs to settle the matter.[4] The right of the local community to deny services to those who refused to pay their assessments was thus upheld by the French administrative and judicial system.[5] Fear of public scandal and the cost of litigation, however, deterred the community from hasty exercise of that right.

Consistorial leaders used the denial of synagogue honors to enforce the acceptance of innovations in ritual and to punish those who deviated from the consistory's social goals. Through the lay commissaires-surveillants, whom they appointed in each community, and through younger communal rabbis the leaders of the departmental consistory in Strasbourg extended their influence throughout the region. Thus, in 1843 the consistory decided "to take measures to bring to an end the disorder that reigns in the funeral processions outside of the departmental seat."[6] Several years later, when two individuals in Benfeld complained that the community was planning an outdoor public celebration in honor of the donation of Torah scrolls, even though the expense involved might be perceived as outrageous given the extent of public misery, the consistory responded by issuing regulations banning "tumultuous ceremonies, all public demonstrations, all street corteges" and noted that it would ask the mayor to enforce the regulation.[7] The same year it reproved the commissaire of Osthausen for allowing a youth to celebrate his bar mitzvah by reading from the Torah in the synagogue, although the youth could not produce a certificate of having taken the exam or participated in the new ceremony of religious initiation.[8] The consistory also advised the rabbi of Bouxwiller how he might abolish the auction of synagogue honors during the services and accepted a commissaire's (in this case, of Ingwiller) right to discipline a community member for reciting his prayers in the synagogue in a loud voice.[9] These cases are examples of traditional forms of discipline used in the interest of modernization, but the Braunschweig incident represented the survival of traditional sanctions with no modernizing intent.

In 1860 the consistory issued detailed instructions to communal rabbis and commissaires on the conduct of funerals and circumcisions. The funeral party was to be organized in a double file, no funds were to be solicited during the procession, designated porters were to be supplied with appropriate black garments, and the rabbi was to preside over the prayers to be recited by the mourners in a low voice.[10] As for circumcision, the consistory demanded that all mohalim (ritual circumcisers) pass a licensing exam before a committee composed of a rabbi, a physician, and a notable The consistory reserved the right to ban elderly mohalim from performing circumcisions. Finally, the ceremony was not to take place within the synagogue.[11]

Although it is not possible to ascertain how strictly these regulations were enforced, after the 1840s there is no evidence of vocal protest against them or of rampant disregard. Certainly these specific rules for ritual behavior generated by the urban elites strengthened the position of villagers who sought to modify traditional Jewish practice. The power to license—applied to rabbis, school-teachers, and mohalim—enabled consistorial leaders to introduce new criteria for professional representatives of the Jewish community Commenting in 1853 in the progressive *Archives israélites* on the consistories and their affiliated communal institutions, Rabbi Samuel Dreyfuss of Mulhouse noted that their leaders "were concerned with only one thing, the approbation of the Christian public. The assimilation of our manners and institutions to those of our Christian fellow citizens, was almost the unique goal of all the official acts of our various consistories from their origin until our days."[12]

Jewish leaders also used the synagogue to promote the economic transformation of the masses. Particularly in the 1820s and 1830s, when the question of Jewish usury was a matter of public debate within Alsace and both national and local Jewish leaders feared exceptional government measures against the Jews, the Central Consistory as well as both Alsatian consistories encouraged their members to report instances of usury to the authorities and ordered communal rabbis and commissaires-surveillants to deny synagogue honors to known usurers. The Central Consistory even voiced the opinion that religious measures against usurers were likely to be more effective than judicial approaches [13] Yet, in spite of consistorial censure, moneylending remained an attractive calling for Alsatian Jews throughout much of the nineteenth century. Only the establishment in 1882, with the support of the German regime, of a network of mutual credit societies to provide cheap credit to peasants undermined the demand for the Jew's financial services in the countryside.[14] To promote artisanry, which it saw as the solution to Jewish poverty and petty commerce in the region, the Strasbourg Consistory mandated the commissaires-surveillants to publicize the Society for the Encouragement of Work, recruiting subscriptions through postings and announcements in the synagogue.[15] The consistories of both Strasbourg and Colmar sought to discourage begging by establishing rationalized systems of philanthropy and by banning assistance to foreign beggars.[16]

Government authorities intervened in Jewish communal affairs to strengthen the hand of progressive forces and promote a leadership favorable to acculturation and integration. The centralized consistorial system established by Napoleon had placed the institutions of the Jewish community under governmental supervision and, with revisions during the nineteenth century, had set the requirements for selection as a notable, for suffrage in consistorial elections, and for the respective proportions of lay and rabbinic membership on the consistories. Departmental consistories were in contact with the prefect; both he and the Central Consistory reported on Jewish matters to the Ministry of Cults.[17] Governmental intervention, however, particularly in the Department of the Upper Rhine, went beyond the measures stipulated by law.

From the Napoleonic era through the 1860s the French government and the Central Consistory perceived the Jewish community of the Upper Rhine as the most backward in France. With several exceptions, its rabbis and lay leaders resisted innovations in ritual matters; indeed, they spearheaded the opposition even to moderate religious reform. They also lagged behind in the modernization of education and showed little enthusiasm for the vocational training so dear to the consistorial leaders of the Lower Rhine. In contrast, the Strasbourg Consistory was composed of successful and acculturated lay leaders and by the 1830s it boasted a rabbi willing to respond with some flexibility to the demands of the times. The prefect of the Lower Rhine was more likely to send to the Ministry of the Interior copies of speeches by consistorial leaders urging the inculcation of patriotic values among the Jews of the department than to interfere directly in the administration of the consistory.[18] The government looked more warily upon the Colmar Consistory, taking energetic steps to direct it on a course more acceptable to state functionaries.

In March 1824 the prefect of the Upper Rhine recommended to the minister of the interior that the consistorial seat of the department be transferred from the town of Wintzenheim to the city of Colmar. This move was originally suggested late in 1823 by a number of Colmar Jews who felt that they were not adequately represented among the Jewish notables of the department because the majority of the notables were required to be selected from the town that housed the departmental consistory. The prefect, who detested the leadership of the Consistory of the Upper Rhine for claiming that the Jews of the department had no need of regeneration, supported the move as a way to transform the consistory. "I persist in thinking," he wrote to the minister, "that one of the first means for introducing useful reforms in the customs and habits of the Jewish population of this department is to reconstitute the consistory, from which must come the most salutary impulse toward the proposed goal . . . The sole means to accomplish this change is to transfer the seat of the consistory to Colmar."[19] The prefect reiterated his position in May, noting that "the transfer is the best means to form a consistory composed of men sufficiently enlightened to regenerate the Jewish population of the Upper Rhine generally given to usury."[20]

Although dissenting from the prefect's negative evaluation of the department's Jews, the Central Consistory supported the transfer and advised the minister of the interior to disregard the opposition of the local notables and of the Consistory of the Upper Rhine itself.[21] The Central Consistory outlined to the departmental consistory the advantages of a move to Colmar. The move would promote closer relations with departmental authorities, who were situated in Colmar. Since the prefect felt that the step would complete the regeneration of the Jews of the department, the transfer would lead to his acquiring a more favorable opinion of the local Jews.[22] The decision to relocate the consistorial seat in Colmar was handed down on June 23, 1824.

The new prefect shared his predecessor's opinion on the need for regeneration and selection of notables with progressive social attitudes. In December 1824 he complained to the minister of the interior that candidates for the college of notables presented by the Central Consistory included Jews whom his predecessor had already deemed unworthy of the confidence of the government. Soon thereafter the prefect began a campaign against the selection of Jacob Brunschwig, a longtime former member of the consistory, although the Central Consistory supported the candidate. According to the prefect, Brunschwig was "one of the most pronounced antagonists of measures aimed at the repression of usury" and was also uneducated.[23] Because the prefect felt Brunschwig to be an influential leader of the party opposed to regeneration, he refused to confirm him as a candidate for the college of notables even though certificates attested to his morality and his not being a usurer. The prefect also objected to another candidate, Leopold Cremnitz, as being too feeble and too poorly educated to cooperate in the measures necessary to regenerate the Jews. The prefect did not seek Cremnitz's elimination because of his irreproachable reputation, however.[24] Although Brunschwig does not appear on membership lists of the college of notables in the years following 1825, the prefect's victory was only partial; Brunschwig was soon elected to the consistory.[25]

In his zeal to reshape the college of notables, the prefect proposed to the minister of the interior those candidates worthy of support and those to be eliminated. In his 1830 report on the college of notables, he characterized four of the twenty-five notables as "religious fanatics," two as "without instruction," and two as "of bad reputation." He suggested replacing all but one of these.[26] In his letters to the minister of the interior that year the prefect stressed the need to select notables who favored efforts at ameliorating the Jews and suggested that he be allowed to draw up the list of candidates at his own discretion—a proposal rebuffed by the minister because it contravened the 1808 decree which allocated that right to the Central Consistory.[27] Nonetheless, because of the prefect's efforts younger and better educated men amenable to governmental and consistorial efforts at "regeneration" were included in the college of notables. In the process, however, he fostered so much turmoil that the Central Consistory sent a fact-finding commission to the department in 1828, and consistorial elections and the preparation of the local budget were suspended (by the prefect) in 1830.[28] The bitter split within the consistory between traditionalists and progressives, exacerbated by the prefect's involvement, characterized consistorial administration of the Upper Rhine for the next generation.

The prefects of the Upper Rhine remained dissatisfied with the state of the Jews of the department, often condemning in sweeping generalizations the moral and economic condition of the entire Jewish population. Even in 1845 when two progressives were elected to the consistory, the prefect reported to the minister of justice that he doubted that this "would lead to any notable change." After all, the two delegates who would represent the departmental consistory in the forthcoming election of the grand rabbi of the Central Consistory were chosen from "among the Jews imbued with all the prejudices of their sect "[29] In spite of their disappointment the prefects did not interfere with the operation of the consistory during the 1840s.

The governance of the consistory, however, became embroiled in crisis after the accession of Salomon Klein to the grand rabbinate of Colmar in 1850 and the coincident emergence of a small faction of progressive laymen. Both the Central Consistory and the prefect sought to undermine the authority of the grand rabbi, who quickly became, despite his relative youth, the most articulate and powerful spokesman for a staunch traditionalism. They perceived Klein's ability to organize the masses and his willingness to disagree with—indeed, to subvert—projects promoted by the Central Consistory as threatening. As he became the symbol of "fanaticism," the Central Consistory and the prefect used the machinery of the state to crush him and destroy what they saw as the most powerful obstacle to the improvement of the Jews of the department. The saga of the confrontation of Klein and the representatives of state and consistorial authority is the most compelling example of the impact of state power, as expressed directly and indirectly through the Central Consistory, on traditional Jewish leadership in France.

Salomon Klein was a formidable opponent. Born in Bischheim in 1814, he combined traditional rabbinic learning with a secular education. According to family tradition, he studied with Rabbi Marx of Durckheim [30] In 1839, after passing an examination administered by the Ecole Rabbinique of Metz "in diverse branches of religious studies," he was awarded the title of "Morhenou Harab." The decision to confer the title upon him took note of his three years' attendance in classes of rhetoric and philosophy at the Collège Royal of Strasbourg and the diploma of Bachelier-des-lettres he had received the previous year [31] Klein was able to call upon the authority due him among Jews as a traditionally learned rabbi while drawing on his secular culture to defend traditional Judaism before the public in French sermons, circulars, and articles in the press. A stubborn man of ironclad convictions, he saw his mission as the spiritual leader of a major Jewish community to demonstrate that traditional Judaism could flourish under conditions of civic equality and to promote policies that would ensure its survival

The bitter controversy that erupted in the Colmar Consistory in the second half of the 1850s stemmed from the Central Consistory's unwillingness to allow any interference with its program. It aimed to improve the economic and moral status of the rural Jews of Alsace by encouraging modern secular education, vocational training for the poor, moderate reform in the public expression of Judaism, and the election of assertive progressive lay leaders to the consistories. As Phyllis Cohen Albert has demonstrated, the Central Consistory limited the role of rabbis in determining the contours of its policies to the narrowest of religious concerns, and, even there, made clear its preference for rabbis who were accepting of reform [32] Klein opposed the Central Consistory in all of these areas.

Although Klein supported the development of modern Jewish public schools in the Upper Rhine and sent at least one of his sons to the Colmar lycée, he publicly declared that the religious instruction offered in these schools was inadequate. As grand rabbi of Colmar he promoted supplemental schools of Jewish learning and established an école talmudique in Colmar to provide training in rabbinics on a secondary school level, ostensibly to prepare youth for careers as rabbis or ministres-officiants. To the Central Consistory his enthusiastic promotion of an illegal Talmudic school came at the expense of support for the vocational training school at Mulhouse and smacked of insubordination.[33]

More important, Klein took the lead in opposing the moderate reforms in public religious ritual promoted by the Central Consistory and its supporters. That opposition came to the fore in 1856 when the Central Consistory convened a conference of rabbis to address such issues as abridging of synagogue services by eliminating *piyyutim* (medieval liturgical poems), reading a French translation of the weekly Torah portion, and introducing new rites of confirmation and the blessing of newborn infants within the synagogue. At the first meeting of the rabbis, on May 15, 1856, Klein took exception to the consistory's plan to make binding the decisions of the rabbinic conference as to the permissibility of the changes. During the week-long conference Klein persistently rejected any change in religious ritual that undermined established custom or suggested imitation of Christian practices. Citing the great sixteenth-century Polish rabbi Moses Isserles, he refused to accept the elimination of any piyyutim and hailed the length of religious services on sabbaths and holidays as "in the spirit of our religion, which wants [these] days to belong 'half to God and half to you.'" Moreover, he suggested, the suppression of piyyutim would inevitably lead to the elimination of other prayers and would therefore be "a first step down a dangerous path." Finally, he reviled the introduction of ceremonies to bless the newborn in the synagogue and to initiate adolescents into their religious community. Both were unprecedented in Judaism, and in Klein's words, "It is dangerous to introduce . . . ceremonies and words strange to Judaism."[34]

What concerned the leaders of the consistory most of all was not Klein's resistance to innovation at the rabbinical conference itself but his later public repudiation of the conference. On October 7, 1856, Klein issued a pastoral letter addressed to the Jews of the Upper Rhine and reprinted in the *Univers israélite,* the journal that represented the traditionalist perspective. In matters of religious authority, Klein argued, majority rule could not govern "It was not in our power to sacrifice anything to the majority of our colleagues, despite the respect which we profess for the members of the conference . . for our opinions, fruit of long and serious meditation, rest on the most grave religious authorities," he stated resolutely. Klein supplemented his argument against majority rule by challenging the composition of the voting majority and calling for recognition of the sentiment of local rabbis in small communities in introducing religious innovations. As Klein commented, "We are profoundly convinced that in deliberations on religious matters, the opinions of communal rabbis must have as much weight as those of grand rabbis." Finally, Klein rejected the notion that Jews in one country alone could make changes in Judaism. "Religion   . is not circumscribed by the boundaries of one place; it forms the mysterious and providential link of that great family of Jacob dispersed to all corners of the earth. The religious interests of [some] Jews do not differ, cannot differ, from the religious interests of other Jews in the world."[35]

Klein refused to be bound by three decisions of the conference: the modification of the piyyutim, the introduction of an organ into the synagogue, and the innovation of a ceremony for blessing infants. Stressing the importance of historical memory and the powerful emotional bonds to Jewish custom evoked from childhood, Klein based his rejection of the organ and the new ritual on his reverence for the past and his fear of the consequences of "imitating the Gentiles." His pastoral letter called for communal leaders and laymen alike to resist the religious mandate of the Central Consistory. Acting on his own advice, Klein and five communal rabbis from the Upper Rhine joined the newly formed Commission of Conservers of Judaism, thereby evoking reprimands from the Central Consistory and several denunciations to the minister of public instruction and cults.[36]

Although Klein had been the frequent target of criticism in the pages of the reformist *Archives israélites* since the 1840s, his public opposition to consistorial-sponsored reforms and his increasing assertion of his prerogatives as spiritual leader seem to have spurred the Central Consistory to intervene more closely in the internal affairs of the departmental consistory with the cooperation of governmental authorities. The lay candidates supported by the Central Consistory had been elected by a highly restricted pool of voters in 1854 and were reelected in November 1856. There were protests that the elections were not conducted freely and that armed police were present in at least one voting hall. Indeed, in October the minister of public instruction and cults had advised the prefect of the Upper Rhine that the Central Consistory was keenly interested in the election of enlightened men to the Colmar Consistory and had urged the departmental authorities to support this goal.[37] Salomon Klein soon found himself on a collision course with the progressive lay members of the Colmar Consistory, the leaders of the Central Consistory, and the departmental administration.

Two notes, dated January and April 1857, written by an assistant to the minister of public instruction and cults stated that Klein's position in his struggle with the Central Consistory on rabbinic independence was on solid legal ground and found the explanations of the Central Consistory insufficient. Indeed, the first memo commented, that "the Central Consistory, in this circumstance as always, had attributed to itself powers that it did not yet enjoy." Although recognizing the validity of Klein's claims, the assistant recommended that the Central Consistory not be censured because the government was seeking to strengthen its position. A note from the minister's cabinet added that "there would perhaps be serious inconveniences to give complete satisfaction to the grand rabbi of Colmar."[38] Whatever the hesitations of his staff, the minister took a firm and negative position in responding to Klein's complaints about his treatment by the Central Consistory and its mobilization of the temporal authorities to promote its candidates in the recent elections [39]

With support from the Central Consistory and the French government, the lay members of the Colmar Consistory sought to undermine Klein's authority through acts of public humiliation. They held meetings to which he was not invited, replaced his authorized ritual slaughterer with another, and summarily lowered his seat in the synagogue, depriving him of a visible position of honor. Klein reacted by supporting the former shoḥet [ritual slaughterer], by publishing a circular letter thanking the Jews of Colmar for their expressions of sympathy, and by supporting a petition campaign against the actions of the Colmar Consistory throughout the countryside By autumn 1857 the conflict between the rabbi and the lay leaders had become so heated and public that the Central Consistory sent a delegate, Louis Halphen, to Colmar to resolve the differences between the parties.[40]

On October 15, 1857, Halphen presided over an extraordinary session of the Colmar Consistory. Although the session was convened to restore peace within the consistory, it did not succeed in doing so. Klein resolutely defended himself against a by-now familiar list of charges—that he did not lend his support to the vocational training school in Mulhouse and instead, without consistorial approval, advertised and solicited funds for his illegal Talmudic school and for its students; that he supported a rival shoḥet to the consistory's choice, thereby depriving the consistory of much-needed revenues; and that he promoted the public outcry over the dismantling of his seat of honor in the Colmar synagogue. Ostensibly the arbitrator, Halphen repeatedly supported the consistory's lay members against Klein, even referring to Klein's opposition to the transfer of the Ecole Rabbinique from Metz to Paris as "the most insubordinate act that I have ever seen."[41]

Within days of this four-hour meeting the conflict erupted again, and the Central Consistory turned to the minister of public instruction and cults to accuse Klein of stirring up trouble.[42] On November 23, the Central Consistory asked the minister for authority to respond to Klein's insubordination. Immediate and severe measures were necessary, added the consistory, because Klein was a bad influence.[43]

The Central Consistory's request prompted the minister of public instruction and cults to solicit from the prefect of the Upper Rhine information on Klein's role, the attitude of the local consistory, and the disposition of the local Jewish population. Clearly influenced by the Central Consistory's version of events, the minister prefaced his request with the comment that "the grand rabbi obstinately refuses to exercise his influence, in the interest of order, on that part of his flock whose religious zeal he has himself enflamed."[44]

The prefect's report confirmed the minister's evaluation of Klein. Although the prefect acknowledged that the conflict stemmed from the government's open support of the Central Consistory's candidates in the elections of November 1856, he blamed Klein for failing to see that "the government, in designating to the Jews the candidates that the Central Consistory deemed most worthy of their confidence, had in view only the well-being of the Jewish population." In the prefect's eyes, Klein's behavior reflected his belonging to "the old Jewish party whose ideas, manners, and tendencies are not of our time and whose influence on the current generation can only be disastrous. It is to combat this influence that the new members of the [departmental] consistory have addressed all their concerns." The prefect recommended that the minister discipline the grand rabbi with a stern warning.[45] In a strongly worded letter, the minister followed the prefect's advice. Holding Klein personally responsible for the conflict, he accused him of failing to cooperate with a "consistory animated by honorable intentions." He stressed the need to end the conflict, which compromised both the consistory's authority and Klein's character, and concluded by threatening to take severe measures should the disorder spread to other communities in the Upper Rhine.[46]

The minister's admonition of Rabbi Klein, who defended himself and his authority as rabbi, failed to end the conflict In the spring the Colmar Consistory lodged new complaints against Klein and publicly censured him. By June 1858 the traditionalist population of the department had organized in support of the popular and beleaguered rabbi. The archives contain petitions, each with dozens of signatures, from Colmar, Mulhouse, and thirty-two other Jewish communities in the Upper Rhine; Jews from Strasbourg, Bischheim, and eight other communities in the Lower Rhine also signed petitions in support of Klein. Even the prefect, no admirer of the grand rabbi, commented in a letter to the minister of public instruction and cults that "everyone, partisan and adversary alike, praises [Klein's] religious spirit, knowledge, and private virtues."[47]

In July the prefect succeeded in mobilizing the president of the Central Consistory, Colonel Max Cerfberr, then in Colmar, to serve as a personal

conciliator between the warring factions After meeting separately with Cerfberr and with the prefect, Klein accepted a compromise. The prefect, Cerfberr,
and the Central Consistory all reported the happy conclusion of the affair to the
minister of public instruction and cults; to his friend and lawyer, Michel
Hemerdinger, Klein expressed his relief and his joy at having preserved the
Talmudic school. Both sides appear to have made concessions.[48]

A possible motivation for the Central Consistory's willingness to make peace
with Klein without requiring his complete submission may have been the
consistorial leadership's fear that Klein was about to disclose publicly that the
grand rabbi of France, Salomon Ulmann, had dissented from the consistory's
decision to censure Klein and had informed him of this fact in personal
correspondence. Klein first learned of this rumor in a letter of the Paris-based
scholar Salomon Munk, who asked him to discredit it.[49] One of Klein's lay
supporters on the Colmar Consistory had already pointed out to the minister of
public instruction and cults that the absence of the grand rabbi's signature on
the Central Consistory's letter of censure to Klein was evidence of the grand
rabbi's disapproval of the stand.[50] To reveal dissension within the Central
Consistory would have undermined its claim of having achieved consensus
with its moderate approach among all of French Jewry (with the exception of
Klein's "fanatic" followers).

Even this resolution of the affair did not proceed smoothly. Klein reacted
with dismay to the prefect's letter of July 10, 1858, which held Klein completely
responsible for the conflict because he resisted the legitimate authority of the
Central Consistory.[51] Carrying his cause to Paris, Klein secured an interview
with the minister of public instruction and cults and shortly thereafter strongly
defended his Talmudic school in a long letter of self-justification to the prefect.[52] Since assuring the survival of that school had been Klein's primary
motivation for compromise, the continued attacks on its legitimacy disturbed
him and reinforced his wariness vis-à-vis the Central Consistory.

Klein's concern was well founded. In the November 1858 elections for lay
members of the Colmar Consistory, the Central Consistory again promoted a
specific list of candidates and received the prefect's support for government
intervention in the elections. The prefect reported to the minister of public
instruction and cults: "This [Central] Consistory is, with regard to the Jewish
cult, in the same situation as the Directory with regard to the Augsburg
confession. These two bodies represent the rationalist tendencies, and they
confront, in the old Jewish party as in the old Lutheran party, an opposition
which grows each day." The government should intervene in these religious

quarrels, advised the prefect, if only to see that the opponents of the Central Consistory "repudiate all separatist doctrines." In conclusion the prefect noted that "this intervention would be more dangerous in Colmar than anywhere else; the candidates for the departmental consistory are evidently directed against the grand rabbi with whom the Consistory has recently had a difference in which, from our perspective, right did not lie with its side."[53]

When the traditionalist candidates prevailed in the elections in spite of the intervention of the Central Consistory and the administration, the government annulled the elections.[54] The government based its decree on "irregularities committed under the influence of the grand rabbi of Colmar."[55]

A government administrator wrote a long note to the minister of public instruction and cults in support of the annulment. This memo reflects the French government's view of Alsatian Jewry at the end of the 1850s as well as its perception of its role in their regeneration. According to the note, the source of the conflict lay in the traditionalists' fear that the Central Consistory nourished secret plans to radically reform Jewish ritual. Although the Central Consistory denied these rumors, one of its administrative tasks was to uplift the Jews of France and ensure their rapprochement with the rest of the French population. It sought to do so by expanding the economic profile of the Jews. These economic reforms frightened the orthodox party, which saw in them "the ruin of the Jewish religion." This was understandable, for, as the administrator who wrote the note saw it, "an orthodox Jew cannot be a worker, neither in the fields, nor in the workshop, nor in the factory. The Central Consistory [was] struck to see that . . . the Jewish population of the Upper Rhine had not furnished one of its own to any profession other than business, dealing in old clothes, and peddling and was living separated [à l'écarte] from the rest of the French population."[56]

Sharing the Central Consistory's view of the situation of the Jews of the Upper Rhine, the author of the note, in agreement with the prefect, strongly endorsed the annulment of the elections:

> In summation, one can predict that if the grand rabbi [Klein] succeeds in electing a consistory of his choice and in sending to the Central Consistory his most active partisan, the lawyer Hemerdinger, the social and moral amelioration of the Jews of the Upper Rhine will be adjourned for a long time, and their community , more separated than ever from the other citizens, will continue to be seen, not without reason, as the plague of the countryside of Alsace. . Must the measures successively adopted by the State with the goal of effacing in France the traces of the ancient and inhumane condition of the Jews, be sacrificed to the scruples of a

self-proclaimed orthodoxy which exists only in the spirit of a pedantic Talmudist? One would not think so. It is too evident that in Alsace the civilizing task, begun in 1808 by Napoleon I, is far from being accomplished. .   Intervening in the elections of Colmar   is in the interest of the State [57]

Government intervention in the consistorial elections of the Upper Rhine persisted into the early 1860s. So overt was the administration's policy that immediately before the elections scheduled for January 13, 1861, government meddling provoked a petition to the emperor from prominent Jews in the department, including a member of the Municipal Council of Colmar and a textile manufacturer They complained that free elections had not been held for eight years and protested against the application of force in religious matters, especially since the emperor had seen fit to accord to Jews in the conduct of their affairs the guarantees of universal suffrage.[58] In spite of the support for free elections articulated by the elite (presumably those whose enlightened interests the government was seeking to serve by influencing the elections), the minister of public instruction and cults mandated the prefect of the Upper Rhine to do what he could to deliver the appropriate results in the election. Indeed, following the minister's instructions conveyed in a telegram of November 30, 1860, the prefect summoned Rabbi Klein for a conversation. As the prefect reported,

After reminding [the grand rabbi] of the difficulties which his claims against the last consistory had caused, I let him know that the Central Consistory did not wish to allow him to compose a local consistory of men of his choice. After protesting against the reproaches of which he has been the target and the attacks of which he claims to have been the object on the part of the Central Consistory, M. Klein assured me that he would remain completely neutral. But as I was informed that the party at whose head the grand rabbi stands was prepared to intervene actively at the time of the elections and even sought toward that end to disturb religious ideas by saying that the Sabbath would be transferred to Sunday, I was obliged to conform to Your Excellency's instructions   to write to the mayors to engage them to recommend to the influential voters the list proposed by the Central Consistory.[59]

The Central Consistory's list prevailed, provoking from the traditionalist president of the Colmar Consistory a protest against this "attack on the liberty of conscience and of religion."[60]

For the rest of the decade a progressive majority prevailed among the lay members of the Colmar Consistory.[61] Yet the conflict within the consistory subsided The emergence of Léon Werth, an acculturated and religiously observant textile manufacturer who was the chief supporter of the Jewish vocational school in Mulhouse, as the dominant lay figure (and president) of the Colmar Consistory seems to have created an opportunity for harmonious relations between Klein and the consistory. Perhaps Werth interpreted the interference of the Central Consistory and the government in the departmental consistory's affairs as an expression of contempt for the ability of "provincials" (like himself) to determine their own fate wisely. Indeed, an antagonist of Klein's in the 1850s because of his lack of enthusiasm for the vocational school, Werth promoted Klein, in both the Alsatian and French Jewish press, as a candidate for grand rabbi of France, when the position became vacant upon the death of Rabbi Salomon Ulmann in 1865. Werth found Klein to be a candidate who combined a number of qualities essential for the spiritual leader of the Jews of France. Widely recognized for his Jewish learning, his writing, and his eloquence as a preacher, he was also broadly educated in secular culture. A vigorous defender of Jews and Judaism, he also demonstrated "the perfect compatibility of the Jewish religion with the philosophical principles that triumphed in 1789." As for the charge that Klein was too scrupulously obser-vant, Werth noted that these rituals, "which are for the most part purely hygienic, in no way disturb the practice of all the social virtues, which M. Klein has always exalted, exercised, and recommended on all occasions. Orthodoxy as understood and practiced by M. Klein has never prevented public opinion from recognizing the great merits that distinguish him and that are as incontest-able as they are uncontested."[62] Thus, ironically, one of the progressive candi-dates promoted by the Central Consistory and the French government to undermine Klein's influence became the key actor in efforts to restore Klein's reputation with the French Jewish public outside of Alsace as well as with the general public and to sponsor him as the most appropriate leader for French Jewry. These attempts failed, however, and Klein died in 1867 without achiev-ing the national leadership that in earlier times would have been his in recogni-tion of his scholarly distinction and popular following [63]

What did the Central Consistory and the French government accomplish in their combined vigorous efforts to shape the acculturation and economic transformation of the Jews of Alsace? They legitimated moderate religious reform and suggested that some forms of Jewish practice, opinion, and eco-nomic behavior were more compatible with good citizenship than others. They linked eligibility for philanthropic assistance with a specific type of religious education and provided a new model of respectable economic activity for the

Jewish poor, recruiting some of their sons into the ranks of productive craftsmen. And, as the experience of Salomon Klein demonstrates, they made those
who dissented from their methods and goals pay a high price. Although it is
difficult to evaluate the impact upon individuals of harassment by government
and communal Jewish authorities, such efforts at intimidation may have tipped
the scales in favor of accommodation on the part of some Alsatian Jews, just as
they provoked at least mild resistance from others.

These measures of social engineering reinforced the broad social and economic trends that spurred the Jews of Alsace to move from village to town and
city, to acquire the accouterments of bourgeois culture, and to embrace the
opportunities offered by French citizenship. In making it clear how they felt
Jews should read and respond to those opportunities, the governmental and
consistorial elites defined the parameters of Jewish modernity for the Jews of
Alsace.

TEN

Conclusion

The experience of the Jews of Alsace in the three generations following their emancipation in 1790–91 illuminates the dynamics of transformation of modern Jewry in general as well as the specific history of French Jewry in the nineteenth century. Although modern Jewish historiography has focused on the ideologies and public discourse of the organized Jewish community, the view from nineteenth-century Alsace demonstrates the collective impact of the activity of anonymous individual Jews, who together determined the pace and patterns of change as they interpreted and responded to their social reality. True, Jewish leaders articulated a vision of the possible and through their access to government power were able to implement their vision at least partially. But the Jewish masses of Alsace proved resistant to manipulation and helped shape a Franco-Jewry that respected Jewish tradition even as it departed from its strict observance.

The political emancipation of the Jews of France during the Revolution was a symbolic turning point in European Jewish history. The Revolution made clear that the Western nation-state of the eighteenth century was moving away from self-governing enclaves such as the traditional Jewish community. The Revolution and subsequent emancipation substituted the model of individual civic equality for political status derived from community of birth. Although the ideal of emancipation that would stimulate Jewish self-improvement and integration into the larger society was embraced by European Jewish leaders virtually without exception until the rise of Zionism, the Jewish masses responded in nonideological fashion to the Revolution's promise.

As the first traditional Jewish population to deal with the consequences of political emancipation, the Jews of Alsace took advantage of new opportunities with some hesitancy. Perhaps the local climate of suspicion and hostility toward Jews as well as Napoleon's restrictive legislation made them doubt the rhetoric of liberty and equality. As the Alsatian Jewish cahiers of 1789 reveal, on the eve of the Revolution the Jews had aspired only to secure redress from discriminatory taxes and restrictions on settlement. It is no surprise, then, that geographic mobility, especially to the cities from which they had been banned, was their predominant response to political emancipation Yet, unlike the Jews of the neighboring southwestern German states, who migrated to America in large numbers in the 1830s, 1840s, and 1850s, in large part because of restrictions on their settlement and economic activity,[1] a much smaller percentage of Alsatian Jews sought their fortune abroad. It can be said, thus, that the French Revolution kept Jews in France in the nineteenth century

Acculturation followed in due course, but the pace of acculturation must be measured in generations, not years. Most Alsatian Jews experienced no traumatic disruption in the first half of the nineteenth century They acculturated gradually, retaining traditional religious and familial patterns and adapting them only when they were perceived as dramatically out of step with the times or with the demands of urban living. Gradual social change cushioned the impact of emancipation on Alsatian Jews.

The acculturation and social integration of the Jews of Alsace in the three generations following their emancipation derived from the interplay of social, economic, and political forces Economics played a primary role in accelerating Jewish acculturation and integration in the 1840s.[2] The decline of the traditional Jewish economy in the countryside stimulated greater urbanization and the investment of Jewish capital in commerce and industry. In the cities upwardly mobile Jews turned to the local bourgeoisie as their model for appropriate behavior and began to be treated, however grudgingly, with tolerance. Increased economic and social contacts between village and small town Jews and their urban cousins served to diffuse bourgeois standards beyond the city's boundaries.

Although economic trends were paramount in stimulating social and cultural change, government and consistorial leaders, working in tandem, had an impact on the Alsatian Jewish population. Through the power of licensing of rabbis, ministres-officiants, and teachers, all of whom functioned under state aegis, they prescribed the requirements for the paid officials of the Jewish community and promoted a model of acculturated Jewish leadership The governmentally recognized modern primary and vocational schools that the consistorial leaders established instilled civic rectitude and a modern Jewish identity along with reading, math, French language and history, and training in the crafts. Through the centrally supervised consistorial system, consistorial leaders were able to reach every Jewish community and disseminate standards for public observance of religious ritual. Because the power of the consistories ultimately resided in the state, which from the time of the Revolution and Napoleon had made clear its interest in assimilating the Jews into the general French populace, the consistorial elite was emboldened to attempt to refashion the Jewish masses in its own image of useful citizenry. Through the power of the purse it made deviance particularly costly for the Jewish poor, who depended on consistorial institutions for philanthropic assistance. And the willingness of the state to intervene in the governance of the Jewish community set limits on the free expression of traditionalists. The role of the state throughout Europe in the adaptation of Jews to the conditions of modernity deserves far more attention than it has hitherto been accorded.

The evidence from Alsace suggests that the processes of acculturation, identity formation, religious reform, and social mobility of nineteenth-century Jews were complex and embedded in specific class and regional contexts. Although the Jewish elite promulgated policy for the entire Jewish community, the masses were not passive objects of manipulation. Nor did the elite or the masses speak with one voice. Recovering the multiplicity of voices within different Jewish communities saves dissent from the historical obliteration that triumphant opponents often impose upon it. The act of historical recovery demonstrates the range of possibilities that existed at different points in the past.

The social and cultural activity of Alsatian Jews in the nineteenth century also contributes to an ongoing reevaluation of the impact of emancipation on the identity of Western and Central European Jews. As Phyllis Cohen Albert, Gary Cohen, Michael Graetz, Marion Kaplan, Robert Liberles, and Shulamit Volkov have suggested in their recent studies of French, German, Prague, and British Jewry,[3] a measure of ethnic solidarity survived even among those European Jewish communities that are depicted, quite rightly, as highly assimilated, as "Germans of the Mosaic persuasion," to give one formulation. Although the conception of the Jew as adherent of a particular religious confession was the dominant societal definition of Jewishness in modern European circles, assimilated Jews saw themselves as more than citizens of their respective countries who happened to profess the Jewish faith. As Alsatian Jews demonstrated in their combination of patriotism, moderate traditionalism, and concern for Jews of foreign lands—whether victims of violence in Damascus,

the poor in Palestine, or wandering beggars from Germany in their own home-
towns—post-emancipation Jews were capable of forging a complex identity
from disparate elements. In 1836 Simon Bloch, the editor of *La Régénération*
and a grateful citizen of France, articulated a sense of French Jewish identity
that recognized the coexistence of Jewish particularism with the universalism of
French citizenship: "The Israelite of France wishes only to be Israelite and
French: he is not obliged to renounce his personality in order to be French in
the fullest extent of the expression."[4] Bloch's assertion of the compatibility of a
specific Jewish "personality" with a French self-conception seems to be an
explicit expression of the identity that most Alsatian Jews realized implicitly in
their daily lives Along with most of their fellow Jews in Central and Western
Europe, the Jews of Alsace demonstrate that the Jewish identity of the generations that struggled for and achieved emancipation cannot be adequately
described with facile generalizations about the subordination of a particularist
Jewish identity to a more comprehensive national one or the contraction of
Jewishness to a private sentiment.

Although the Jews of Alsace faced challenges of acculturation and redefini-
tion of identity as well as opportunities of economic mobility similar to those
that confronted other Jewish communities in Western and Central Europe, the
French context left its mark upon the Jewish responses to emancipation. First,
the role of France as pioneer in emancipation mitigated some of the pressure for
self-improvement, and the inevitable self-flagellation, that emerged within the
Jewish leadership in the German states and the Habsburg Empire. Like their
counterparts in other European societies, French Jewish leaders called upon
their constituents in Alsace to abandon their "vicious practices," but in recognition of their obligations as citizens, not as a means of proving their worthiness.
Indeed, responding to a statement by the Society for the Encouragement of
Education among Poor Jews of the Lower Rhine that linked worthiness for
citizenship with learning an artisan trade, the *Univers israélite*, edited by a Jew
from Alsace, wrote: "That question of worthiness is good fortune for the . . .
philosophers of Germany, who refuse the sun and liberty to Jews on the
external pretext. 'You are not yet worthy.' But in France, thank God, the
secondhand dealers . . . deserve just as much to be free as all the students of
your vocational school."[5] Contrasting their situation with that of German Jews,
Jewish spokesmen in Alsace frequently commented, both explicitly and implicitly, that they were "more happy" than their cousins in Germany.[6] In spite of
public criticism by Gentiles and the persistence of discrimination, Jews in
Alsace apparently felt that the ideal of equality emblazoned by the Revolution

on France's public insignia, however inadequately realized on a day-to-day basis, would not be rescinded.

The sense of relative security in their citizenship was linked not only to the legacy of the Revolution but also to the power of the centralized French state. The activist state promoted assimilation and constrained the more formidable traditionalist leaders like Salomon Klein, but it also served as the defender of Jewish equality both at home and abroad. When incidents of discrimination occurred in Alsace, when the French press ran articles vilifying Alsatian Jews as usurers, when Jewish citizens doing business in Switzerland were not accorded the same rights as other French citizens, through the mechanism of the consistorial system Alsatian Jewish leaders felt comfortable in turning to the central government for redress of their grievances. Indeed, perhaps because the Jewish milieu of Alsace fostered a particularly strong sense of Jewish pride, the two departmental consistories were vigorous in protesting cases of discrimination and urging the more cautious Central Consistory to intervene with government authorities.[7]

Because the state—with its seat of authority in Paris and its representative, the prefect, in residence locally—was the guarantor of their equality, the Jews of Alsace were stimulated to acquire French culture as a badge of their civic status. Their good fortune as citizens derived, after all, from the French polity located in Paris and not from local authorities. No surprise, then, that Alsatian Jews reportedly taught French in their schools with greater enthusiasm than did their Gentile neighbors.

The system of confessionally based public primary education that derived from the Guizot Law of 1833 was also a special feature of the Alsatian Jewish experience. The concentration of Jews within the province, combined with their preference for education conducted under Jewish auspices, enabled Jewish youth in Alsace from the time of the July Monarchy to acquire French culture in an environment that facilitated the synthesis of civic duty and French patriotism with ethnic pride. The encounter of Alsatian Jewish youth with Western culture was, therefore, less traumatic than was the case in other social contexts.

The impact of the village experience of Alsatian Jewry transcended the borders of Alsace, for the province was the biological and cultural reservoir of French Jewry and, even with outmigration, dominated France's Jewish population demographically until the loss of the province to Germany in 1870. Even thereafter, until the mass migration of Jews from Eastern Europe inundated the native Jewish community, the majority of French Jews traced their origins to the

villages and small towns of Alsace. The concentration of the Jewish population
of Alsace in a rural and conservative social context prevented radical assimilation. As the major source of opposition to the reformist tendencies of the
leadership of the Central Consistory, Alsatian Jews acted as a brake upon
ideological religious reform The traditionalism of village Jews was also reflected in the French rabbinate, for Alsace and Lorraine were the virtually
exclusive recruiting ground for the rabbinate until the arrival of East European
immigrants at the turn of the twentieth century. The Jewish community of
Alsace, remembered with heightened nostalgia and patriotism after 1870 because its soil was now under foreign control, also served French Jews in two
ways. It was a symbol of nationalist yearning shared with their fellow citizens
and a reminder of their humble origins and the distance traveled from them.
Finally, a residue of the solidarity of the traditional Jewish culture of Alsace
expressed itself in the twentieth century in support for Zionism far surpassing
that of the rest of French Jewry.[8]

    In the first generations following the Revolution it fell to the Jews of Alsace to
decide how to respond both to the promises of political equality and economic
opportunity and to the demands for acculturation and economic change that
accompanied their emancipation. They had to define the relationship between
the French and Jewish components of their identity and determine how much
Jewish particularity was consonant with French universalism. The history of
the Jews of Alsace, with its patterns of acculturation and resistance to assimilation, contributes to our understanding of the transformation of Jewish socioeconomic characteristics and identity in modern Western societies.

Abbreviations
Used in Notes

───────

AI	*Archives israélites*
ADBR	Archives Départementales du Bas-Rhin
ADHR	Archives Départementales du Haut-Rhin
AMVS	Archives Municipales de la Ville de Strasbourg
A N	Archives Nationales (Paris)
CAHJP	Central Archives for the History of the Jewish People (Jerusalem)
JTS	Archives of the Jewish Theological Seminary of America (New York)
LBI	Archives of the Leo Baeck Institute (New York)
LBIYB	*Leo Baeck Institute Yearbook*
REJ	*Revue des études juives*
UI	*Univers israélite*

Notes

Chapter One. Introduction

1 For the best general treatment of the political and ideological aspects of Jewish emancipation in Europe, see Jacob Katz, *Out of the Ghetto* (Cambridge, Mass , 1973), Reinhard Rurup, "Jewish Emancipation and Bourgeois Society," *LBIYB*, 14 (1969), 67–91, and Salo Baron, "Ghetto and Emancipation," *Menorah Journal*, 14 (June 1928), 515–26, and "Newer Approaches to Jewish Emancipation," *Diogenes*, 29 (Spring 1960), 56–81 For the history of the terminology of emancipation, see Katz, *Emancipation and Assimilation* (Westmead, Eng , 1972), pp 21–45

2 Henri Grégoire, *Essai sur la régénération physique, morale et politique des juifs* (Metz, Paris, and Strasbourg, 1789), p 31

3 Notable examples of this new trend include Jacob Toury, "Der Eintritt der Juden ins deutsche Burgertum," in *Das Judentum in der deutschen Umwelt, 1800–1850,* ed Hans Liebeschutz and Arnold Paucker (Tübingen, 1977), pp 139–242, Steven M Lowenstein, "The Pace of Moderni- sation of German Jewry in the Nineteenth Century," *LBIYB*, 21 (1976), 41–56, and "The Rural Community and the Urbanization of German Jewry," *Central European History*, 13, no 3 (1980), 218–36, Monika Richarz, ed , *Judisches Leben in Deutschland, 1780–1871* (n p , Germany, 1976), *Im Kaiserreich* (Stuttgart, 1979), and "Emancipation and Continuity German Jews in the Rural Economy," in *Revolution and Evolution 1848 in German-Jewish History*, ed Werner E Mosse, Arnold Paucker, and Reinhard Rürup (Tübingen, 1981), pp 95–115, Avraham Barkai, "The German Jews at the Start of Industrialization—Structural Change and Mobility, 1835–1860," in *Revolution and Evolution*, ed Mosse et al , pp 123–49, David Cohen, *La Promotion des juifs en France à l'époque du Second Empire, 1852–1870*, 2 vols (Aix-en-Provence, 1980), Christine Piette, *Les Juifs de Paris (1808–1840) la marche vers l'assimilation* (Quebec, 1983), and Marsha Rozenblit, *Assimilation and Identity The Jews of Vienna, 1867–1914* (Albany, 1984) For a social anthropological perspective, see Werner Cahnman, "Village and Small-Town Jews in Ger- many—A Typological Study," *LBIYB*, 19 (1974), 107–31 For a schematic sociological and demographic analysis of the problem, see Calvin Goldscheider and Alan S Zuckerman, *The Transformation of the Jews* (Chicago, 1984)

4 For the village locus of much of German Jewry, see Toury, "Der Eintritt der Juden," pp 139–40, and Lowenstein, "Rural Community," pp 219–21 and table 3

5 For Baron, see "Ghetto and Emancipation", for Katz, see *Emancipation and Assimilation,* for Michael Meyer, see his *The Origins of the Modern Jew* (Detroit, 1967), and for David Sorkin, see his *The Transformation of German Jewry, 1780–1840* (New York, 1987)

6 Cited in Ismar Schorsch, "From Wolfenbuttel to Wissenschaft The Divergent Paths of Isaak Markus Jost and Leopold Zunz," *LBIYB,* 22 (1977), 110

7 On the slow pace of modernization of the masses of French citizens, see Eugen Weber, *Peasants into Frenchmen* (Stanford, 1976)

8 On prerevolutionary Alsatian Jewry, see Elie Scheid, *Histoire des juifs d'Alsace* (Paris, 1887), Georges Weill, "Recherches sur la démographie des juifs d'Alsace du xvie au xviiie siècle," *REJ*, 130 (1971), 51–89, and his "L'Alsace," in *Histoire des juifs en France*, ed Bernhard Blumenkranz (Toulouse, 1972), pp 137–92 (population estimate on p 166), Freddy Raphael and Robert Weyl, *Juifs en Alsace culture, société, histoire* (Toulouse, 1977), and *Regards nouveaux sur les juifs d'Alsace* (Strasbourg, 1980), and Arthur Hertzberg, *The French Enlightenment and the Jews* (New York, 1968), pp 164–70

9 Raphael and Weyl, *Regards nouveaux*, pp 133–34, Simon Schwarzfuchs, *Du juif à l'israélite* (Paris, 1989), pp 26–27

10 For a comprehensive analysis of the Jewish consistories in the nineteenth century, see Phyllis Cohen Albert, *The Modernization of French Jewry Consistory and Community in the Nineteenth Century* (Hanover, N H , 1977)

Chapter Two· The Status of Jews in Alsace

1 For a discussion of the impact of "regeneration" on nineteenth-century French Jewry, see Jay Berkovitz, *The Shaping of Jewish Identity in Nineteenth-Century France* (Detroit, 1989) On the concept of regeneration, see Mona Ozouf, "Regeneration," in *A Critical Dictionary of the French Revolution*, ed François Furet and Monica Ozouf, trans Arthur Goldhammer (Cambridge, Mass , 1989), pp 781–91

2 On the demography of Alsatian Jewry during the ancien régime, see Weill, "Recherches sur la démographie des juifs," pp 51–89

3 Scheid, *Histoire des juifs d'Alsace*, pp 248–59, S Posener, "Les Juifs sous le Premier Empire," *REJ*, 93 (1932), 203 For a recent description of the status of Jews in Alsace under the ancien régime, see Michael Burns, "Emancipation and Reaction The Rural Exodus of Alsatian Jews, 1791–1848," in *Living with Antisemitism Modern Jewish Responses*, ed Jehuda Reinharz (Hanover, N H , 1987), pp 22–23

4 Weill, "Recherches sur la démographie des juifs," pp 63–89

5 The citation is from Daniel Stauben, *Scènes de la vie juive en Alsace* (Paris, 1860), p 9 Useful information on the economic activity of Alsatian Jews may be found in Zosa Szajkowski, *The Economic Status of the Jews in Alsace, Metz, and Lorraine, 1648–1789* (New York, 1953), and, for the end of the ancien régime in Roland Marx, *Recherches sur la vie politique de l'Alsace prérévolutionnaire* (Strasbourg, 1966), a more reliable source than Szajkowski On the Jewish peddler, see Raphael and Weyl, *Juifs en Alsace*, pp 36–68, and Freddy Raphael and Dominique Lerch, "Enracinement et errance le colportage juif en Alsace au xixe siècle," in Raphael and Weyl, *Regards nouveaux*, pp 215–34 Raphael and Lerch draw on applications for licenses, required from 1849, to provide interesting information particularly on Jews who peddled books, almanacs, and prints, largely to fellow Jews

6 On Cerf Berr and his political activities, see the privately printed history of his descendant Roger Levylier, *Notes et documents concernant la famille Cerf Berr*, 3 vols (Paris, 1902–6), and, more recently, Renée Neher-Bernheim, "Cerf Berr de Medelsheim et sa famille," *Saisons d'Alsace*, nos 55–56 (1975), 47–61, Georges Weill, "Cerf Berr de Medelsheim, militant de l'émancipation," *Nouveaux cahiers*, 45 (1976), 30–42, Robert Weyl and Jean Daltroff, "Le Cahier de doléances des juifs d'Alsace," *Revue d'Alsace*, 109 (1983), 65–80, and Michael Graetz, ed and trans , *The French Revolution and the Jews The Debates in the National Assembly, 1789–1791* [Hebrew] (Jerusalem, 1989), pp 29–34, 120

7 Cited in S Posener, "The Immediate Economic and Social Effects of the Emancipation of the Jews in France," *Jewish Social Studies*, 1, no 3 (1939), 271

8 Baruch Hagani, *L'Emancipation des juifs* (Paris, 1928), p 167, and Boruch Szyster, *La Révolution française et les juifs* (Toulouse, 1929), pp 28–29

9 Hertzberg, *French Enlightenment*, pp 52–54, 219–20

10 Posener, "Immediate Economic and Social Effects," p 280, Zosa Szajkowski, "The Jewish

Problem in Alsace, Metz, and Lorraine on the Eve of the Revolutions of 1789," reprinted in his *Jews and the French Revolutions of 1789, 1830, and 1848* (New York, 1970), pp 311–21, originally published in 1954

11 Szajkowski, *Economic Status*, pp 123–40, Hertzberg, *French Enlightenment*, p 184, Schwarzfuchs, *Du juif a l'israélite*, pp 48–51

12 Szajkowski, *Economic Status*, p 92

13 Szajkowski, "Anti-Jewish Riots during the Revolution of 1789, 1830, and 1848" [Hebrew], *Zion*, 20 (1955), 83–86

14 Szyster, *Révolution française*, p 28

15 Roland Marx, "De la Pré-Révolution à la Restauration," in *Histoire de l'Alsace*, ed Philippe Dollinger (Toulouse, 1970), p 364

16 Joseph de Lataulade, *Les Juifs sous l'ancien régime* (Bordeaux, 1906), p 273

17 Ibid , p 296

18 Achille-Edmond Halphen, *Recueil des lois, décrets, ordonnances, avis du Conseil d'Etat, arrêtés et règlements concernant les israélites depuis la Révolution de 1789* (Paris, 1851), pp 10–11 For a full discussion of this episode see Lataulade, *Juifs*, pp 254–55, and Hertzberg, *French Enlightenment*, pp 348–49, 354–59

19 *La Révolution française et l'émancipation des juifs*, vol 5 *Addresses, mémoires et petitions des juifs, 1789–1794* (Paris, 1968) See Hagani, *L'Emancipation*, p 166, and Hertzberg, *French Enlightenment*, pp 343–45

20 Zosa Szajkowski, *Autonomy and Jewish Communal Debts during the French Revolution of 1789* (New York, 1959), p 28

21 Ibid The tax collection mechanism and the tracing of Jewish descendants of indebted communities continued until the 1880s On the prerevolutionary history of the Jewish "nations" of France, see Simon Schwarzfuchs, "Les Nations juives de France," *Dix-huitième siècle*, 13 (1981), 127–36, and Gérard Nahon, *Les "Nations" juives portugaises du sud-ouest de la France (1684–1791) Documents* (Paris, 1981)

22 Szajkowski, *Jews and the French Revolutions*, pp 785–825, J Godechot, "La Révolution française et les juifs (1789–1799)," in *Les Juifs et la Révolution française*, ed Albert Soboul and Bernhard Blumenkranz (Toulouse, 1976), pp 60–63

23 Posener, "Immediate Economic and Social Effects," pp 282–87

24 Maurice Liber, "Napoléon et les juifs la question juive devant le Conseil d'Etat en 1806," *REJ*, 71 (1920), 134–38

25 Henri Lucien-Brun, *La condition des juifs en France depuis 1789* (Paris and Lyon, 1901), p 22 For the most comprehensive treatment of Napoleon's relations with French Jewry, see Robert Anchel, *Napoléon et les juifs* (Paris, 1928)

26 Marx, "De la Pré-Révolution à la Restauration," in *Histoire de l'Alsace*, ed Dollinger, p 379, and his "La Régénération économique des juifs d'Alsace à l'époque révolutionnaire et Napoléonienne," in *Juifs et la Révolution française*, ed Soboul and Blumenkranz, pp 115–16, Zosa Szajkowski, *Agricultural Credit and Napoleon's Anti-Jewish Decrees* (New York, 1953), p 65 Szajkowski estimates that only 6 4 percent of mortgage debts in Alsace were owed to Jews, an extremely low figure

27 The quotation is from Michael Burns, "Emancipation and Reaction," p 25, and is drawn from reports from the communes of Guebwiller, Giromagny, and Belfort, all in the Department of the Upper Rhine

28 Anchel, *Napoléon*, pp 26, 62–70, Liber, "Napoléon et les juifs," p 144

29 Liber, "Napoléon et les juifs," p 142 For the characterization of de Bonald, see François Delpech, "La Révolution et l'Empire," in *Histoire des juifs en France*, ed Bernhard Blumenkranz (Toulouse, 1972), p 289

30 Philippe Sagnac, "Les Juifs et Napoléon (1806–1808)," *Revue d'histoire moderne et contemporaine*, 2 (1900–1901), 472

31 On the Napoleonic Sanhedrin, see Anchel, *Napoléon*, pp 128–225, as well as Barukh Mevorakh, *Napoleon utekufato* (Jerusalem, 1968), Frances Malino, *The Sephardic Jews of Bordeaux Assimila-*

tion and Emancipation in Revolutionary and Napoleonic France (Birmingham, Ala , 1978), Simon Schwarzfuchs, *Napoleon, the Jews and the Sanhedrin* (London, 1979), and *Le Grand Sanhedrin de Napoléon,* ed Bernhard Blumenkranz (Toulouse, 1979) The proceedings of the Sanhedrin originally appeared in English as *Transactions of the Paris Sanhedrin,* trans. and ed Diogène Tama (London, 1807)

32 Anchel, *Napoléon,* pp 251–429, Lataulade, *Juifs,* p 271, Sagnac, "Juifs et Napoléon," p 462

33 Moche Catane, "Les Juifs du Bas-Rhin sous Napoléon I leur situation démographique et économique" (Ph D diss , Université de Strasbourg, 1967), p 262

34 "Au ministère secrétaire d'état au Département de l'Intérieur," memo from Central Consistory, Feb 17, 1818, A.N F¹⁹ 11 028, Conseil Général du Haut-Rhin, July 5–20, 1816, A N F¹⁹ 11 007, *Moniteur,* Nov 14, 1817

35 "Rapport à son excellence   ," Central Consistory, 1810, A N F¹⁹ 11 031

36 Erckmann-Chatrian, *Le Blocus,* ed with intro and notes, Arthur Ropes (Cambridge, Eng , 1905), p 12 As literary collaborators from the end of the 1840s into the 1880s, Emile Erckmann and Alexandre Chatrian devoted their popular fiction to the society and culture of the Alsatian countryside For a comprehensive discussion of the image of the Jew in the work of Erckmann-Chatrian, see Freddy Raphael and Robert Weyl, "Présence du juif dans l'oeuvre d'Erckmann-Chatrian," in their *Regards nouveaux,* pp 150–207

37 Paul Leuilliot, *L'Alsace au debut du xixe siècle,* 3 vols. (Paris, 1959–60), 2 182, "A son excellence Mssr le ministre secrétaire d'état, Département de l'Intérieur," from Consistory and Notables of Circonscription of Wintzenheim (Upper Rhine), 1823, ZF 973, CAHJP

38 "A son excellence," p 23

39 Letter from Consistory of Lower Rhine to M le procureur général près la Cour Royale à Colmar, Oct 12, 1823, AR-C 1088 2863, #627–28, LBI, "A son excellence," ZF 973, CAHJP The citation of the Wintzenheim report is from Burns, "Emancipation and Reaction," p 30

40 Berkovitz, *Shaping of Jewish Identity,* pp 48–51

41 Michel Betting de Lancastel, *Considérations sur l'état des juifs dans la société chrétienne et particulièrement en Alsace* (Strasbourg, 1824) I differ with Berkovitz's interpretation (p 51) of this text as calling for exceptional legislation against Jews Although Betting de Lancastel discusses such legislation as an option, he rejects it as unfair to the innocent among the Jews (p 115)

42 M Tourette, *Discours sur les juifs d'Alsace* (Strasbourg, 1825)

43 ADBR V 511 The report was solicited by the French government in response to a request of the Prussian government, which was seeking to formulate new legislation regarding its own Jewish population For a summary of the prefects' reports see David Cohen, "L'Image du juif dans la société française en 1843, d'après les rapports des préfets," *REJ,* 136 (1977), 163–69 On the Prussian connection, see Herbert Strauss, "Pre-Emancipation Prussian Policies towards the Jews, 1815–1847," *LBIYB,* 11 (1966), 107–36

44 ADBR V 511

45 See *AI,* 4 (1843), 460, and below, chapter 7, for numerous examples

46 Letter from A Ratisbonne to editor of *Le Droit,* Mar 11, 1859, AR-C 1088, 2863, #3153, LBI

47 Yves, avocat, "Mémoire pour la commune de Bergheim, appelante, contre le sieur Israel-Gabriel Sée, intime" (manuscript, Houghton Library, Harvard University) Sée was one of the wealthiest Jews in Bergheim

48 *AI,* 24 (1863), 7–8

49 Letter of June 27, 1864, JTS, French Documents, consistorial correspondence, Box 10, 1863–69 For one incident, see *AI,* 25 (1864), 595–97

50 Minutes of Strasbourg Consistory, 1853–58, meeting of Sept 8, 1853.

51 *AI,* 10 (1847), 558–60 For other examples, see Zosa Szajkowski, *Jewish Education in France, 1789–1939* (New York, 1980), p. 28

52 *AI,* 11 (1850), 612, 648–51; letter of Jérôme Aron, Paris, Oct 20, 1850, with copies of favorable letter from the headmaster of the lycée of Strasbourg and letter of consolation from the inspector general promising his assistance in securing another position and adding that "despite the difficulties of position to which your quality as an Israelite can lead you, you can offer real

services in public instruction" (Brandeis University Library, Special Collections, French Documents, 6 26 Varia 1750–1929)

53 Letter from prefect to Consistory of Strasbourg, Mar 22, 1837, ADBR V 512

54 Letter from Schwartz, avocat, copied by Consistory of Strasbourg and countersigned by A Ratisbonne, 185–, AR-C 1088 2863, #635, LBI, letter of Central Consistory to Consistory of Strasbourg, Jan 26, 1857, HM 1060, CAHJP

55 Cited in AI, 3 (1842), 102–3

56 Cited in AI, 6 (1845), 159.

57 AI, 12 (1851), 435

58 Erckmann-Chatrian, Maître Daniel Rock, 2nd ed (Paris, 1873), p 32

59 Leuilliot, L'Alsace au debut du xixe siècle, 3 243; Burns, "Emancipation and Reaction," p 29; F L'Huillier, "L'Evolution dans la paix," in Histoire de l'Alsace, ed Dollinger, p 401

60 Letter of subprefect, with anonymous note attached, July 1, 1832, Sélestat, ADBR V 513

61 Letter of prefect, June 13, 1832, to lieutenant general commandant of 5th division, ADBR V 513

62 Letter of prefect, July 3, 1832, ADBR V 513

63 Letter of subprefect of Sélestat to prefect of Lower Rhine, July 5, 1832, ADBR V 513

64 Police générale de Strasbourg to ministre de l'Intérieur, July 3, 1832, and July 31, 1832, ADBR V 513

65 Police générale de Strasbourg to ministre de l'Intérieur, July 31, 1832, ADBR V 513.

66 Szajkowski, "Anti-Jewish Riots," p 94 Patrick Girard states that sixty Jewish communities in Alsace were attacked but cites neither sources nor the names of the communities See his Les Juifs de France de 1789 à 1860 de l'émancipation à l'égalité (Paris, 1976), p 123. For an analysis of the social strains—agricultural crisis, transition to a capitalist economy, and peasant indebtedness—that led to attacks on Jews, see Reinhard Rürup, "The European Revolutions of 1848 and Jewish Emancipation," in Revolution and Evolution, ed Mosse et al , pp 33–37 For a general discussion of peasant problems and revolutionary violence, see Albert Soboul, "Les troubles agraires de 1848," in his Problèmes paysans de la Révolution, 1789–1848 (Paris, 1976), pp 293–334

67 AI, 9 (1848), 186–89, 214–15, 227–29, 259–62, 297–301, 465–70 See also Moïse Ginsburger, "Troubles contre les juifs d'Alsace en 1848," REJ, 62 (1912), 109–17, and Jacob Toury, Mehumah um'vukhah b'Mahpekhat 1848 (Tel Aviv, 1968), pp 24–31 On the response of the Alsatian press to the events, see Shulamit Catane, "The Local Alsatian Press on the Anti-Jewish Riots in 1848," [Hebrew] Zion, 33 (1968), 96–98

68 Introductory page of mohel book of Raphael Brunschwig, 1870, HM 5508, CAHJP

69 Transcript of court decision, Mar. 25, 1851, JTS, French Documents, Box 1 The Jews lost the case because the town was not held responsible for the seditious behavior of some of its inhabitants and could not be sued by its own mayor See AI, 12 (1851), 221–22 Rürup's claim that "the excesses were directed as a rule against individual Jews accused of 'usury' or other practices harmful to the economic life of the Christian population" is not borne out in Alsace See his "European Revolutions," p 37

70 Szajkowski, "Anti-Jewish Riots," p 96

71 Raphael and Weyl, Regards nouveaux, pp 103–4

72 Cited in David Cohen, La Promotion des juifs en France à l'époque du Second Empire (1852–1870), 2 vols (Aix-en-Provence, 1980), 2 676 For several expressions of anti-Semitic tension in Alsace in the 1850s, see Albert, Modernization of French Jewry, pp 159–60.

73 Report of procuror general of the court of Colmar, March 1853, as cited in Cohen, La Promotion, 2 677

74 Felix Ponteil, "En manière de conclusion l'Alsace en 1848," in Deux siècles d'Alsace française, 1648, 1798, 1848 (Strasbourg, 1948), p. 506, letter of Jonas Ennery resigning as secretary of Consistory of Strasbourg because of his election, May 20, 1849, ZF 323, CAHJP; list of candidates "proposés par une réunion d'ouvriers et de cultivateurs extra-muros dans leur réunion du 15 avril 1849" and results of elections from Strasbourg and the Department of the Lower Rhine, LBI, AR-C 1088 2863, #942, 945, 946, 952, billet de garde of "le citoyen Abraham Israel,"

Haguenau, Jan 2, 1849, JTS, French Documents, Box 26, *AI,* 10 (1849), 297–98, 16 (1855), 592, 25 (1864), 177, *UI,* 19, (1863–64), 286

75 *AI,* 25 (1864), 403

76 *AI,* 21 (1860), 474, 478–79, 25 (1864), 41, 327 The reelection of Simon Sée as a judge in Colmar prompted the *Univers israélite* to reflect that "in this province of the Upper Rhine, where there still exist numerous and strong prejudices against us, nevertheless the important and lofty functions of judge have been entrusted to one of ours," 23 (1867–68), 9

77 See, for example, the reports on the inauguration of new synagogues in Trimbach and Biesheim, built with substantial government subsidy *UI,* 21 (1865–66), 45–46

78 *UI,* 22 (1866–67), 374–76

79 *Enquête agricole,* 2nd ser , enquêtes départementales, 13e circonscription, Bas-Rhin and Haut-Rhin (Paris, 1867), pp 125–26 For a lengthy discussion of the Enquête agricole, see Cohen, *La Promotion,* 2 687–98

80 Xavier Mossmann, *Etude sur l'histoire des juifs à Colmar* (Colmar and Paris, 1866), p 51

81 *AI,* 22 (1861), 108, 153–57

Chapter Three: The Economic Matrix

1 P Vidal de la Blache, *La France de l'Est* (Paris, 1917), p 20

2 Etienne Juillard, *Atlas et géographie de l'Alsace et de la Lorraine* (n p , 1977), pp 36–39, 77, and photographs

3 Weill, "Recherches sur la démographie des juifs," pp 63–67

4 Figures are from census data in A N F^{19} 11 023

5 Consistorial censuses, Upper Rhine, 1851, JTS, French Documents, Box 26, Lower Rhine, 1854, LBI, AR-C 1088 2863, #34–39

6 *Statistique générale de la France,* 1866, as cited in Cohen, *La Promotion,* 1 86–87

7 Minutes of Strasbourg Consistory, Mar 15, 1853, Registre des procès-verbaux, 1853–58 Still, the Jewish community of Quatzenheim, which wrote to the Strasbourg Consistory to complain about the misery of its population and to seek help in eliminating begging, increased from 299 to 305 persons between 1854 and 1863 Ibid , Mar 24, 1853

8 Figures are from 1851 Upper Rhine consistorial census and 1854 Lower Rhine consistorial census

9 In the Upper Rhine, the results were 38 percent of the Jewish communities had a Jewish population density of <10 percent, 38 percent were in the range of 10 to 25 percent; and 24 percent had a population density > 25 percent, in the Lower Rhine, the figures are 40 percent of the Jewish communities had a Jewish population density of <10 percent, 52 percent were in the range of 10 to 25 percent, and 8 percent had a population density of >25 percent

10 Théophile Hallez, *Des juifs en France de leur état moral et politique* (Paris, 1845), p 240

11 Marx, "La Régénération économique," in *Les Juifs et la Révolution,* ed Soboul and Blumenkranz, p 113

12 L'Huillier, "L'Evolution dans la Paix," in *Histoire de l'Alsace,* ed Dollinger, pp 398–99, quotation on p 399 *Histoire de l'Alsace rurale,* ed Jean-Michel Boehler, Dominique Lerch, and Jean Vogt (Strasbourg, 1983), pp 305–7, 334–35

13 L'Huillier, "L'Evolution dans la Paix," in *Histoire de l'Alsace,* ed Dollinger, p 402.

14 Ibid , pp 402–7, Roger Price, *An Economic History of Modern France* (London, 1981), p. 126

15 *Histoire de l'Alsace rurale,* ed Boehler et al , p 305

16 On Dreyfus père and grandpère, see Michael Burns, "The Dreyfus Family," in *The Dreyfus Affair Art, Truth, Justice,* ed Norman Kleeblatt (Berkeley, 1987), pp 145–46, and his "Emancipation and Reaction," pp 38–39

17 Marriage records used include ADBR 4E 330, Niederroedern (1793–1830), 4E 226, Itterswiller (1793–1830), and 5M1 852 and 853, Bischheim (1813–32); 5M1 1663, Strasbourg, (1823–24) (1825–26) (1827–28), and ADHR 5E 105, Colmar (1822–28)

18 Tax lists, Lower Rhine communities, LBI, Alsatian Collection, Frais du culte israélite du département du Bas-Rhin, #226–509 Villages and towns selected were Bischheim, Bouxwiller, Dettwiller, Haguenau, Ingwiller, Itterswiller, Lingolsheim, Niederroedern, Obernay, Odratzheim, Quatzenheim, Saverne, Stotzheim, Wissembourg, and Wolfisheim

19 1843 prefect's report, ADBR V 511, p 2

20 Tax records, LBI, Alsatian Collection, AR-C 1088, tax records, JTS, French Documents, Box 24, calculations from 1846 census, ADBR 7 M 719, 726, 733, 740 (Strasbourg)

21 Etienne Juillard, *La Vie rurale dans la plaine de Basse-Alsace* (Paris, 1953), pp 447–48

22 Edmond Uhry, "Galleries of Memory," unpublished memoir, LBI, pp 14–15 Uhry emigrated from Alsace to the United States

23 Tax records, LBI, Alsatian Collection, AR-C 1088, #226–509

24 Jean-Paul Aron, Paul Dumont, and Emmanuel Le Roy Ladurie, *Anthropologie du conscrit français* (Paris and The Hague, 1972), pp 94–137

25 Prefect's report on the situation of the Jews, June 18, 1843, ADBR V 511

26 ADBR U 2300 (1826), U 2310 (1836), U 2320 (1846), U 2330 (1856), U 2340 (1866) Every ten years all cases involving Jews (as determined by onomastic criteria) were noted, and 25 percent were then sampled Many cases listed in the annual register were missing from the files

Year	No Cases	No Involving Jews	Percent Involving Jews
1826	779	138	17 7
1836	ca 675	187	27 7
1846	1,021	236	23 1
1856	827	228	27 6
1866	1,352	336	24 7

27 Sources used include Patentes des juifs d'Alsace, HM 2 782a and 782b, 1808–13, manuscript censuses, 1846 and 1866, Bischheim, Niederroedern, and Itterswiller, ADBR 7 M 459, 7 M 266 and 267, 7 M 562, and liquidation of debts, 1880, ZF 869, CAHJP

28 For a fine discussion of the problematics of occupational classification in social history, see Michael B Katz, "Occupational Classification in History," *Journal of Interdisciplinary History*, 3, no 1 (1972), pp 63–88

29 Liste des chefs de famille juifs, domiciliés en la ville de Bergheim, contenant leurs facultés pecuniaires, 1808, en Horbourg, 1808, HM 2/4941, CAHJP

30 Report of prefect of Upper Rhine, 1828, HM 2/4673, CAHJP The tax lists of the following Jewish communities of the Lower Rhine were analyzed Bischheim, Bouxwiller, Dettwiller, Haguenau, Ingwiller, Itterswiller, Lingolsheim, Niederroedern, Obernay, Odratzheim, Quatzenheim, Saverne, Stotzheim, Wissembourg, and Wolfisheim Frais du culte israélite du département du Bas-Rhin, #226–509, Alsatian Collection, AR-C 1088 2863, LBI

31 This scale, derived from Michael Katz's work on social mobility in nineteenth-century North America, avoids a sharp white-collar, blue-collar distinction, which was not characteristic of the reality of nineteenth-century economic life In light of the preponderance of mercantile professions (and of merchants who were not affluent) in the Jewish population, I have adapted Katz's scale by splitting his top category in two, thereby demoting ordinary merchants to a secondary rank The problem of the merchant in the Jewish economy, however, remains unsolved Clearly the status ranking of the Jewish population as a whole is artificially inflated vis-à-vis other groups by including all merchants in high-level categories, when many lived on the edge of poverty For an elaboration of the scale, see Michael Katz, *The People of Hamilton, Canada West* (Cambridge, Mass , 1975), pp 343–48

32 Report of Central Consistory, Jan 9, 1809, A N F[19] 11 034

33 Liste des vingt-cinq candidats pour le renouvellement intégral du collège des notables 1823, ADBR V 517, 1823 Frais du culte israélite du département du Bas-Rhin, Alsatian Collection, LBI, AR-C 1088 2863, letter of police commissioner, Aug 12, 1823, AMVS 71/402 Ref 9 (1823–24), Liste des cinquante israélites les plus imposés dans la circonscription de Strasbourg établie d'après le cens de 1829, ADBR V 517

34 Notables, Circonscription de Colmar, 1828, ZF 745, CAHJP Prefect's report, Department of

Upper Rhine, listing twenty-five Jewish notables, October 1830, HM 2/4673, CAHJP, "Notes sur les degrés de parenté qu'offre la liste des cinquante israélites les plus imposés aux frais généraux dans le Département du Haut-Rhin pour 1828," French Archival Documents, Box 4, Yeshiva University Library In 1831 thirteen of the notables of the Upper Rhine were related by blood or marriage Letter of prefect of Upper Rhine to minister of justice and cults, Nov 23, 1831, HM 2/4673, CAHJP The prefect claimed that this situation was very common

35 List of notables, Consistory of the Lower Rhine, 1845, ADBR V 517 On the Ordinance of 1844, see Albert, *Modernization of French Jewry*, pp 66–77

36 For the case history of an eighteenth-century Alsatian Jewish moneylender, see Jean Daltroff, "Samuel Levy de Balbronn prêteur d'argent en Basse-Alsace au 18e siècle," in *Archives juives*, 24, nos 1–2 (1988), 3–9 For a description and maps of the economic activity of two Jewish moneylenders from Bergheim, one from 1808 and the other from 1833, see *Histoire de l'Alsace rurale*, ed Boehler et al , pp 310–11

37 On the lack of adequate credit facilities, see L'Huillier, "L'Evolution dans la paix," in *Histoire de l'Alsace*, ed Dollinger, p 401 and Paul Klein, *L'Evolution contemporaine des banques alsaciennes* (Paris, 1931), pp 31–35 On Jewish moneylending see Wahl, *Confession et comportement*, 1 556–60, the citation is from p 556 For a general description of how Jewish moneylenders conducted their business as they bought and sold livestock and property, see Wahl, pp 550–58 Wahl has the annoying habit of referring to all Jewish moneylenders as usurers even when there is no evidence that the interest they received contravened the law

38 E Tisserand and Léon Lefebure, *Etude sur l'économie rurale de l'Alsace* (Paris and Strasbourg, 1869), p 217

39 Notarial records, court of Mutzig, ADBR

40 Sefer Heshbonot, Altkirch, ZF 154, CAHJP The account book had six pages torn out I deduced the name of its owner from a page in French at the end listing the expenses of Salomon Brunschwig and from several loans to "Moritz Brunschwig, my brother."

41 Zosa Szajkowski, *Poverty and Social Welfare among French Jews (1800–1880)* (New York, 1954), p 84 The results of the inquiry are found in ADBR X 372 and served as the source of L P Reboul-Deneyrol's study, *Paupérisme et bienfaisance dans le Bas-Rhin* (Paris and Strasbourg, 1858)

42 ADBR X 372.

43 Ibid

44 Paul Leuilliot, for example, discusses begging as a general social phenomenon but then singles out the Jews for special mention See his *L'Alsace au debut du xixe siècle,* 3 vols (Paris, 1959–60), 2 21

45 See Anchel, *Napoléon et les juifs* (Paris, 1928), pp 532–36

46 Consistory of the Upper Rhine, draft of report to the prefect, ca 1827, JTS, French Documents, Box 18, part 1, letter of Central Consistory to the minister of the interior, May 21, 1827, #2521, HM 1056, CAHJP

47 Letter of Consistory of Lower Rhine to mayor of Strasbourg, including extracts from Minutes of the Consistory, Oct 24, 1822, AMVS 71–402 Ref 8 (1821–22) Minutes of the Consistory of the Lower Rhine, Oct 24, 1822, Registre des délibérations, 1819–26, HM 5515, CAHJP

48 Letter from sixty wealthy Jews of Upper Rhine to minister of interior, ca 1829, HM 2/4673, CAHJP; Consistory of the Upper Rhine, draft of report to prefect, ca 1827, JTS, French Documents, Box 18, part 1, letter of Central Consistory to minister of the interior, May 21, 1827, #2521, HM 1056, CAHJP

49 Minutes of Comité d'administration de la communauté israélite de Strasbourg, Dec 14, 1839, HM 5526, CAHJP

50 Ibid , Sept 3, 1846, HM 5526, CAHJP

51 Ibid , Nov 26, 1846, Jan 14, 23, Apr 4, 1847, May 29, 1848, HM 5526, CAHJP

52 ADBR Y2 °, Registre des prisons civiles, 1847–52

53 Consistoire israélite de Strasbourg, Registre des procès-verbaux, 1853–58, sessions of Mar 15, 24, May 19, 1853 See also Albert, *Modernization of French Jewry,* pp. 136–40

54 See, e g , *AI*, 1 (1840), 315–17, 2 (1841), 118–20, 4 (1843), 614–15, 14 (1853), 433–34, 15 (1854), 273–79, 318–27, 383–91, 459–68, 507–11, 19 (1858), 325–27

55 *Lien d'Israèl*, 3, no 10 (1858), 435–39, and 3, no 11 (1858), 485–88

56 Wealthy Jews often invested in property In a survey of the economic activity of Jews in the area supervised by the Consistory of the Upper Rhine, conducted at the initiative of the consistory in 1820, the mayors of Belfort, Biesheim, Cernay, Wintzenheim, Niederhagenthal, Grussenheim, Horbourg, Hobsheim, Wettolsheim, Herabsheim, Bollviller, and Zillisheim commented that some Jews in their communes were cultivating land JTS, French Documents, Box 1 The census data from the mid-nineteenth century reveal, however, that Jews engaged in agriculture were even rarer than the 1820 report would indicate See Albert, *Modernization of French Jewry*, pp 141–42

Chapter Four· On the Domestic Scene

1 Henri Grégoire, *Essai sur la régénération physique, morale et politique des juifs* (Metz, 1789), p 36

2 Ibid

3 For a discussion of the ways in which nineteenth-century Western Jews viewed the Jewish family and of the centrality of the family in debates about assimilation, see my "The Modern Jewish Family Image and Reality," in *The Jewish Family Myth and Metaphor*, ed David Kraemer (Oxford, 1989), pp 179–93

4 Cahun, *La Vie juive* (Paris, 1886), pp 97–98

5 Stauben, *Scènes*, p 87 Stauben's stories on Alsace were published in a number of general as well as Jewish journals in the late 1840s and 1850s before their collective publication in 1860

6 An article about the travails of Jewish education in the Upper Rhine, written by a schoolteacher, mentions in passing that "ordinarily the father is absent the entire week " See *UI*, 17 (1861–62), 33–34 See also Stauben, *Scènes*, pp 223–25, and Raphael and Weyl, *Juifs en Alsace*, pp 336–38

7 Coypel, *Le Judaisme*, p 188

8 Ibid , pp 185–86, Weill, *Ma jeunesse*, 1 41–42, Raphael and Weyl, *Juifs en Alsace*, pp 302–3, 336

9 Cahun, *La Vie juive*, pp 21–22, Stauben, *Scènes*, Raphael and Weyl, *Regards nouveaux*, pp 209–10, Raphael and Weyl, *Juifs en Alsace*, p 338 For other descriptions of the traditional Sabbath observance prevalent in Alsatian villages through the 1870s, also see Coypel, *Le Judaisme*, pp 173–79, and Debré, *L'Humour judéo-alsacien*, p 291

10 My calculations from census taken in 1808, A N F¹⁹ 11 009, F¹⁹ 11 010 Estimation of age at marriage calculated from age at birth of first child

11 My calculations from marriage records, ADBR 4E 330, Niederroedern (1793–1830) (1831–62), 4E 226, Itterswiller (1793–1830) (1831–62), 5M1 852 and 853, Bischheim (1813–32) (1833–42) (1843–52) (1853–62), 5M1 1663, Strasbourg (1823–24) (1825–26) (1827–28) (1844–45) (1846–47) (1860–62), ADHR 5E 105, Colmar (1822–28) (1845–48), 5M1 66R 50, Colmar (1860–62)

12 Etienne Van de Walle, "Marriage and Marital Fertility," *Daedalus*, 97, no 2 (1968), 497 In 1866 the Alsatian departments of Haut-Rhin and Bas-Rhin had a mean age at first marriage (of both women and men) of 27 9 and 27 3, respectively These figures were considerably higher than the French norm

13 My calculations from marriage records cited in n 11, above

14 Pierre-Yves Touati, "Le Registre de circoncisions de Moshe et Simon Blum," *REJ*, 142, nos 1–2 (1983), 119–21 In Alsace after mid-century the Protestant rate of illegitimate births was approximately 7 percent See *Histoire de l'Alsace rurale*, ed Boehler et al , p 424

15 Mouvement de population, Colmar, 1860, ZF 953, CAHJP As is traditionally the case with illegitimate births, more than half of the illegitimate children (eight in fifteen) were stillborn

16 My calculations from marriage records cited in n. 11, above

17 Ibid

18 5M1 1663, Strasbourg (1823–24) (1825–26) (1827–28) (1844–45) (1846–47) (1860–62)

19 Stauben, *Scènes*, pp 41–53, 179–80, Coypel, *Le Judaïsme*, p 110, Weill, *Couronne*, p 117, Cahun, *La Vie juive*, pp 33, 87, Raphael and Weyl, *Juifs en Alsace*, pp 249–50 For a description and analysis of Jewish marriage customs in Alsace, also see Freddy Raphael, "Le Mariage juif dans la campagne alsacienne dans la deuxième moitié du xixe siècle," Folklore Research Center Studies, 4, *Studies in Marriage Customs*, ed Issachar Ben-Ami and Dov Noy (Jerusalem, 1974), pp 181–98 Raphael's sources, however, reflect the first half of the century better than the second half

20 Arnaud Aron, *Prières d'un coeur israélite* (Strasbourg, 1848), p 278

21 Examples of t'naim from the second half of that period 1826, Wissembourg, P90i, CAHJP, 1834, Strasbourg, JTS, French documents, Box 23, #23; and 1840, Ettersbach, LBI, Prenuptial agreement between Marc Dreyfuss and Minette Coblentz, Nov 27, 1867, from a private collection, displayed in the exhibition entitled "Memories of Alsace Folk Art and Jewish Tradition," The Jewish Museum, New York, May 18, 1989–Aug 14, 1989

22 "Procès-verbal de l'affaire Samuel Braunschweig," Yiddish with French translation, 1834, Hegenheim, JTS, French Documents, Box 18, part 1

23 David Schornstein, "La Dîme," *AI*, 25 (1864), 617–24, 718–24, 758–64, 804–9, 944–49, 992–97 Schornstein (1826–79) later assumed the pen name of Georges Stenne See also Stauben, *Scènes*, p 46, and Alexandre Weill, *Histoires de village* (Paris, 1860), p 219

24 Prenuptial contract of Marc Dreyfuss and Minette Coblentz, 1989 Jewish Museum exhibit

25 Freddy Raphael, "Le Mariage juif," in *Studies in Marriage Customs*, ed Ben-Ami and Noy, p 183, *Lien d'Israël*, 4 (1858–59), 74, *AI*, 29 (1868), 715

26 Raphael, "Le Mariage juif," in *Studies in Marriage Customs*, ed Ben-Ami and Noy, pp 182–83, Raphael and Weyl, *Juifs en Alsace*, pp 248–49

27 Marion Kaplan's fine study of the dowry among German Jews demonstrated the persistence of the custom through the Wilhelmian period See her "For Love or Money The Marriage Strategies of Jews in Imperial Germany," *LBIYB*, 28 (1983), 263–300

28 Household census data were drawn from ADBR 7 M 719, 726, 733, 740 (Strasbourg), 7 M 266 (Bischheim), 7 M 459 (Itterswiller), 7 M 562 (Niederroedern), all 1846, and CAHJP, ZF 478 (Uffheim) and ZF 683 (Herrlisheim), both 1850 Household census data cannot, of course, provide accurate age-specific fertility because children who have died or moved away are not reflected in the data, but they are useful for comparative purposes, as here

29 See my "Jewish Fertility in Nineteenth-Century France," in *Modern Jewish Fertility*, ed Paul Ritterband (Leiden, 1981), pp 78–93

30 The discussion of household size and structure is based on analysis of all the Jewish households of Strasbourg, Bischheim, Niederroedern, and Itterswiller located in the manuscript censuses of 1846, which listed the religion of each individual, and traced in the censuses of 1856 and 1866, which did not The sources are ADBR files listed in n 28, as well as 7 M 267 (Bischheim) and 7 M 720, 727, 734, 741 (Strasbourg, 1856), 7 M 722, 729, 736, 743 (Strasbourg, 1866)

31 Uffheim, ZF 478, and Herrlisheim, ZF 683, CAHJP

32 For a stimulating survey of the literature on family history, see Lawrence Stone, "Family History in the 1980s Achievements and Future Trends," *Journal of Interdisciplinary History*, 12, no 1 (1981), pp 51–87

33 Uffheim, ZF 478, Herrlisheim, ZF 683, and Hochfelden, ZF 695, CAHJP

34 Burns, "Dreyfus Family," in *Dreyfus Affair*, ed Kleeblatt, pp 145–46

35 See chapter 3 and Dreyfus Family Archives, P90f, CAHJP

36 Joan W Scott and Louise A Tilly, *Women, Work, and Family* (New York, 1978), p 124

37 Schornstein, "La Dîme," *AI*, 25 (1864), 619

38 Burns, "Dreyfus Family," in *Dreyfus Affair*, ed Kleeblatt, pp 143, 146

39 Schornstein, "La Dîme," *AI*, 25 (1864), 623

40 Notarized document with stamp "Emp Fran ," Dreyfus Family Archives, P90/b1, CAHJP The documents in this family archive indicate that Hirtzl [Henry] Dreyfuss, born in 1755, had

emigrated from France in 1793 but had returned by 1808, when he and his wife and children registered their new names Sometime thereafter they were removed from the list of émigrés In 1816 the mayor of Wissembourg certified that Henry Dreifus [sic], the father of eight children, had lost the major part of his fortune as a result of his emigration He is listed in documents variously as a négociant (large-scale businessman or wholesaler, 1776), marchand (1800), commerçant (the document cited, during the First Empire), butcher (1825), and marchand juif (1826)

41 Statement of mayor of Wissembourg, July 25, 1816, Dreyfus Family Archive, P90/b, CAHJP

42 See my "Modern Jewish Family," in Jewish Family, ed Kraemer, pp 179–93

43 Lien d'Israël, 4 (1858–59), 73–74

44 See, e g , UI, 20 (1864–65), 274–76, 598

45 AI, 14 (1853), 415 The editor of this journal sees the Jewish delight in luxury as a long-standing abuse Attributing this abuse to women also has a long history, as Jewish communal sumptuary legislation reveals

46 See, e g , L'Ami des israélites· revue mensuelle, religieuse, morale et littéraire, 1 (1847–48), 41–44

47 Quotation is from Aron, Prières d'un coeur israélite Joel Anspach, editor of the Rituel des prières, which was first published in Metz in 1820 and went through four editions by 1848, mentions in the introduction to the first edition (p 1) that the situation of his wife and sisters, who were constrained to pray mechanically in a language they did not understand, stimulated him to correct this "abuse," which, he admitted, also affected "a large sector of men who haven't studied the holy tongue "

48 Commission de la propagation des livres de morale et religion, Strasbourg Consistory, 1846, JTS, French Documents, Box 19

49 Extracts of Minutes of Strasbourg Consistory, Sept 17, 1846, and Dec 9, 1846, JTS, French Documents, Box 18, part 2

50 Aron, Prières d'un coeur israélite, p 263

51 Ibid , pp 264–65

52 Ibid , pp 266–67 There was also a prayer for a widow, pp 268–69, but none for a widower It seems that dependency was presumed to motivate prayer

53 Ibid , pp 260–62. This concept of the importance of the mother's educational role, a staple of nineteenth-century bourgeois thought, found expression some decades later in French Jewry's educational project among the Jews of North Africa and the Ottoman Empire through the Alliance Israélite Universelle See Aron Rodrigue, French Jews, Turkish Jews (Bloomington, 1990), pp 78–79

Chapter Five· The Social Foundations of Cultural Conservatism

1 For a stimulating discussion of the relationship between social reality and religious culture, see Peter Berger, The Sacred Canopy (Garden City, N Y , 1969)

2 Académie de Strasbourg, Université de France, Nov 6, 1821, A N F¹⁹ 11 028

3 Cited in Zosa Szajkowski, "The Struggle against Yiddish in France" [Yiddish], YIVO Bleter, 14, nos 1–2 (1939), 71–72

4 "Observations sur les écoles israélites," AI, 4 (1843), as cited in Szajkowski, "Struggle," p 77

5 "Souvenirs d'un voyage en Alsace," AI, 5 (1844), 469–70

6 Szajkowski, "Struggle," pp 64–69

7 Stauben, Scènes pp. 79–80.

8 Ibid , pp 221–22

9 Ibid , pp. 112–13

10 Weill, Couronne, pp 42, 151

11 ADBR 4E 330, Niederroedern (1793–1830) (1831–62), 4E 226, Itterswiller (1793–1830) (1831–62), and 5M1 852 and 853, Bischheim (1813–32) (1833–42) (1843–52) (1853–62)

All Jewish marriages in these three communes were coded The grooms figuring in these marriage lived in sixty-three locales in Alsace

12 JTS, French Documents, Box 18, Folio 177

13 ZF 306, CAHJP

14 Copies of letters from the community of Bischheim (1837–47), HM 5519 and pinkas (minute book) of the community (1836–57), HM 5520, CAHJP

15 Colmar Consistory, Inquiry concerning community of Hattstatt, 1847, ZF 212, CAHJP

16 The Odratzheim pinkas is MS 3834, JTS, the Bouxwiller pinkas, HM 5506, CAHJP

17 My calculations The Strasbourg marriage files used were 5M1 1663 (1823–24) (1825–26) (1827–28) (1844–45) (1846–47) (1860) (1861) (1862) I found and coded a total of 176 Jewish marriages in Strasbourg in those years The statistics on the Lower Rhine may be found in *Histoire de l'Alsace rurale,* ed Boehler et al , p 326

18 On the innovation among women's names and the greater traditionalism in men's names, see Paul Lévy, *Les noms des israélites en France* (Paris, 1960), p 73 The marriage records listed above were used, as were the following census records ADBR 7 M 719, 726, 733, 740 (Strasbourg, 1846), 7 M 720, 727, 734, 741 (Strasbourg, 1856), 7 M 722, 729, 736, 743 (Strasbourg, 1866)

19 Marriage records, as listed in nn 11 and 17, above

20 *Histoire de l'Alsace rurale,* ed Boehler et al , p 366

21 Freddy Raphael, "Les Juifs d'Alsace et la conscription au xixe siècle," in *Juifs et la Révolution française,* ed. Soboul and Blumenkranz, p 127, and Raphael and Weyl, *Regards nouveaux,* p 239 For other references to this phenomenon, see Weill, *Couronne,* p 76, and Stauben, *Scènes,* p. 184 One lithograph of Rabbi Seckel Loeb, produced in Strasbourg in the mid-nineteenth century, appeared in the Jewish Museum exhibit "Memories of Alsace "

22 Raphael and Weyl, *Juifs en Alsace,* pp 239, 289–90, Weill, *Ma jeunesse,* 1 73, and *Couronne,* pp 5–7

23 Cahun, *La Vie juive,* pp. 10–11, Coypel, *Le Judaïsme,* p 43, Debré, *L'Humour judéo-alsacien,* p 40

24 JTS, French Documents, Box 18 The Central Consistory shared the opinion of the prefect of the Department of the Upper Rhine that such a ban would not work and instead suggested that the commissaire surveillant report incidents of this "scandalous behavior" to governmental authorities Letter of Central Consistory to the Wintzenheim Consistory, #2419, Nov 30, 1823, HM 1055, CAHJP

25 Weill, *Couronne,* p 197

26 Originals are in the LBI, West European Collection, AR-C 1638–4099, #3–19 and ZF 276 (the signed and dated version) in the CAHJP In one version in the LBI West European Collection the mother recited the prayer for her son. For Raphael's analysis of similar documents, see his "Juifs d'Alsace et la conscription," pp 122–23, and Raphael and Weyl, *Regards nouveaux,* pp 235–39

27 Raphael and Weyl, *Juifs en Alsace,* pp 190–92, and Weyl and Raphael, *L'Imagerie juive d'Alsace* (Strasbourg, 1979), p 31 The Torah binder, or wimpel, was the swaddling cloth used during an infant's circumcision and donated to the synagogue to wrap the Torah scroll, especially at the time of the boy's bar mitzvah In light of the contradictory evidence in literary sources, it seems to me that Raphael and Weyl attribute too much to the few nineteenth-century Torah wimpels they have found in red, white, and blue or with patriotic symbols As the Jewish Museum 1989 exhibit suggests, most of the patriotic Torah binders date from after 1870, during the period of the German annexation The exhibit also included a "Composite Souvenir Conscription Number and Decoration for the Eastern Wall" (shiviti), made for Leopold Bauer of Strasbourg in 1855.

28 Cahun, *La Vie juive,* p 53

29 Honel Meiss, *Traditions populaires alsaciennes à travers le dialecte judéo-alsacien* (Nice, n d), p 207 In his collection of Judeo-Alsatian humor, Debré attributes no pejorative connotation to the term *rek* but claims that it refers only to the soldier's impoverished condition This seems to be an apologetic reading of the term See Debré, *L'Humour judéo-alsacien,* p 239.

30 On the Jewish adaptation of general Alsatian images, see Weyl and Raphael, *L'Imagerie juive,* and the brochure of the 1989 Jewish Museum exhibition, "Memories of Alsace," pp 2–3 The

exhibit included a watercolor mizraḥ of an Alsatian bouquet of roses, a Torah crown of paper flowers (reproduced in Raphael and Weyl, *Juifs en Alsace*, opp p 289), and three lithographs of biblical scenes. For a discussion of lower-class Jews' adoption of the cultural patterns of the urban poor in London, see Todd Endelman, *The Jews of Georgian England, 1730–1830 Tradition and Change in a Liberal Society* (Philadelphia, 1979), pp 166–226

31 *AI*, 6 (1845), 879, *Lien d'Israel*, 1 (1855), 101.

32 On the dedication of new synagogues, see *Lien d'Israël*, 7 (1861), 152, *AI*, 29 (1868), 887, and 30 (1869), 572

33 Stauben, *Scènes*, pp. 148–49

34 Uhry, "Galleries of Memory," p 75

35 Stauben, *Scènes*, p 160, Cahun, *La Vie juive*, p 96

36 Isaac Lévy, *Les Veillées du vendredi* (Verdun, 1863), p. 158. See also Debré, *L'Humour judéo-alsacien*, p. 84, Weill, *Histoires de village* (Paris, 1860), p 300, Cahun, *La Vie juive*, p 102, and Raphael and Weyl, *Juifs en Alsace*, p 309.

37 For a representative sample of quotations expressing this point of view, see Robert Liberles, "Emancipation and the Structure of the Jewish Community in the Nineteenth Century," *LBIYB*, 31 (1986), 51–52

38 For a list of gabbaim in the Department of the Lower Rhine, see the letter of 22 Ellul 5598 (1838) to Grand Rabbi Aron and the Strasbourg Consistory, *Iggrot Paquam*, 8, 108 b See also Jonathan Helfand, "The Contacts between the Jews of France and of the Land of Israel in the First Half of the Nineteenth Century" [Hebrew], *Cathedra*, 36 (1985), 37–54

39 Cahun, *La Vie juive*, p 80, Raphael and Weyl, *Juifs en Alsace*, pp 388–89, Debré, *L'Humour judéo-alsacien*, p 276, *AI*, 1 (1840), 315–17, 2 (1841), 118–20, 4 (1843), 614–15, 14 (1853), 433–34, 15 (1854), 273–79, 318–27, 383–91, 459–68, 507–11, 19 (1858), 325–27

40 HM 5010, CAHJP

41 *UI*, 1 (1844–45), 16

42 *UI*, 12 (1856–57), 105

43 On Christian birth customs, see Freddy Sarg, *La Naissance en Alsace* (Strasbourg, 1974) On Jewish birth customs, see Coypel, *Le Judaïsme*, p 94, Raphael and Weyl, *Juifs en Alsace*, pp 234–35, Raphael, "Rîtes de naissance et médecine populaire dans le judaïsme rural d'Alsace," *Ethnologie française* 1, nos 3–4 (1971), 83–87 The 1989 Jewish Museum exhibit displayed several amulets for women in childbirth as well as an amuletic knife, a *krasmesser*. For an incantation directed against Lilith and her cohorts, see P/102, CAHJP For an analysis of the historical development of one Jewish birth custom, see Elliott Horowitz, "The Eve of the Circumcision A Chapter in the History of Jewish Nightlife," *Journal of Social History*, 23, no 1 (1989), 45–69

44 Raphael and Weyl, *Juifs en Alsace*, pp 236–37, Raphael, "Rîtes de naissance," pp 88–90

45 Stauben, *Scènes*, pp 11–12, Weill, *Histoires de village*, p 308, Coypel, *Le Judaïsme*, p 134

46 *AI*, 5 (1844), 661

47 On the confrontation with the rabbi of Haguenau, see Minutes of Strasbourg Consistory, Mar 27, 1847, HM 5503, CAHJP. The quotation is from Coypel, *Le Judaïsme*, p 34

48 Stauben, *Scènes*, pp 89–95, Coypel, *Le Judaïsme*, pp 146–62 For an extensive discussion of Jewish death and mourning customs in Alsace, see Raphael and Weyl, *Juifs en Alsace*, pp 266–87, and Consistoire Israélite de Strasbourg, "A MM les rabbins communaux et commissaires administrateurs des synagogues, 1 nov 1860," p 1, Houghton Library, Harvard University

49 Yiddish manuscript will of Yeckel bar Yitzchak Schwartz of Balbronn, dated 28 Shvat, 5631 (1871), HM 5513, CAHJP

50 *AI*, 15 (1854), 529

51 Ibid , 5 (1844), 284

52 LBI, West European Collection, AR-C 1638–4099, #3–15

53 On Rabbi Loeb Sarassin, see *UI*, 16 (1860–61), 85–86. Sarassin studied in Mainz, Mannheim, and Frankfurt am Main; *Tableau du personnel des ministres du culte israélite*, 1864, LBI, AR 10882863, #80–101

•

54 Albert, *Modernization of French Jewry,* pp 242–55

55 LBI, AR-C 1088 2863, #80–101, Albert, *Modernization of French Jewry,* pp 255–58

56 *AI,* 5 (1844), 78–79

57 Ibid , p 737

58 *AI,* 1 (1840), 562–63

59 *AI,* 5 (1844), 610, 8 (1847), 477 Even in 1858 the Strasbourg Consistory issued an ordinance banning the sale of honors throughout the Department of the Lower Rhine "A MM les commissaires administrateurs des synagogues," Mar 20, 1858, Houghton Library, Harvard University

60 Letter of Salomon Ulmann to Nordmann, October 1850 replying to Nordmann's letter of Sept 30 Ulmann agreed with Nordmann's position Letters of Rabbi Salomon Ulmann, December 1843–August 1857, MS 8488, pp 185–86, JTS, S Bloch, "Nouvelle excursion en Alsace," *UI,* 5 (1849–50), 481

61 Steven M Lowenstein, "The 1840s and the Creation of the German-Jewish Reform Movement," in *Revolution and Evolution,* ed Mosse et al , pp 251, 265–66

62 For a general discussion of traditional hevrot in Alsace, see Raphael and Weyl, *Juifs en Alsace,* pp. 271–74

63 Letter from Central Consistory to departmental consistories, Nov 20, 1862, #9151, HM 1061, CAHJP A pre-Passover circular from Rabbi Aron of Strasbourg refers to the numerous philanthropic *confréries* and *associations pieuses* as hevrot *UI,* 9 (1853–54), 373 An earlier document of 1810 from the Hevra d'Talmud Torah of Wissembourg demanded payment of membership dues from Jona Treyfus [sic] even though he was then in the army P90/h, CAHJP

64 Letter from Central Consistory to Colmar Consistory, May 13, 1828, #2651, HM 1056, CAHJP

65 *UI,* 2 (1845–46), p 323 The *Archives israélites* also mentioned the existence of hevrot in Scherviller *AI,* 4 (1843), 286

66 *L'Ami des israélites* (1847), pp 127–28

67 Ibid , p 218

68 Takonos shel Hachevro d'Shocharei Hatov, Riedseltz, 5697 [Yiddish], in manuscript, HM 5521, and Pinkas Cheshbonos shel Chevras Shocharei Hatov b'Riedseltz (1837–49) [Yiddish], HM 5528, CAHJP

69 Pinkas, HM 5528, CAHJP

70 Albert, *Modernization of French Jewry,* p 186 For a full description of the post, see pp 182–87, 612

71 Ibid , pp 186–87

72 Letter, Strasbourg Consistory, Feb 21, 1830, ZF 295, CAHJP

73 JTS, French Documents, Box 18, Folios 236–37

74 *AI,* 5 (1844), 796

75 JTS, French Documents, Box 18

76 Albert, *Modernization of French Jewry,* pp 183–84, 186

77 Letter from the Central Consistory to the Strasbourg Consistory, Apr 12, 1867, JTS, French Documents, Box 10, Consistorial correspondence, 1863–69, *AI,* 29 (1868), 283–84

78 Petition, June 10, 1846, JTS, French Documents, Box 18, petition from Luemschwiller, Houghton Library, Harvard University

79 Archives of the Strasbourg Consistory, uncataloged, Minutes, May 13, 1858 See Albert, *Modernization of French Jewry,* p 191

80 *AI,* 1 (1840), 520–21

81 Ibid , pp 580–81

82 Ibid , p 665, 3 (1842), 26, 6 (1845), 46–47

83 *AI,* 6 (1845), 46–47

84 *AI,* 2 (1841), 612–15, 5 (1844), 206–7

85 *AI,* 7 (1846), 505–9 On the 1846 selection process for the position of grand rabbi of France, see Albert, *Modernization of French Jewry,* pp 274–75, 298–301

86 Petitions, JTS, French Documents, Box 18, *AI,* 7 (1846), 292–96, 505–9

87 The *Archives israélites* condemned Klein's critique See "Un rabbin plus orthodoxe que le Talmud," *AI*, 8 (1847), 313–17 The article dismisses Klein as "a village rabbi" (p 313)

88 Salomon Klein, *Sermon*, Imprimée à la demande de plusieurs notables (Paris, 1847), 12 pp , citations are from pp 8 and 11

89 *AI*, 11 (1850), 291

90 Ibid , p 292

91 *AI*, 12 (1851), 348–49, 15 (1854), 28–29

92 Salomon Klein, *Ma 'aneh Rakh* (Mulhouse, 1846), p 1

93 Ibid , p 4

94 Ibid , p 12

95 Salomon Klein, *Ha-emet v'hashalom āhavu* (Frankfurt am Main, 1861), p 7

96 Salomon Klein, *Mipne Koshet Bikoret Sefer Darkhei HaMishnah* (Frankfurt am Main, 1861)

97 Ibid , p 2

98 Ibid , pp 2–3

99 Ibid., p 3

100 Ibid , p 32

101 Ibid , p 13

102 Ibid , p 30

103 Minutes of the 1856 meeting of the rabbis of the consistories of the east, JTS, French Documents, Box 19

Chapter Six: Migration

1 Doris Ben Simon-Donath, *Sociodémographie des juifs de France et d'Algérie, 1867–1907* (Paris, 1976), p 94

2 My calculations, based on governmental census data found in A N F¹⁹ 11 024 and consistorial censuses located in the LBI Archives, AR-C 1088 2863, Folios 34–39, 80–101 See also Albert, *Modernization of French Jewry*, pp 18, 328, 334

3 *Histoire de l'Alsace rurale*, ed Boehler, et al , pp 307–8, Marx, "De la Pré-Révolution à la Restauration," in *Histoire de l'Alsace*, ed Dollinger, p. 359; Weill, "L'Alsace," in *Histoire des juifs en France*, ed Blumenkranz, p 166, Albert, *Modernization of French Jewry*, pp 324, 339, *Statistique générale de la France;* A N F¹⁹ 11 023 and F¹⁹ 11 024

4 My calculations, notarial records of the court of Mutzig, 1855–64, ADBR

5 See Judith Laikin Elkin, *Jews of the Latin American Republics* (Chapel Hill, N C , 1980), pp 34, 37, 39, 44–46, 50, and Robert Levinson, *The Jews in the California Gold Rush* (New York, 1978), pp 6, 146. On Aron Dreyfus and the contract of sale for the Metz house, see the Dreyfus Family Papers, P90 g, CAHJP

6 "Emigration en Amérique d'habitants du Bas-Rhin—états numériques et nominatives, 1828–37," ADBR 3M 703 Since I selected only emigrants whose names were distinctively Jewish, it is likely that the total of Jewish emigrants considerably exceeded fifty I wish to thank Vicki Caron for bringing this source to my attention On general Alsatian emigration in the first half of the nineteenth century, see *Histoire de l'Alsace rurale* ed Boehler, et al , pp 308–9 For a stimulating discussion of the evolution of emigration from Alsace after the German annexation, see Caron, *Between France and Germany Jews and National Identity in Alsace-Lorraine, 1871–1918* (Stanford, 1988)

7 Strasbourg Consistory, Minutes, 1853–58 See also Albert, *Modernization of French Jewry*, pp 139–40

8 Marriage records include information on place of birth and domicile of the bride and groom as well as the domicile of their parents It is therefore possible to ascertain whether the bride and groom or the parents have migrated. One-third of the 544 grooms in my sample from the Lower Rhine were domiciled in a locale different from their place of birth, indicating that they, or their parents (and sometimes both) had migrated Forty-one of the sixty-three grooms in my sample from Colmar were also from migrating families Yet, my figures from marriages taking

place in Alsace understate the real extent of migration because emigrants from the region tended not to return for the purpose of marriage Notarial records list the domiciles of surviving heirs, more than 40 percent of them had migrated ADBR 4E 330, Niederroedern (1793–1830) (1831–62); 4E 226, Itterswiller (1793–1830) (1831–62); and 5M1 852 and 853, Bischheim (1813–32) (1833–42) (1843–52) (1853–62); 5M1 1663, Strasbourg (1823– 24) (1825–26) (1827–28) (1844–45) (1846–47) (1860) (1861) (1862), ADHR 5E 105, Colmar (1822–28) (1845–48), and 5M1 66R.50 (1860–62) ADBR, notarial records of the court of Mutzig, 1855–64

9 My calculations, notarial records of the court of Mutzig, 1855–64, ADBR

10 Membership lists of mutual aid societies, French Archival Collection, Box 2, Yeshiva University Library

11 Uhry, "Galleries of Memory," pp 1–10

12 Burns, "Dreyfus Family," pp 142–45, and "Emancipation and Reaction," in Living with Antisemitism Modern Jewish Responses, ed Jehuda Reinharz (Hanover, N H , 1987), pp 38–39

13 My calculations from marriage records listed above Of the migrating grooms 0 9 percent were illiterate as compared with 2 2 percent of the nonmigrants Although 1 8 percent of the fathers of the migrants were illiterate, 4 2 percent of the fathers of the stationary grooms were illiterate

14 Lowenstein, "Rural Community and Urbanization of German Jewry," pp 219, 221–23, 226– 28, 235 Unlike the situation in France, however, legal barriers kept Jews in villages and small towns in several German states in the first half of the nineteenth century Lowenstein has evidence for educational and cultural change preceding migration that is not available for the Alsatian Jewish setting

15 "Etat nominatif des notables de la circonscription consistoriale de Strasbourg," 1828, ZF 659, and "Etat nominatif des notables de la circonscription consistoriale de Colmar," 1828, ZF 745, CAHJP

16 Letter of the Administrative Committee of Bischheim, Feb 20, 1848, HM 5520, CAHJP

17 Ben Simon-Donath, Sociodémographie des juifs de France, p 150 I have modified my occupational classification in order to permit comparison with Ben Simon-Donath's figures

18 List of electors from Lille, 1861, French Archival Collection, Box 2, Yeshiva University Library

19 List of departments containing Jews originally from the Lower Rhine and who were obligated to contribute to the extinction of the debt of the former Jewish community of Alsace, 1868, Alsace-Lorraine Collection, Box 1, Folder 8, Hebrew Union College Library

20 For a discussion of migration within France, see Leslie Page Moch, Paths to the City Regional Migration in Nineteenth-Century France (Beverly Hills, Calif , 1983)

21 Cahun, La Vie juive, p 108

22 Ibid , p 73

23 Stauben, Scènes, p 96

24 For a similar analysis of East European Jewish immigrants to the United States, see Charles Liebman, "Religion, Class and Culture in American Jewish History," Jewish Journal of Sociology, 9, no 2 (1967), 227–41

25 Coypel, Le Judaïsme, p 158

26 Debré, L'Humour judéo-alsacien, p 291

27 See, for example, Todd Endelman's fine discussion of behavioral assimilation among the urban Jewish lower classes in his Jews of Georgian England Although Endelman does not stress the immigrant origins of the Anglo-Jewish community of that period, his evidence supports our argument On the erosion of the traditional culture of Jewish immigrants from Eastern Europe in New York City, see Moses Rischin, The Promised City. New York's Jews (Cambridge, Mass., 1962)

28 Burns, "Emancipation and Reaction," pp 32–33.

29 Membership lists of mutual aid societies, French Archival Collection, Box 2, Yeshiva University Library

30 Letter, Sept 4, 1848 In this letter, however, the influx was not attributed to the revolutionary unrest HM 5533, CAHJP

31 AI, 25 (1864), 598–99

32 My calculations from my sample of 607 Jewish marriages from Strasbourg, Bischheim, Itterswiller, Niederroedern, and Colmar, as cited above, n 7

33 "Souvenirs d'un voyage en Alsace," *AI*, 5 (1844), 468 Population statistics on Mulhouse derive from A N F¹⁹ 11 023 and F¹⁹ 11 024 and from Statistics, Colmar Consistory, 1851, JTS, Box 26, letter from Central Consistory to Ministry of Cults, May 28, 1838, HM 1058, CAHJP

34 A N F¹⁹ 11 023 and F¹⁹ 11 024, List of communities, Consistory of the Lower Rhine, 1854 and 1863, LBI AR-C 10882863, 34–39. Analysis of geographical origins of Strasbourg's adult Jewish population derived from ADBR 7 M 719, 726, 733, 740 (Strasbourg, 1846)

35 *Lien d'Israel*, 3 (1857–58), 253–54

Chapter Seven: Education and the Modernization of Alsatian Jews

1 Citation from *Précis de l'examen qui a eu lieu, le 18 janvier 1824, à l'école primaire israélite de Strasbourg* (Strasbourg, 1824), p 27 On Enlightenment attitudes toward moral and civic education, see Harvey Chisick, *The Limits of Reform in the Enlightenment· Attitudes toward the Education of the Lower Classes in Nineteenth-Century France* (Princeton, 1981), pp 157–60 On the general moral thrust of primary education in nineteenth-century France, see R D Anderson, *Education in France, 1848–1870* (London, 1975), pp 15, 170–71, and Maurice Crubellier, *L'enfance et la jeunesse dans la société française, 1800–1950* (Paris, 1979), p 92 On Haskalah attitudes toward education, see Mordecai Eliav, *Jewish Education in Germany in the Period of Enlightenment and Emancipation* [Hebrew] (Jerusalem, 1961), and Michael A Meyer, *Response to Modernity A History of the Reform Movement in Judaism* (Oxford, 1988), pp 13–17, 23 On the linkage of regeneration and Jewish education in France, see Berkovitz, *Shaping of Jewish Identity*, pp 150–91

2 *Précis de l'examen*, p 17

3 Ibid , pp 25–26

4 Ibid., p 28

5 On this pattern in Jewish education at the end of the eighteenth century and the beginning of the nineteenth, see Eliav, *Jewish Education in Germany*, pp 15, 74

6 Posener, "Immediate Economic and Social Effects," p 310

7 Moche Catane, "The Education and Culture of the Jews of Alsace at the End of the Eighteenth Century and the Beginning of the Nineteenth Century" [Hebrew], *Proceedings of the Fifth World Congress of Jewish Studies,* vol 2 (Jerusalem, 1972), p 309 On the basis of signatures of the 1808 registers of name changes, Catane found an illiteracy rate of 8 percent for Jewish men and 38 percent for Jewish women

8 Consistory of the Lower Rhine, Register of deliberations, Sept 9, 1819, HM 5515, CAHJP The initial decision preceded this meeting for in July the Central Consistory had congratulated the Strasbourg Consistory on its plan to establish schools, especially for the poor The Central Consistory described the establishment of schools as "the only and unique way to bring about the moral amelioration of those under our administration " Letter of Central Consistory to the Strasbourg Consistory, July 2, 1819, #1926, HM 1055, CAHJP

9 Comité cantonal, Délibérations, Nov 13, 1820, HM 5516, CAHJP

10 Letter of Central Consistory to Consistory of Wintzenheim, Dec 12, 1821, #2554, HM 1055, CAHJP

11 Letter of Central Consistory to Consistory of Colmar, Aug 2, 1826, #2718, HM 1056, CAHJP

12 Consistory of the Lower Rhine, Session of Dec 31, 1823, HM 5515, CAHJP

13 Letter to rector, Mar 2, 1826, Copie de lettres du Comité cantonal des israélites du ressort de l'Académie de Strasbourg, 1825–32, HM 5529, CAHJP

14 Weill, *Ma jeunesse*, 1 67–69, 73–75 For a critical biography of Weill, see Joe Friedemann, *Alexandre Weill Ecrivain contestaire et historien engagé, 1811–1899*, Société Savante d'Alsace et des Régions de l'Est, vol 29 (Strasbourg, 1980)

15 Letter to Consistory, July 18, 1826, letter to rector, Aug 18, 1826, Copie de lettres du Comité cantonal, HM 5529, CAHJP

16 For example, in Zellwiller in 1825 Délibérations of Comité cantonal, Mar 28, 1825, Nov 27, 1825, HM 5516, letter to rector, Nov 28, 1825, HM 5529, CAHJP

17 Letter of May 25, 1831, ibid

18 On Goudchaux's relocation to Colmar, see letters of Central Consistory, #3603 to Colmar Consistory, Dec 10, 1833, and #3630 to Strasbourg Consistory, Jan 28, 1834, HM 1057, CAHJP

19 Letter of Cantonal Committee, May 25, 1831, HM 5529, CAHJP By 1843 one elderly teacher of calligraphy turned to the Consistory of the Lower Rhine for assistance because he had lost all his students since the establishment of academic schools Letter from Ephraim Grosmuth, May 10, 1843, HM 5503, CAHJP

20 Deliberations of Comité cantonal, Jan 2, 1826, HM 5516, CAHJP, and Maurice Bloch, "L'Alsace juive depuis la Révolution de 1789" (Colmar, 1907), p 12

21 Letter of June 8, 1832, Comité d'instruction primaire pour les écoles du Bas-Rhin, 1832–33, HM 5518, CAHJP

22 Letter to prefect of Lower Rhine, Aug 31, 1833, ibid

23 On the Guizot Law see Antoine Prost, Histoire de l'enseignement en France, 1800–1967 (Paris, 1968), pp 92, 166 and Anderson, Education in France, p 30 For the 1833 inquiry, see Paul Lévy, "Les écoles juives d'Alsace et de Lorraine d'il y a un siècle," La Tribune juive, no 32 (Aug 11, 1933), p 520

24 Lévy, ibid , no 33 (Aug 18, 1933), p 540

25 Ibid , no 38 (Sept 15, 1933), p 624

26 Ibid , no 34 (Aug 25, 1933), p 569, and no. 36 (Sept 8, 1933), p 600

27 Anderson, Education in France, p 29

28 La Régénération, 1 (1836), 20

29 Victor Treshan, "The Struggle for Integration The Jewish Community of Strasbourg, 1818–1850" (Ph D thesis, University of Wisconsin, 1979)

30 For complaints about the reluctance of municipal councils to provide funds for Jewish primary schools, see 1846 consistorial census with survey of educational facilities, circonscription of Strasbourg, JTS, #8599, UI, 2 (1845–46), 338, 469, and L'Ami des israélites (1847), 278 As late as 1862 the Central Consistory noted instances of abuse in the Department of the Upper Rhine, letter to minister of public instruction and cults, July 4, 1862, A N F¹⁹ 11 034

31 Letter of June 2, 1834, as cited in Treshan, Struggle for Integration, p 100

32 Szajkowski, Jewish Education in France, p 10 In 1846 the Jews of Obernai complained that their municipal council refused support to the local Jewish school with the claim that the Christian school was sufficient for all children Census, 1846, JTS, #8599

33 Letter of Central Consistory to minister of public instruction and cults, Dec 8, 1841, HM 1058, CAHJP The Central Consistory complained that only three of the forty primary schools in the Upper Rhine received any subvention

34 Strasbourg Consistory, Minutes, June 15, 1842, HM 5503, CAHJP

35 For example, see letter of May 31, 1825, from Comité cantonal to Strasbourg Consistory, HM 5529, CAHJP, and AI, 4 (1845), 246–47

36 Letter of minister of justice and cults, Mar 12, 1841, A N F¹⁹ 11 028 It was a direct grant from the Ministry of Public Instruction that enabled Bischheim's Jewish school to become an école communale Letter from the administrator of the Jewish community of Bischheim to Col Max Cerfberr, deputy from the Lower Rhine, July 12, 1847, JTS, French Documents, Box 25

37 HM 1058, CAHJP

38 Report of prefect of the Lower Rhine, June 18, 1843, ADBR V 511

39 AI, 4 (1843), 280–88

40 My calculations from figures provided by Aron in ibid Girls also accounted for about one-third of primary school pupils in France in general at this time See Anderson, Education in France, p 31

41 1846 census, Strasbourg Consistory, JTS, #8599 A number of communities complained about the conditions of the schools and the fact that the local teacher, often the cantor, was not licensed

42 Statistics, Consistory of the Lower Rhine, 1854, LBI, AR-C 10882863, #34–39

43 *L'Ami des israélites* (1847), 278 The paper counted fifty-seven schools, twenty-four public and thirty-three private, in comparison with fifty-eight schools—twenty-eight public and thirty private—in 1854

44 Statistics, Consistory of the Upper Rhine, 1851, JTS, French Documents, Box 26

45 *UI*, 9 (1853–54), 277; *Lien d'Israël*, 3 (1857–58)

46 Statistics, Consistory of the Upper Rhine, 1851, JTS, French Documents, Box 26, *AI*, 8 (1847), 241, 243

47 In 1842 six Jewish students were studying in the Ecole Normale of Strasbourg, although the number of Jewish students was not supposed to exceed one for each twenty-five Jewish schools Minutes, Strasbourg Consistory, Nov 15, 1842, HM 5503, CAHJP The *Archives israélites* of 1841 mentions a graduate of the Ecole Normale who was directing the Jewish school in Mutzig *AI*, 2 (1841), 699 The quotation is cited in *AI*, 8 (1847), 74

48 Stauben, *Scènes*, pp 79–80

49 Letter of Salomon Klein to M Vurmser, June 21, 1858, private collection, Moche Catane, Jerusalem

50 *AI*, 21 (1860), 563–65

51 *UI*, 21 (1865–66), 385

52 *UI*, 15 (1859–60), 65

53 *AI*, 21 (1860), 562

54 *UI*, 23 (1867–68), 386–87

55 Prost, *Histoire de l'enseignement en France*, pp 106–7, and Anderson, *Education in France*, p 160

56 Figures are calculated from signatures of marriage documents in the following files ADBR 4E 330, Niederroedern (1789–1830) (1831–62), 4E 226, Itterswiller (1793–1830) (1831–62), and 5M1 852 and 853, Bischheim (1813–32) (1833–43) (1843–52) (1853–62), 5M1 1663, Strasbourg (1823–24) (1825–26) (1827–28) [note, none from the 1830s] (1844–45) (1846–47) (1860) (1861) (1862), ADHR 5E 105, Colmar (1822–28) (1845–48) and 5M1 66R 50 (1860–62) A total of 606 marriages were recorded Average age of grooms—ca 30, average age of brides—ca. 27

57 Letter of Cantonal Committee, May 25, 1831, HM 5529, CAHJP

58 The citation is from Bloch, "L'Alsace juive," p 9 On the attitude of Alsatians and their clergy to the teaching of French in this period see Paul Lévy, *Histoire linguistique d'Alsace et de Lorraine*, 2 vols (Paris, 1929), 2 158–63

59 On the Haskalah approach to the teaching of religion and on the relation of the mission theory to nineteenth-century religious reform, see Meyer, *Response to Modernity*, pp 16, 23, 78, 137–38 On Ennery, see letter of Comité local de surveillance, May 6, 1835, HM 5517, CAHJP

60 *UI*, 9 (1853–54), 372 One Jewish primary school inspector commented of catechism, "This study, embracing the divine principles of our religion, reminds us at the same time of our moral and social duties," letter of Cantonal Committee, May 25, 1831, HM 5529, CAHJP On the development of Jewish catechisms in the nineteenth century, see Jacob Petuchowski, "Manuals and Catechisms of the Jewish Religion in the Early Period of Emancipation," in *Studies in Nineteenth-Century Jewish Intellectual History*, ed Alexander Altmann (Cambridge, Mass , 1964), pp 47–64 On the need for consistorial approval, see *UI*, 9 (1853–54), 372 The school books that I consulted include Ben-Lévi's, *Les Matinées du samedi* (Paris, 1843), S Ulmann, *Recueil d'instructions morales et religieuses à l'usage des jeunes israélites français* (Strasbourg, 1843), L Sauphar, *Gan Raveh Manuel d'instruction religieuse et morale*, trans and annotated by L Wogue (Paris, 1850), J Ennery, *Le Sentier d'Israel, ou Bible des jeunes israélites* (Paris, Metz, and Strasbourg, 1843), Isaac Lévy, *Les Veillées du vendredi, morale en exemples* (Verdun, 1863), and *Isaïe, ou le travail*, 2nd ed. (Paris, 1865), Elie Lambert, *Les Premices ou Abregé de l'histoire sainte à l'usage des jeunes israélites*, 4th ed (Metz and Paris, 1862), S Hallel, *L'Encens du coeur ou prières de premier ordre avec traduction interlinéaire et accompagnées de courtes notes explicatives et de notes littéraires étendues sur la source, l'age, l'auteur, et l'objet de chaque prière* (Metz, 1867) On the role of Jewish teachers, see Jay Berkovitz, "Jewish Educational Leadership in Nineteenth-Century

France—The Role of Teachers," *Proceedings of the Ninth World Congress of Jewish Studies,* division B, vol 3· *The History of the Jewish People (The Modern Times)* (Jerusalem, 1986), pp 47–54, and his *The Shaping of Jewish Identity,* pp 167–72

61 Ulmann, *Recueil d'instructions,* p 13, Sauphar and Wogue, *Gan Raveh,* pp 71–157

62 Ulmann, *Recueil d'instructions,* p 13

63 Ibid, p. 45

64 Sauphar and Wogue, *Gan Raveh,* p 43

65 Hallel, *L'Encens du coeur,* p 15

66 Ulmann, *Recueil d'instructions,* p 105

67 See, for example, the stories in Lévy, *Les Veillées du vendredi*

68 Ulmann, *Recueil d'instructions,* pp. 104–6; see, also, Lambert, *Les Prémices,* pp 72–73

69 Hallel, *L'Encens du coeur,* pp 28–29

70 Ibid, p 29

71 On the professionalization of Jewish teachers, see Berkovitz, *Shaping of Jewish Identity,* pp 168–71

72 Sauphar and Wogue, *Gan Raveh,* p 43

73 Hallel, *L'Encens du coeur,* pp 68, 75

74 Ben-Lévi, *Les Matinées du samedi;* Louis Cottard, *Souvenirs de Moise Mendelssohn, ou le second livre de lecture des écoles israélites* (Paris, 1832).

75 Stauben, *Scènes,* p. 281

76 *AI,* 16 (1855), 278–81 The citation is from p 278 Lambert, *Les premices,* p 73.

77 Frequent complaints were registered on this issue See *AI,* 3 (1842), 121–22, 9 (1849), 71–72; 16 (1855), 278–81, *L'Ami des israélites* (1847), 217, 262–63 The citation is from "Souvenir d'un voyage en Alsace," *AI,* 5 (1844), 545

78 *UI,* 12 (1856–57), 324

79 Letter from Central Consistory, July 4, 1862, A N F[19] 11 034.

80 *UI,* 2 (1845), 271–72

81 *UI,* 11 (1855–56), 275

82 *UI,* 9 (1853–54), 230–32, circular appeal of Grand Rabbi Klein, printed in *UI,* 12 (1856–57), 420–22 The pastoral letter of the Consistory of the Upper Rhine that called for the establishment of a preparatory school for the Metz Ecole Rabbinique, dated Oct 7, 1850, is in Brandeis University Libraries, Special Collections, Consistoire Israélite de France, II 12a Klein repeatedly defended his work on behalf of the Ecole Talmudique, or Beth Hamedrash "I have no need to tell you how necessary this institution is, given the ignorance of our cantors, and to a colleague I can even say, of our young rabbis, who enter the Metz [Rabbinical] School insufficiently prepared" Letter from Grand Rabbi Klein to grand rabbi of Bordeaux, July 2, 1858, private collection, Moche Catane, Jerusalem Although in 1856 opponents labeled Klein's school a rival to the Ecole Rabbinique, the documents that I examined do not lend credence to this charge For the charge, see Albert, *Modernization of French Jewry,* pp 254–55

83 On the closing of the Sierentz school, see Achilles Nordmann, *Der Israelitische Friedhof in Hegenheim in geschichtlicher Darstellung* (Basel, 1910), p 36 In 1831 the Central Consistory had advised the Colmar Consistory to seek financial assistance from the Ministry of Religion to support the existing "theological schools" of Bergheim, Ribeauvillé, and Sierentz, which had no legal authorization but could serve as preparatory schools for the Ecole Rabbinique Letter of Central Consistory to Colmar Consistory, May 8, 1831, HM 1056, CAHJP

84 Letter of Central Consistory to minister of religion, #7919, Nov 23, 1857, HM 1060, CAHJP The Colmar Consistory, under the leadership of Léon Werth, had initially supported the idea of establishing a preparatory school for the Ecole Rabbinique See *L'Ami des israélites* (1847), 279

85 Circular appeal, *UI,* 12 (1856–57), 421

86 Zosa Szajkowski, "Jewish Vocational Schools in France in the Nineteenth Century" [Yiddish], *YIVO Bleter,* 42 (1962), 89 See the letter from the rabbi of Niederhagenthal of December 1861 complaining of the lack of schools in the Upper Rhine properly teaching Judaism, *UI,* 17 (1861–62), 224–26

87 "Discours prononcé par M le Rabbin Bloch à l'occasion de la distribution des prix du Talmud-Torah au temple de Wissembourg," *UI*, 20 (1864–65), 282–85

88 On this debate see Katz, *Out of the Ghetto*, pp 60–61, 176– 90 and Berkovitz, *Shaping of Jewish Identity*

89 See *La Régénération*, 1 (1836), 24–28. A letter dated Aug 25, 1837, from Moses Nordmann, rabbi in Hegenheim, suggesting the establishment of a model Jewish agricultural school in Alsace appeared in ibid , 2 (1837) pp 149–52 In the 1850s and 1860s Léon Werth was the key figure promoting agricultural training for Jewish youth in Alsace See, for example, his letter soliciting assistance in founding an agricultural colony, to M. Cerfberr, Mar 19, 1869, JTS, French Documents, Box 25 On opposition to agricultural training by the directors of the Ecole de Travail of Strasbourg, see M Ginsburger, *L'Ecole de Travail israélite à Strasbourg* (Strasbourg, 1935), pp 38–40

90 Szajkowski, "Jewish Vocational Schools," pp 113–14, "Renseignements demandés sur l'Ecole israélite d'Arts et Métiers par M le Conseiller d'Etat," 1867, LBI, Alsace-Lorraine Collection, AR-C 10882863, #2820–21, Anderson, *Education in France*, pp 196, 203 For a consideration of the Jewish vocational schools within the context of nineteenth-century French vocational training, see Lee Shai Weissbach, "The Jewish Elite and the Children of the Poor Jewish Apprenticeship Programs in Nineteenth-Century France," *AJS Review*, 12, no 1 (1987), pp 123–42.

91 Ginsburger, *L'Ecole de Travail.*

92 Ibid , pp 8, 11–25

93 *UI*, 2 (April 1845), 39, "Renseignements demandés," LBI; Szajkowski, "Jewish Vocational Schools," p 96

94 *UI*, ibid , *L'Ami des israélites* (1847), 278, letter of Central Consistory to minister of religion, Feb 21, 1848, HM 1059, CAHJP

95 *UI*, ibid , 40, 14 (1858–59), 556; 16 (1860–61), 564–65, Szajkowski, "Jewish Vocational Schools," p. 96

96 Cited in Bloch, "L'Alsace juive," p 15

97 Société d'encouragement au travail   , *Compte de 1862* (Strasbourg, 1863), pp 16–18 In 1845, too, 80 percent of the masters to which the students were apprenticed were Christians *Compte de 1845* (Strasbourg, 1846), p 19

98 Ginsburger, *L'Ecole de Travail*, p 42, "Renseignements demandés," LBI

99 Ginsburger, ibid , p 41, Szajkowski, "Jewish Vocational Schools," p 95

100 *UI*, 1 (1844–45), 35.

101 *AI*, 10 (1849), 189; letter of Adolphe Franck, May 5, 1841, JTS, French Documents, Box 25

102 *UI*, 14 (1858–59), 557, 15 (1859–60), 363

103 On the modest backgrounds of secondary school students, see Robert Anderson, "Secondary Education in Mid-Nineteenth Century France Some Social Aspects," *Past and Present*, 53 (November 1971), 122, 127 On the disappointed career aspirations of lycée graduates, see Patrick J. Harrigan, "Secondary Education and the Professions in France during the Second Empire," *Comparative Studies in Society and History*, 17, no. 3 (1975), 351–52, 355–58.

104 Cited in Anderson, "Secondary Education," p 142

105 *AI*, 5 (1844), 671, *UI*, 15 (1859–60), 65

106 For a persuasive analysis of the Ratisbonnes and other nineteenth-century French Jewish converts to Catholicism, see Jacob Katz, "Religion as a Uniting and Dividing Force in Modern Jewish History," in *The Role of Religion in Modern Jewish History*, ed Jacob Katz (Cambridge, Mass., 1975), pp 6–9 See also François Delpech, *Sur les juifs études d'histoire contemporaine* (Lyon, 1983), pp 321–55, Natalie Isser and Lita Linzer Schwartz, "Sudden Conversion. The Case of Alphonse Ratisbonne," *Jewish Social Studies*, 45 (1983), 17–30, and Jonathan Helfand, "Passports and Piety Apostasy in Nineteenth-Century France," *Jewish History*, 3, no 2 (1988), 62–63

107 The *Archives israélites* contrasted the happy situation of Jewish students in lycées in 1860 with the prejudice that even the three sons of Abraham Javal, one of the wealthiest Jews in Colmar,

had suffered as students in the local lycée at the end of the second decade of the century When Javal complained to the authorities, he was reportedly told, "Have yourself baptized along with your children, then you will be respected " *AI*, 21 (1860), 608

108 *AI*, 8 (1847), 241–42, Minutes, Strasbourg Consistory, Jan 5, 1847, HM 5503, CAHJP

109 For example *AI*, 17 (1856), 538–39, 19 (1858), 535–36, 21 (1860), 563, 608, *UI*, 15 (1859–60), 53–54; 16 (1860–61), 44, 17 (1861–62), 44, 19 (1863–64), 115

110 *AI*, 17 (1856), 539, 21 (1860), 608

111 *UI*, 12 (1856–57), 288 See also *AI*, 21 (1860), 607–8, and *Halevanon*, 2, no 2 (1865), 23–24

112 *AI*, 19 (1858), 535

113 Klein's son is mentioned as a prize winner *UI*, 17 (1861–62), 44

114 A N F[17] 6849 Jewish students were determined by onomastic criteria. Where a name was doubtful, it was excluded Because the survey is not complete and not all students are listed by name, it was not possible to determine the total number of Jewish secondary school students in Alsace in the 1860s

115 A N F[17] 6849 Nationwide, 15 percent of lycée students took the special course as did 36 percent of those in collèges See Anderson, "Secondary Education," p 129

116 Harrigan, "Secondary Education and the Professions," pp 351–52

117 A N. F[17] 6849

118 *Iggrot hapeqidim v'amarkalim meAmshterdam*, manuscript letters, library of Makhon Ben-Zvi, Jerusalem Letters to lay leaders in Colmar, Mulhouse, and Strasbourg were written in Hebrew

119 For a compelling statement of the centrality of the 1840s in the development of modern France, see David Pinkney, *The Decisive Years in France, 1840–1847* (Princeton, 1986)

Chapter Eight. Acculturation and Social Mobility

1 For one example, see *La Régénération*, 1 (1836), 182, which asked whether, in comparison with their Alsatian compatriots, there were more seeds of civilization among the Jews or the Christians

2 François-Georges Dreyfus, *Histoire de l'Alsace* (Paris, 1979), pp 240–41

3 On the Torah binders, see Weyl and Raphael, *L'Imagerie juive*, p 31 The Seder show towel, from the late 1820s, was displayed in the 1989 Jewish Museum exhibit

4 On the influence of German Jewish Haskalah and religious reform on French Jewry in this period, see Jonathan I Helfand, "The Symbiotic Relationship between French and German Jewry in the Age of Emancipation," *LBIYB*, 29 (1984), 344–45

5 Commission report, Sept 6, 1831, Strasbourg Consistory, JTS, French Documents, Box 18 All citations in the following paragraphs are from this document

6 Letter of June 27, 1837, from Comité administratif to Strasbourg Consistory, ZF 300, CAHJP In 1839 the Strasbourg Consistory discussed means of compensating for the loss of revenue due to the abolition of the sale of honors Minutes, Strasbourg Consistory, June 25, 1839 JTS, French Documents, Box 18

7 Minutes, Consistory of the Lower Rhine, Oct 19, 1842, and Nov. 8, 1842, HM 5503, CAHJP

8 Ibid , May 10, 1843, and July 17, 1845 Letter, Aug. 10, 1845, from G Z Blum in response to consistory's denial of the petition Blum claimed that he acted simply as a paying member of the consistory and could have collected 120, rather than 66, names on his petition had the consistory not intervened An organ, he noted, "could not but elevate the pomp and eclat of the worship" HM 5525, CAHJP For the petition and the exchange of letters between Blum and the consistory, see *UI*, 2 (1845), 390–98, and *AI*, 6 (1845), 692, 706–9 On Blum, a businessman born in Reichshoffen and a migrant to Strasbourg, see his obituary in *AI*, 10 (1849), 574–78

9 Minutes, Strasbourg Consistory, June 23, 1853, and Nov 11, 1853, Archives of Strasbourg Jewish Community Similar communal conflicts between reformers and their more conservative opponents occurred throughout Western Europe, especially in Germany See, for example, Michael A Meyer, *Response to Modernity* (Oxford, 1988), pp 119–31

10 Minutes of the reunion of the consistories of Metz, Nancy, and Strasbourg, January 1846, LBI, AR-C 1088 2863, #629–30, report of rabbinical conference in Colmar, February 1854, *Lien d'Israël*, 2 (1856), 258–67, on Niederroedern, Sierentz, and Wintzenheim (Haut-Rhin), see *L'Ami des Israélites* (Strasbourg), no 2 (June 1847), 77–79, on Bieswiller and Diemeringen, see Minutes of Consistory of the Lower Rhine, Apr 22, 1843, and Aug 28, 1843, on Rosheim and Bouxwiller, see Apr 20, 1847, HM 5503, CAHJP, on Wissembourg and Mulhouse, see *Lien d'Israel*, 3 (1857), 233 and 204–5, on Habsheim, see *Lien d'Israel*, 4, no 3 (1858), 138, on Hegenheim, see *AI*, 4 (1843), 190–91, on Niedernai, see *AI*, 5 (1844), 866, on Issenheim, see *AI*, 6 (1845), 171, on Strasbourg, Colmar, Haguenau, Sarre-Union, Sierentz, and Wissembourg, see *AI*, 8 (1847), 373, on Mulhouse, see *AI*, 18 (1857), 668–69, on Thann, see *AI*, 24 (1863), 448, on the Department of the Upper Rhine in general, see *AI* 27 (1866), 92–93, and on Duttlenheim, see *UI*, 21 (1866–67), 42 On the organ, see *AI*, 18 (1857), 669, 26 (1865), 1018, and 29 (1868), 624 On Lévy's installation, see *AI*, 30 (1869), 107–8 On opposition to introduction of religious initiation in Bieswiller and Diemeringen and to new cantorial music in Strasbourg, see Apr 22, 1843, HM 5503, CAHJP

11 *UI*, 16 (1860–61), 310

12 Pinkas of the Jewish Community of Bouxwiller, 1828–1948, HM 1067, CAHJP, pp 32–33 For examples of nineteenth-century German synagogue regulations, see Jacob Petuchowski, ed, *Prayerbook Reform in Europe* (New York, 1968), pp 105–27 On changing attitudes toward menstruants in the synagogue, see Shaye Cohen, "The Concept of Impurity Halacha and 'Minhag,'" in *Daughters of the King. Women in the Synagogue*, ed Susan Grossman and Rivka Haut (Philadelphia, in press)

13 *Lien d'Israel*, 1 (1855), 101, 2 (1856), 107, 3 (1857), 232, Rabbi Samuel Dreyfuss, *AI*, 14 (1853), 250–55

14 Letters from Rabbi Salomon Ulmann of Nancy, a future grand rabbi of France, to rabbis Aron and Dreyfuss discuss their agreement on the need for moderate reform under the auspices of rabbinic leadership See letters of early 1844 (undated), Dec 28, 1844, Dec 25, 1846, JTS, MS #8488

15 *AI*, 24 (1863), 907, 25 (1864), 346, 395, *UI*, 19 (1863–64), 392–94, M Ginsburger, *Der Israelitische Friedhof in Jungholz* (Gebweiler, 1904), p 58

16 Rabbi Samuel Dreyfuss, "Quelque reflexions sur l'état actuel des israélites de l'Alsace," *La Régénération*, 1 (1836), 181

17 "Renseignements sur la situation des israélites," June 18, 1843, ADBR, V 511

18 *La Régénération*, 2 (1837), 159 The paper noted that the mayor and members of the municipal council honored the deceased Sée by accompanying his funeral convoy a certain distance outside the town, *AI*, 27 (1866), 195, *UI*, 19 (1863–64), 286

19 On the election of Aaron Blum as mayor of Rosheim, see Raphael and Weyl, *Regards nouveaux*, p 104

20 *AI*, 8 (1846), 546–47 Georges Livet and Francis Rapp, ed, *Histoire de Strasbourg des origines à nos jours* (Strasbourg, 1982), 4 145

21 New synagogues were dedicated in Belfort, Bischwiller, Huningue, Mertzwiller, Mulhouse, Phalsbourg, Seppois, Thann, Westhausen, Westhoffen, and Wissembourg, and the synagogues of Hegenheim and Uffholtz were renovated On the new synagogues, see *Lien d'Israel*, 2 (1856–57), 452–53, 3 (1858), 451–52, 4 (1858), 38, 168–69, 496–99, 5 (1859), 115, 7 (1861), 152, *UI*, 17 (1861–62), 522–23, 18 (1862–63), 93, *AI*, 11 (1850), 51, 29 (1868), 887, 30 (1869), 516–17, 572, and Salomon Klein, *Recueil de lettres pastorales et de discours de 1861, 1862 et 1863, et des discours d'inauguration des synagogues de Belfort, d'Huningue et de l'Hospice Hôpital de Mulhouse* (Colmar, 1863) This list is not a comprehensive one For visual evidence, see the painting "Dedication of a Synagogue in Alsace," ca 1828, attributed to Georg Opitz, in the collection of the Jewish Museum, New York, and the 1857 watercolor "Dedication of a Torah scroll in Reichshoffen," signed Stern, in the 1989 Jewish Museum exhibit and in the permanent collection of the Musée Alsacien, Strasbourg A photograph of an engraving made to commemorate the occasion appears in Raphael and Weyl, *Juifs en Alsace*, p 320

22 *Lien d'Israel*, 7 (1861), 152 The first citation, referring to Mertzwiller, is from ibid , 4 (1858), 17 The second citation is from ibid , 2 (1856–57), 453

23 *UI*, 17 (1861–62), 522; *AI*, 5 (1844), 661

24 *UI*, 18 (1862–63), 91

25 On prizes to teachers in the Lower Rhine, see *AI*, 15 (1864), 633, and in Upper Rhine and Lower Rhine, 26 (1865), 456, 546, 926, 29 (1868), 811 On students, see *AI*, 28 (1867), 839–41, 29 (1868), 904, 31 (1870), 571, and *Lien d'Israël*, 5 (1859), 114 On M Auscher, see *AI*, 27 (1866), 553 On Rabbi Aron's receiving a decoration as a chevalier of the Legion of Honor, see *AI*, 29 (1868), 809 On others decorated as knights of the Legion of Honor, see *Histoire de Strasbourg*, ed Livet and Rapp, 4·145

26 The first citations are from *Lien d'Israël*, 3 (1857–58), 292–93 An earlier report on the funeral appeared in ibid., 268 *AI*, 28 (1857), 685

27 See chapter 6 On the centrality of the 1840s as a period of economic takeoff, see Pinkney, *The Decisive Years*

28 ADBR X 372 A table derived from this source may be found in Zosa Szajkowski, *Poverty and Social Welfare among French Jews* (New York, 1954), p 84 See chapter 3

29 William Sewell, Jr , "Social Mobility in a Nineteenth-Century European City Some Findings and Implications," *Journal of Interdisciplinary History*, 7, no 2 (1976), 224–25

30 On the reluctance of Jews to apprentice their sons to Gentile masters, see *La Régénération*, 1 (1836), 10 Subsequently, about 80 percent of the students in the Ecole du Travail were apprenticed to Christian masters Société d'encouragement, *Compte de 1845*, p 19, and *Compte de 1862*, pp 16–18

31 Thomas Kessner, *The Golden Door Italian and Jewish Immigrant Mobility in New York City, 1880–1915* (Oxford, 1977), pp 60–61, 110 and Stephen Thernstrom, *The Other Bostonians Progress and Poverty in the American Metropolis* (Cambridge, Mass , 1973), pp 145–75

32 Ben Simon-Donath, *Sociodémographie des juifs de France*, p 143.

33 M Tourette, *Discours sur les juifs d'Alsace* (Strasbourg, 1825), p 9

34 See, for example, Richarz, *Jüdisches Leben in Deutschland*, pp 31–44, and Toury, "Eintritt der Juden," in *Das Judentum in der deutschen Umwelt*, ed Liebeschutz and Paucker, pp 139–242

35 Weill, *Couronne*, and *Histoires de village*, Stauben, *Scènes*, Georges Stenne [David Schornstein] *Perle* (Paris, 1877), and Cahun, *La Vie juive* Cahun's book, in particular, is also informed by nostalgia for the provinces lost as a result of the military defeat in the Franco-Prussian War On the Dreyfuses' festival cloth, see Kleeblatt, ed , *Dreyfus Affair*, p 271 For a broader discussion of the subject of cultural nostalgia among European Jewry, with a special focus on the visual arts, see Richard I Cohen, "Nostalgia and 'Return to the Ghetto' as a Cultural Phenomenon in Western and Central Europe in the Nineteenth Century," in *Assimilation and Community*, ed Jonathan Frankel and Steven Zipperstein (Cambridge University Press, 1991)

Chapter Nine· Political Power and Social Engineering

1 Copy of speech of M Isaac Goudchaux, Feb 11, 1819, A N F[19] 11 042

2 Letter, Feb 14, 1853, from the Administrative Commission of the Strasbourg Consistory to Israel Dreyfus, P90/K1, CAHJP, letter from Rosheim commissaire, Apr 20, 1847, HM 5503, CAHJP See also letter, Strasbourg Consistory to Alfred Auch, Oct 22, 1847, HM 5533, CAHJP

3 "Copy of minutes relative to the affair Samuel Braunschweig in Hegenheim, translated from the German" [sic, Yiddish], the first of Selihoth [penitential period immediately before the Jewish New Year], 5594 [1834], JTS, French Documents, Box 18

4 Letter, Sept 16, 1838, from Samail son of Rabbi Salomon Wahl to the Consistory of Colmar, "translated from the German" [sic], JTS, French Documents, Box 18 The final outcome of the case is unknown

5 In the Braunschweig case the court ultimately accepted the right of the community to deny access to the Jewish burial ground In a letter to the minister of cults regarding complaints that

the commissaire surveillant of Sélestat "literally excommunicated" a number of community members by denying them kosher meat, excluding them from synagogue honors and their wives from the ritual bath, and inscribing their names on a black tablet hung in the synagogue, the Central Consistory defended the commissaire, claiming that he deprived his opponents only of synagogue honors, apparently an acceptable form of discipline Letter from Sélestat to minister of cults, Dec 5, 1848, letter from Central Consistory to minister of cults, Dec 3, 1848, HM 2/4673, CAHJP

6 Minutes, Strasbourg Consistory, Apr 22, 1843, HM 5503, CAHJP

7 Ibid , Oct 21, 1846

8 Ibid , Dec 30, 1846

9 Letters, Strasbourg Consistory to Rabbi Wolff of Bouxwiller, June 15, 1847, HM 5533, CAHJP, Minutes, Strasbourg Consistory, Sept 8, 1846, HM 5503, CAHJP

10 Strasbourg Consistory, "A MM les rabbins communaux et commissaires administrateurs des synagogues," Nov 1, 1860, four-page document on funerals, written in French and German, Houghton Library, Harvard University

11 Strasbourg Consistory, Nov 1, 1860, four-page document on circumcision, written in French and German, Houghton Library On the attempts of the consistories to regulate circumcision, see Albert, *Modernization of French Jewry*, pp 232–33 The first efforts were made in the 1840s

12 *AI*, 14 (1853), 253

13 Letter, Central Consistory to M Waller of Regisheim, July 11, 1820, HM 1055, CAHJP Letter, Central Consistory to Strasbourg Consistory, Jan 28, 1833, letter, Central Consistory to Colmar Consistory, June 25, 1837, HM 1057, CAHJP

14 Vicki Caron, *Between France and Germany The Jews of Alsace-Lorraine, 1871–1918* (Stanford, 1988), pp 124–26, Alfred Wahl, *Confession et comportement dans les campagnes d'Alsace et de Bade, 1871–1939*, 2 vols (Metz, 1980), 1 546–63, and Juillard, *Vie rurale*, p 255

15 Strasbourg Consistory, "A MM les commissaires-surveillans près les temples israélites du departement du Bas-Rhin," July 23, 1834, two-page document written in French and German, Houghton Library See chapter 7

16 See chapter 3

17 For the development of the consistories during the nineteenth-century, see Albert, *Modernization of French Jewry*, pp 45–239

18 As in the case with Isaac Goudchaux's speech (in n 1, above), which was forwarded to the Ministry of the Interior by a prefectural councillor A N F¹⁹ 11 042 On occasion the prefect of the Lower Rhine did suggest the replacement of particular Jewish notables See letter of Central Consistory to minister of the interior, complying with such a request, Feb 11, 1824, HM 1055, CAHJP Such requests, however, were rare

19 Letter of the prefect of the Upper Rhine to the minister of the interior, Mar 31, 1824, A N F¹⁹ 11 042 The information on the source of the suggestion is reported in a letter from the Central Consistory to the minister of the interior, Dec 9, 1823, found in HM 1055, CAHJP as well as in A N F¹⁹ 11 042

20 Letter of prefect of the Upper Rhine to minister of the interior, May 20, 1824, A N F¹⁹ 11 019

21 Letter from the Central Consistory to the minister of the interior, Dec 9, 1823, HM 1055, CAHJP, letter from the Central Consistory to the minister of the interior, May 6, 1824, A N F¹⁹ 11 019

22 Letter of Central Consistory to the Consistory of Winzenheim [Upper Rhine], Feb 4, 1824, HM 1055, CAHJP The Central Consistory substituted its own language, "completing the regeneration," found in its letter of Dec 9, 1823, for the prefect's much stronger negative language

23 Letters of prefect of the Upper Rhine to minister of the interior, Dec 22, 1824, and Feb 3, 1825, A N. F¹⁹ 11 041 On the Central Consistory's support of Brunschwig, see its letter to the minister of the interior, Mar 14, 1825, HM 1056, CAHJP, letter of prefect of the Upper Rhine to minister of the interior, May 14, 1825, and letter of minister of the interior to the prefect of the Upper Rhine, May 26, 1825, both in A N F¹⁹ 11 041.

24 Letter of prefect of the Upper Rhine to the minister of the interior, May 14, 1825, A N F¹⁹ 11 041

25 List of notables, Department of the Upper Rhine, HM 2/4763, CAHJP Brunschwig's name appears as a member of the Colmar Consistory in a letter to the minister of public instruction and cults of Dec 18, 1830, JTS, French Documents, Box 18

26 Letters of 1830 from prefect of the Upper Rhine to minister of the interior, prefect's report of October 1830 with comments on each notable, HM 2/4763, CAHJP

27 Letter of minister of the interior to the prefect of the Upper Rhine, Sept 7, 1830, HM 2/4763, CAHJP

28 Letters of the minister of the interior to the prefect of the Upper Rhine, Apr 17, 1828, and June 6, 1828, letter of the Central Consistory to the minister of the interior, Oct 16, 1828, HM 2/4763, CAHJP, letter from the grand rabbi of Colmar and three members of the consistory to the minister of public instruction and cults, Dec 18, 1830, JTS, French Documents, Box 18, letter from the Central Consistory to the minister of public instruction and cults, September 1831, and letters of prefect to the minister of public instruction and cults, Oct 13, 1831, and Nov 23, 1831, HM 2/4763, CAHJP

29 Letter of prefect of the Upper Rhine to minister of justice, July 15, 1845, A N F^{19} 11 045

30 Personal communication, June 1986, from Dr Moche Catane, Jerusalem, the great-grandson of Salomon Klein

31 Commission administrative de l'Ecole Centrale Rabbinique, Metz, July 23, 1839, report on conferral of diploma of second rabbinic degree (Morhenou Harab) on Salomon Klein, JTS, French Documents, Box 18 Klein had begun his secular studies at the age of eighteen

32 Albert, *Modernization of French Jewry*, pp 265–70, 274–75, 298–302

33 Lettre pastorale du consistoire israélite de la circonscription du Haut-Rhin, Oct 7, 1850, Brandeis University, Special Collections, French Documents, 2, 12a, letter from S Lévy, rabbi of Niederhagenthal, calling for end of criticism of the newly established preparatory rabbinical school in Colmar, first day of Hanukkah 5614 (December 1853), UI, 9 (1853–54), 230–32, for complaints leveled against Klein on this subject, see letter of Colmar Consistory to Central Consistory, Nov 1, 1857, HM 2/4674, and letter of Central Consistory to minister of public instruction and cults, Nov 23, 1857, HM 1060

34 Minutes of the rabbinical conference, May 15–22, 1856, JTS, French Documents, Box 19 A summary of the decisions appears in AI, 17 (1856), 306–13 Extracts of minutes of a conference of rabbis from the two Alsatian departments, which preceded the national conference, also demonstrate the greater traditionalism of the rabbis of the Upper Rhine, JTS, French Documents, Box 19

35 "Lettre pastorale," UI, 12 (1856–57), 104–17 The quotations are from p 105

36 Ibid , pp 105, 106, 107, 111–13, the pastoral letter may be found in full in HM 2/4674, CAHJP, which is a microfilm of A N F^{19} 11 037, an entire file entitled "Conflit du grand-rabbin de Colmar avec son consistoire et le Consistoire Central, 1857", letter of Central Consistory to the vice-president of the Colmar Consistory, Dec 30, 1856, letter of Klein to the minister of public instruction and cults, Dec 31, 1856, and twelve-page printed brochure of Commission des conservateurs du judaisme entitled "A nos coreligionnaires de France, 14 Tischri 5617, in ibid , letter of Central Consistory to minister of public instruction and cults, Apr 7, 1857, HM 1060, CAHJP

37 Prefect of Upper Rhine's reports, Nov 11, 1854, Nov 2, 1856, Nov 22, 1856, memorandum from minister of public instruction and cults to the prefect, Oct 15, 1856, A N F^{19} 11 045

38 Note for minister of public instruction and cults, Jan 5, 1857, and Apr 14, 1857, note from cabinet of minister of public instruction and cults, Apr 18, 1857, HM 2/4674, CAHJP

39 Letter of Salomon Klein to minister of public instruction and cults, Apr 17, 1857, and draft letter from cabinet of minister of public instruction and cults to Klein, Apr 30, 1857, HM 2/4674, CAHJP

40 Salomon Klein, "A Messieurs les membres de la communauté israélite de Colmar," Aug 31, 1857, letter from the Colmar Consistory to the Central Consistory, Sept 25, 1857, JTS, French Documents, Box 19 Klein's circular letter is also in HM 2/4674, CAHJP Petition against the new members of the Colmar Consistory for their maltreatment of Klein, Aug 26, 1857, HM 2/4674,

CAHJP Letter from the Central Consistory to the president of the Colmar Consistory, Oct 13, 1857, HM 1060, CAHJP

41 At least two copies of the forty-two page transcript of the session exist, one in JTS, French Documents, Box 19, and the other in A N F¹⁹ 11 037

42 Letter of Central Consistory to minister of public instruction and cults, Oct 27, 1857, HM 2/4674, CAHJP

43 Letter of Central Consistory to minister of public instruction and cults, Nov 23, 1857, letter of Louis Halphen to minister, Nov 3, 1857, sent by Central Consistory, letter of Salomon Klein to minister, Nov 2, 1857, defending himself against charges leveled against him and protesting his treatment, all in HM 2/4674, CAHJP

44 Letter of minister of public instruction and cults to prefect of the Upper Rhine, Dec 7, 1857, HM 2/4674, CAHJP

45 Letter of prefect of the Upper Rhine to minister of public instruction and cults, Jan 23, 1858, HM 2/4674, CAHJP

46 Letter of minister of public instruction and cults to Rabbi Salomon Klein, Feb 13, 1858, HM 2/4674, CAHJP

47 Petitions and letter of prefect of the Upper Rhine to minister of public instruction and cults, July 11, 1858, HM 2/4674, CAHJP

48 Letter of prefect of the Upper Rhine to minister of public instruction and cults, July 11, 1858, letter of Max Cerfberr to minister, July 11, 1858, letter from Central Consistory to minister, July 14, 1858, all in HM 2/4674, CAHJP Letter of Salomon Klein to M Hemerdinger, July 11, 1858, private collection, Moche Catane, Jerusalem

49 Letter of Salomon Klein to M Hemerdinger, June 29, 1858, letter of Salomon Klein to Salomon Munk, June 29, 1858, letter [in Hebrew, among letters of June 1858] to Salomon Ulmann, thanking him for his support, all in private collection, Moche Catane, Jerusalem

50 Letter of A Meyer, member of Colmar Consistory, to minister of public instruction and cults, June 23, 1858, HM 2/4674, CAHJP

51 Letter of Salomon Klein to the prefect of the Upper Rhine, July 23, 1858, private collection, Moche Catane, Jerusalem

52 Letter of Salomon Klein to M Hemerdinger, July 13, 1858, letter to prefect of the Upper Rhine, July 23, 1858, private collection, Moche Catane, Jerusalem

53 Note for the minister of public instruction and cults, Nov 4, 1858, A N F¹⁹ 11 045

54 Decree annulling the elections, Mar 14, 1859, two appeals and final rejection of both, June 18, 1860, all in A N F¹⁹ 11 045

55 "Note pour son excellence le ministre sur les élections israélites de Colmar de 14 XI 1858," n d , A N F¹⁹ 11 045

56 Ibid

57 Ibid In a letter of Jan 18, 1860, to Hemerdinger, Klein took exception to the Central Consistory's repeated interventions in the Jewish affairs of the Department of the Upper Rhine, which he saw as having made no less progress than the Lower Rhine He concluded with advice to Hemerdinger to let the minister of public instruction and cults know that "we also favor progress " Private collection, Moche Catane, Jerusalem

58 "A sa majesté l'empéreur des français," Colmar, Jan 6, 1861, twenty-five signatories, A N F¹⁹ 11 045

59 Letter of prefect of the Upper Rhine to minister of public instruction and cults, Jan 21, 1861 A letter was also sent by two of the Central Consistory's candidates—Lantz, a member of the Municipal Council of Mulhouse, and A Sée, a lawyer at the Imperial Court in Colmar—to the mayors of all the communes in the Upper Rhine with a Jewish population soliciting their intervention in favor of their candidature and those of their colleagues, Jan 7, 1861 A copy of that letter and the prefect's letter are in A N F¹⁹ 11 045 There is no evidence to support the prefect's allegations about the grand rabbi's party

60 Letter of Mannheimer, president of the Colmar Consistory, Jan 15, 1861, A N F¹⁹ 11 045, letter

from Salomon Klein to Prosper Lunel, Jan 9, 1861, noting that the mayors had intervened in the elections by distributing bulletins, private collection, Moche Catane, Jerusalem

61 Election returns, January 1861, December 1862, and February 1867, A N F¹⁹ 11 045

62 The *Univers israélite* reprinted a letter of Werth's of Dec 18, 1865, addressed to the Jews of the two Alsatian departments, that had appeared in the *Courrier du Bas-Rhin, UI*, 21 (1865–66), 218–20 The quotation is from p 220 The *UI* also reprinted a letter that Werth had sent to a Paris newspaper defending Klein from charges of obscurantism and praising him as a distinguished grand rabbi *UI*, 21 (1865–66), 261–63

63 See Klein's obituary in *UI*, 23 (1867–68), pp 146–51

Chapter Ten. Conclusion

1 For a statistical analysis of Jewish emigration from Germany in the first half of the nineteenth century, see Avraham Barkai, "The German Jews at the Start of Industrialization," in *Revolution and Evolution*, ed Mosse et al , pp 146–49

2 Pinkney, *Decisive Years in France*

3 See Phyllis Cohen Albert, "Ethnicity and Solidarity in Nineteenth-Century France," in *Mystics, Philosophers, and Politicians Essays in Jewish Intellectual History in Honor of Alexander Altmann*, ed Jehuda Reinharz and Daniel Swetschinski (Durham, N C , 1982), pp 249–74; Gary Cohen, "Jews in German Society Prague, 1860–1914," in *Jews and Germans from 1860 to 1933 The Problematic Symbiosis*, ed David Bronsen (Heidelberg, 1979), pp 306–37, Michael Graetz, *Haperiferya hay'ta l'merkaz* (Jerusalem, 1982), Marion Kaplan, "Priestess and Hausfrau Women and Tradition in the German-Jewish Family," in *The Jewish Family*, ed. Steven M Cohen and Paula E Hyman (New York, 1986), pp 62–91, Robert Liberles, "Emancipation and the Structure of the Jewish Community in the Nineteenth-Century," *LBIYB*, 31 (1986), 51–67, and Shulamit Volkov, "Distinctiveness and Assimilation The Paradox of Jewish Identity in the Second Reich" [Hebrew], in *Crises of German National Consciousness in the Nineteenth and Twentieth Centuries* [Hebrew], ed Moshe Zimmermann (Jerusalem, 1983), pp 169–85

4 *La Régénération* (1836), 1 37

5 Ibid , p 8 The citation is from *UI*, 1 (1845), 35–36

6 *La Régénération*, Prospectus, p 3

7 On the Alsatian consistories' vigorously protesting incidents of discrimination, see letter from Schwartz, avocat, copied by Strasbourg Consistory and countersigned by A Ratisbonne, 185–, AR-C 1088 2863, #635, LBI, letter of the Central Consistory to the Strasbourg Consistory, Jan 26, 1857, HM 1060, CAHJP, letter of Strasbourg Consistory July 12, 1858, HM 5533, CAHJP, and letter of June 27, 1864, JTS, French Documents, consistorial correspondence, Box 10, 1863–69 For the Central Consistory's criticism of the Strasbourg and Colmar Consistories for complaining directly to the minister of public instruction and cults about a *Le Monde* article accusing the Jews of Alsace of usury, see letter of Nov 18, 1861, HM 1061, CAHJP On the petition of the Colmar Consistory to the Central Consistory to protest the treatment of Jews in Switzerland, see letter of Central Consistory to Colmar Consistory, Jan. 29, 1863, HM 1061, CAHJP; letter of Strasbourg Consistory, July 23, 1852, JTS, French Documents, Box 4, letter of Strasbourg Consistory, n d , to the prince-president of the Republic, JTS, French Documents, Box 4, petition from individual Jews of several communes of Upper Rhine to the Colmar Consistory, Mar 22, 1857, JTS, French Documents, Box 4 On the French-Swiss negotiations, see David Feuerwerker, *L'Emancipation des juifs en France de l'ancien régime à la fin du Second Empire* (Paris, 1976), pp 651–702

8 On the rabbinate, see Albert, *Modernization of French Jewry*, p 258 On Alsatian Jews and Zionism see Michel Abitbol, *Les Deux terres promises Les juifs de France et le sionisme* (Paris, 1989), pp 203–6, 271–72; Paula Hyman, *From Dreyfus to Vichy The Transformation of French Jewry, 1906–1939* (New York, 1979), p 173 For a different perspective, see Raphael and Weyl, "La Double demeure les juifs d'Alsace et le sionisme," in their *Regards nouveaux*, pp 255–74

Selected Bibliography

Archival Documents

Archives Départementales du Bas-Rhin (ADBR)

Notarial records, court of Mutzig, 1855–64

U 2300 (1826) U 2310 (1836) U 2320 (1846) U 2330 (1856) U 2340 (1866) Fonds du Greffe du Tribunal de Commerce de Strasbourg

V 511 Rapport au préfet du Bas-Rhin sur les israélites du département et les moyens de les régénérer (1832) Rapport du préfet Sers au ministre de l'Intérieur sur l'émancipation des juifs dans le Bas-Rhin (1843) Application par le consistoire du Bas-Rhin des dispositions de l'ordonnance du 29 juin 1819 relative à l'organisation du culte (1819). Instructions diverses données par le consistoire aux fidèles (1812–19)

V 512 Décret concernant les sépultures (1806). Autorisation d'exercer le culte à Sélestat et Stotzheim (1811–37). Scissions dans les communautés et manifestations d'indiscipline à l'égard du consistoire Haguenau, Itterswiller, Pfaffenhoffen, Riedseltz, Strasbourg, Wissembourg (1812–66).

V 513

V 517 Collège des notables des israélites de la circonscription consistoriale du Bas-Rhin, 1823–45.

V 518 Collège des notables des israélites de la circonscription consistoriale du Bas-Rhin, 1850.

V 560 Projet anonyme de statuts d'une "Société pour la régénération des juifs," précédé de considérations sur leur état moral et intellectuel

V 561 Société d'encouragement au travail des israélites du Bas-Rhin.

V 564 Ecole israélite d'arts et métiers, 1849–70.

V 565 Ecoles israélites primaires, 1819–61.

X 318

X 372 Rapports des rabbins sur la pauvreté, 1856–57, liste des familles pauvres, 1857

Y2° Registre des prisons civiles, 1847–52.

3 M 703 Emigration en Amérique d'habitants du Bas-Rhin—états numériques et nominatives, 1828–37

4 E 226 Marriage records, Itterswiller, 1793–1830, 1831–62

4 E 330 Marriage records, Niederroedern, 1793–1830, 1831–62.

5M1 852 and 853 Marriage records, Bischheim, 1813–32, 1833–42, 1843–52, 1853–62

5 M 1 1663 Marriage records, Strasbourg 1823–24, 1825–26, 1827–28, 1844–45, 1846–47, 1860, 1861, 1862.

7 M 266 Manuscript censuses, Bischheim, 1836–46.

7 M 267 Manuscript censuses, Bischheim, 1856–66.

7 M 459 Manuscript censuses, Itterswiller, 1836–66

7 M 562 Manuscript censuses, Niederroedern, 1836–66.

7 M 719, 726, 733, 740 Manuscript censuses, Strasbourg, 1846.

7 M 720, 727, 734, 741 Manuscript censuses, Strasbourg, 1856.

7 M 722, 729, 736, 743 Manuscript censuses, Strasbourg, 1866

Archives Départementales du Haut-Rhin (ADHR)

5 E 105 Marriage records, Colmar, 1822–28, 1845–48

5 M 1 66R 50 Marriage records, Colmar, 1860–62

Archives Municipales de la Ville de Strasbourg (AMVS)

Police 71–402 Juifs

Archives Nationales, Paris (A.N)

F^{12} 938 Liste des principaux négociants sous l'Empire

F^{17} 6849 Rapport sur la situation de l'enseignement secondaire, 1864

F^{19} 11 013 Dettes des juifs d'Alsace, 1796–1905

F^{19} 11 019

F^{19} 11 023 Statistique. Dénombrement de la population juive Réponses et états fournis par les préfets en reponse à la circulaire de l'Intérieur du 29 mars, 1808.

F^{19} 11 028 Délibérations et correspondance du consistoire central au sujet de la création d'écoles primaires et autres (1809–17). Secours aux écoles primaires israélites

F^{19} 11 029 Police du culte. Règlements intérieurs, troubles à l'exercice du culte (an XI-1861) Réunions de prières illicites, ouvertures et fermeture d'oratoires (an XI-1905).

F^{19} 11.030 Coutumes et usages. Mariages et divorces (an XIII-1906) Costume des officiants (1810). Serment more judaïco (1807–12). Circoncision (1813–45) Pains azymes, boucheries et nourritures spéciales (1811–93) Culte dans les prisons (1840–1904).

F^{19} 11.031 Prières publiques, actions de grâces, fêtes, réceptions officielles, préséances (1809–90). Plaintes et réclamations contre faits d'intolérance (1820–1902)

F^{19} 11.034 Organisation des consistoires (1808–11) Correspondance relative aux notables et à l'organisation des consistoires, tableaux de circonscriptions, désignations des notables (1808–9) Procès-verbaux des assemblées de notables du consistoire de Paris (1809) Installation des consistoires, délibérations et circulaires (1809–10) Organisation du culte israélite dans les nouveaux départements de Hollande (1811) Réunions de rabbins (1856)

F¹⁹ 11 036 Plaintes contre des consistoires, des commissaires surveillants, des administrations de temples, 1810–95

F¹⁹ 11.037 Conflits entre le consistoire de Colmar et le consistoire central (1849–57). Conflit entre consistoire et commissaire administrative de la synagogue de Besançon (1888–89), à Nancy (1838) Conflit entre les consistoires de Colmar et de Mulhouse (1849)

F¹⁹ 11.038 Conflits entre les consistoires (1838–1903).

F¹⁹ 11 041

F¹⁹ 11.042 Rapports au ministère de l'intérieur, 1818–42.

F¹⁹ 11.045

F¹⁹ 1849a Liquidation des dettes de la nation juive de la province d'Alsace.

Central Archives for the History of the Jewish People, Jerusalem (CAHJP)

ZF 153 Account book of Chevras Bikkur Cholim, 1844–94, Haguenau

ZF 154 Account book, 1835–50, Altkirch.

ZF 212 Colmar Consistory, inquiry in Hattstatt, 1847.

ZF 213 Colmar, 1826

ZF 276 Strasbourg, 1857, ritual prayer for draft lottery of Abraham Lévi

ZF 277 Marriage contract, Lower Rhine, 1860.

ZF 278 Legal documents, 1840–42

ZF 284 Strasbourg, 1810, ban on Haman klopfen in synagogues on Purim.

ZF 296 Strasbourg, 1831, consistory, complaint against the rabbi

ZF 297 Strasbourg, synagogue

ZF 298 Rosheim, 1836, letter of prefecture refusing a subvention for the reconstruction of the synagogue.

ZF 299 Strasbourg, 1836, letter of the prefecture announcing a subvention for the Société pour l'encouragement des jeunes israélites du Bas-Rhin

ZF 300 Strasbourg, 1837, communal affairs

ZF 301 Strasbourg, 1837, ritual slaughter.

ZF 304 Strasbourg, 1832, consistory, rabbinate

ZF 306 Strasbourg, regarding ministre-officiant Loewe

ZF 307 Strasbourg, 1834, denial of subvention for reconstruction of synagogue.

ZF 310 Lingolsheim, 1834, complaint against administrators.

ZF 311 Strasbourg, 1838, correspondence with prefect

ZF 312 Strasbourg, 1839, correspondence with Consistory of Lower Rhine.

ZF 313 Strasbourg, letters of mayor.

ZF 314 1840, oath moré judaico

ZF 315 Strasbourg, 1840, consistory

ZF 316 Strasbourg, 1841, consistory.

ZF 317 Strasbourg, 1842, consistory

ZF 318 Strasbourg, 1843, consistory.

ZF 319 Strasbourg, 1844, consistory.

ZF 322 Strasbourg, 1849, documents regarding the ministre-officiant.

ZF 323 Strasbourg, 1849, consistory

ZF 324 Strasbourg, reconstruction of synagogue, 1856–68

ZF 327 Strasbourg, regarding ritual slaughter

ZF 328 Strasbourg, règlement

ZF 329 Strasbourg, 1865, communal offices.

ZF 330 Strasbourg, 1864, choir.

ZF 331 Strasbourg, consistory, 1868–69.

ZF 335 Strasbourg, 1835–37, statutes of Chevra Bikkur Cholim

ZF 336 Rosenweiler, 1865, cemetery

ZF 449 1835, *La Régénération*.

ZF 451 Strasbourg, 1810–63, miscellaneous documents.

ZF 464 Colmar, 1843, notables

ZF 478 Uffheim, 1850, census.

ZF 486 Strasbourg, 1831, rabbis and notables

ZF 521 Lille, 1869, electors

ZF 653 Strasbourg, 1809, repartition

ZF 654 Strasbourg, 1825, notables

ZF 655 Strasbourg, 1823, notables.

ZF 659 Strasbourg, 1828, notables

ZF 673 Bischwiller, 1863, census.

ZF 683 Herrlisheim, 1850, census

ZF 685 Dornach, 1849, census

ZF 686 Dornach, 1848, census

ZF 694 Hochfelden, 1833, census.

ZF 695 Hochfelden, 1860, census

ZF 702 Lixheim, 1830

ZF 703 Mutzig, 1828, tax list

ZF 712 Ribeauvillé, 1843, census.

ZF 730 Sélestat, 1859, census

ZF 739 Upper Rhine, 1828, list of wealthiest Jews

ZF 742 Upper Rhine, 1826, tax lists

ZF 744 Colmar, 1841, notables

ZF 745 Colmar, 1828, notables.

ZF 746 Colmar, 1844, notables

ZF 748 Upper Rhine, list of fifty wealthiest Jews.

ZF 749 Upper Rhine, 1850

ZF 750 Colmar, 1850, electoral list.

ZF 869 Lower Rhine, 1880, list of Jews obliged to pay debt of nation juive d'Alsace.

ZF 875 Lower Rhine, 1858, movement of population.

ZF 876 Lower Rhine, 1859, movement of population.

ZF 942 Pfastatt, 1845, census.

ZF 943 Dornach, 1846, census

ZF 944 Wittenheim, 1845, census.

ZF 953 Colmar, 1860, movement of population

ZF 959 Colmar, 1859, movement of population

ZF 967 1861, diploma of a mohel

ZF 973 Upper Rhine, 1833, petition of notables to minister of the interior regarding usury.

P/90 Papers of Dreyfus family of Wissembourg, eighteenth to twentieth centuries.

P/102 Birth incantation, Hebrew and Yiddish.

On Microfilm

HM 1055 Registre de Correspondance du Consistoire Central, 1818–24.

HM 1056 Registre de Correspondance du Consistoire Central, 1824–31.

HM 1057 Registre de Correspondance du Consistoire Central, 1831–37.

HM 1058 Registre de Correspondance du Consistoire Central, 1837–43.

HM 1059 Registre de Correspondance du Consistoire Central, 1843–50.

HM 1060 Registre de Correspondance du Consistoire Central, 1850–59.

HM 1061 Registre de Correspondance du Consistoire Central, 1859–66.

HM 1062 Registre de Correspondance du Consistoire Central, 1866–70.

HM 1066 Procès-verbaux du Consistoire Central, 1832–48

HM 1067 Procès-verbaux du Consistoire Central, 1848–71

HM 5503 Strasbourg Consistory, minutes, 1842–47.

HM 5506 Pinkas of the Jewish Community of Bouxwiller, 1828–1948

HM 5508 Introductory page of mohel book of Raphael Brunschwig, 1870.

HM 5509 Sefer Hashulia shel Moshe Halévi Meir, Wintzenheim, 1839–74.

HM 5513 Will of Yeckel bar Yitzchak Schwarz, with instructions on observance of mourning rituals, 1871.

HM 5515 Consistory of the Lower Rhine, minutes, 1819–26

HM 5516 Register of deliberations of Comité cantonal des écoles du culte hébraïque, 1820–26.

HM 5517 Letters of Comité cantonal des écoles (surveillance of schools), 1831–43.

HM 5518 Comité d'instruction primaire pour les écoles du Bas-Rhin, 1832–33

HM 5519 Bischheim, letters of Jewish community, 1834–47.

HM 5520 Bischheim, pinkas of Jewish community, 1836–57.

HM 5521 Riedseltz, Statutes of Chevro d'Shocharei Hatov

HM 5523 Strasbourg, 1849, correspondence regarding election to National Assembly.

HM 5524 Strasbourg, budget, 1838.

HM 5525 Strasbourg, dossiers of ministres-officiants, 1837–58.

HM 5526 Strasbourg, Comité d'administration, 1830–49 (mislabeled as Comité cantonal israélite de l'Académie de Strasbourg, 1825–32)

HM 5527 Assembly of Notables of Jews of Lower Rhine, 1821–30

HM 5528 Riedseltz, pinkas of Chevro d'Shocharei Hatov

HM 5529 Letters of Comité cantonal des israélites du ressort de l'Académie de Strasbourg, 1825–32 (mislabeled as Deliberations of Comité cantonal des écoles, 1821–32).

HM 5532 Strasbourg, register of petitions, 1815–21

HM 5533 Strasbourg, letters, 1847–60.

HM 2/759, 2/761, 2/767, 2/769, 2/772 Declarations of family names by Jews of Lower Rhine, 1808.

HM 782a and 782b Patents certifying bearer as nonusurer, Lower Rhine, 1808–13.

HM 2/4672 = A.N. F^{19} 11 030 and 11 031

HM 2/4673 = A.N. F^{19} 11 036

HM 2/4674 = A N. F^{19} 11.037

HM 2/4941

HM 2/5010 Memorbukh of the Jewish Community of Haguenau, eighteenth and nineteenth centuries

HM 2/5095 R. Levylier, *Notes et documents concernant la famille Cerf-Berr*

Brandeis University Library, Special Collections, Waltham, Mass

Consistoires israélites de France, Boxes 1, 2, 3, 6, 7

Hebrew Union College Library, Cincinnati

Documents on Jews in Alsace (1781–1866)

French Miscellanea

Houghton Library, Harvard University, Cambridge

Circulars of Strasbourg Consistory

Jewish Theological Seminary, New York

French Documents, Boxes 1–28

MS # 3834 Pinkas of Jewish community of Odratzheim

MS # 8488 Letters of Rabbi Salomon Ulmann, December 1843–August 1857

MS # 8599 Census of French Jewish communities, 1846

Leo Baeck Institute, New York (LBI)

West European Collection, AR-C 1638–4099

Alsace-Lorraine Collection, AR-C 1088–2863

Typescript memoir of Edmond Uhry, "Galleries of Memory," 2 vols.

Makhon Ben-Zvi, Jerusalem

Iggrot hapeqidim v'ha'amarkalim me-amshterdam, manuscript letters, vols. 3, 4, 7, 8, 11, 12, 13

Strasbourg, Jewish Community

Consistoire israélite, Registre des procès-verbaux, 1853–58.

Yeshiva University Library, New York

French Archival Documents, Boxes 1–4

Private Collection, Dr. Moche Catane, Jerusalem

Two copy books of letters of Salomon Klein, grand rabbi of Colmar

Newspapers

L'Amı des israélıtes, Strasbourg, 1847–48

Archives ısraélites, Parıs, 1840–70

Halevanon, Parıs, 1865–71.

Lıen d'Israel, Mulhouse and Strasbourg, 1855–61

La Régénération, Strasbourg, 1836–37.

Unıvers israélite, Paris, 1844–70

Prınted Prımary Sources

Anspach, Joel, ed. *Rıtuel des prıères journalıères* Metz Imprımerıe E. Hadamard, 1820.

Aron, Arnaud *Prıères d'un coeur ısraélıte· recueil de prıères et de médıtations pour toutes les cırconstances de la vie.* Publıé par la Socıété consistorıale des bons lıvres. Strasbourg Imprımerıe de G. Sılbermann, 1848

Ben-Lévı, G. [Godchaux Weıl] *Les Matınées du samedı.* Parıs: Bureau des "Archıves ısraélites de France," 1843.

Bettıng de Lancastel, Mıchel. *Consıdérations sur l'état des juifs dans la société chrétienne et partıculıèrement en Alsace* Strasbourg. F.-G Levrault, 1824.

Cahun, Léon *La Vie juıve.* Parıs. E Monnıer, de Brunhoff et cıe , 1886.

Cerfberr de Medelsheım, A[lphonse] *Ce que sont les juifs de France.* Parıs and Strasbourg Mansut, 1844.

———— *Bıographıe alsacıenne-lorraıne* Parıs A Lemerre, 1879.

Consıstoire de Strasbourg, "A MM les commıssaıres admınıstrateurs des synagogues," 20 mars, 1858.

Cottard, Louıs *Souvenırs de Moïse Mendelssohn, ou le second lıvre de lecture des écoles ısraélites.* Parıs· F.-G. Levrault, 1832

Coypel, Edouard. *Le Judaısme· esquısse des moeurs juıves.* Mulhouse Imprımerıe Brust-leın et cıe., 1876

Ennery, J(onas) *Le Sentıer d'Israël, ou Bıble des jeunes ısraélıtes* Parıs· n p , 1843

Enquête agrıcole, 2nd ser., enquêtes départmentales, 13e cırconscrıptıon, Bas-Rhın et Haut-Rhın [Rapport de M. Eugène Tısserand]. Parıs. Imprımerie ımpériale, 1867.

Erckmann-Chatrıan. *Le Blocus.* Parıs. J. Hetzel, 1867 Eng. ed wıth ıntro and notes by Arthur Ropes) publıshed ın Cambrıdge, Eng., 1905

————. *Maître Daniel Rock* Parıs 1873.

Grégoıre, Henrı *Essai sur la régénératıon physıque, morale et polıtıque des juifs.* Metz and Parıs, 1789

Hallel, S *L'Encens du coeur, ou prières de premier ordre avec traduction ınterlınéaıre et accompagnées de courtes notes explıcatives et de notes lıttéraıres étendues sur la source, l'âge, l'auteur, et l'objet de chaque prière.* Metz: J Mayer, 1867.

Hallez, Théophıl. *Des juifs en France de leur état moral et politique.* Parıs: G. A. Dentu, 1845.

Halphen, Achılle-Edmond. *Recueıl des loıs, décrets, ordonnances, avıs du Conseıl d'Etat, arrêtés et règlements concernant les israélites depuis la Révolution de 1789.* Paris Archives israélites, 1851

Iggerot hapeqidim v'ha'amarkalım me'amshterdam, 5586–5587, ed Yosef Yoel and Bınyamin Rıvlın Jerusalem: Yad Yızḥak Ben-Zvı, 1965.

Iggerot hapeqidim v'ha'amarkalım me'amshterdam, 5588, ed. Yosef Yoel and Bınyamın Rıvlın. Jerusalem: Yad Yizḥak Ben-Zvi, 1970.

Iggerot hapeqidim v'ha'amerkalim me'amshterdam, 5589, ed Bınyamın Rivlin. Jerusalem. Yad Yızḥak Ben-Zvı, 1979.

Kleın, Salomon Wolf *Ha-emet v'hashalom ahavu.* Frankfurt am Maın. J. Kauffmann, 1861

———. *Le judaïsme, ou la verité sur le Talmud.* Mulhouse: J. P. Rısler, 1859.

——— *Ma ʿaneh Rakh* Mulhouse J. P. Rısler, 1846

———. *Mipne Koshet. Bikoret Sefer Darkhei HaMishnah.* Frankfurt am Main: J Kauffmann, 1861

———. *Recueil de lettres pastorales et de discours de 1861, 1862 et 1863, et des dıscours d'inauguration des synagogues de Belfort, d'Huningue et de l'Hospice-Hôpital de Mulhouse.* Colmar· C Decker, 1863.

———. *Réponses de M. le rabbin Klein aux questions de la Commission Consistoriale.* Parıs. Lacrampe Fils et Comp., 1847

——— *Sermon,* Imprımée à la demande de plusıeurs notables. Parıs, 1847.

Lambert, Elie *Les Prémıces, ou abrégé de l'hıstoire saınte à l'usage des jeunes ısraélıtes,* 4th ed. Metz and Parıs. Alcan, 1862 [Fırst edıtıon 1849.]

Lévy, Isaac. *Les Veıllées du vendredı, morale en exemples.* Paris: Librairie israélite, 1863.

Levy, Michel. *Coup d'oeil historique sur l'état des ısraélites en France, et particulièrement en Alsace* Strasbourg G Sılbermann, 1836

Mossmann, Xavıer *Etude sur l'hıstoıre des juifs à Colmar.* Colmar and Parıs: E. Barth, 1866

Précis de l'examen quı a eu lıeu le 18 janvıer 1824, à l'école primaıre ısraélıte de Strasbourg. Strasbourg, 1824.

Reboul-Deneyrol, L. J. *Paupérısme et bienfaısance dans le Bas-Rhın* Parıs and Strasbourg: Vve Berger-Levrault et fils, 1858.

La Révolutıon française et l'émancıpatıon des juifs, 8 vols Parıs: Edıtıons socıales, 1968

Sauphar, L[ıpmann] A. *Gan Raveh (Jardin fertile)· manuel d'ınstruction relıgıeuse et morale.* Traduıt et annoté par L. Wogue. Approuvé par MM les grands-rabbıns de France, et admis par le Consistoire Central pour l'usage des écoles ısraélıtes Parıs· Typ de Wıttersheim, 1850

Société d'encouragement au travail en faveur des ısraélıtes ındıgents du Bas-Rhın, *Compte de 1845.* Strasbourg, 1846

———. *Compte de 1862* Strasbourg, 1863

Soultz, Jewısh communıty of. *Hesped* [Eulogy] (n p., 1867)

Stauben, Daniel [Auguste Wıdal]. *Scènes de la vie juıve en Alsace* Parıs· Mıchel Lévy frères, 1860.

Stenne, Georges [Davıd Schornsteın] *Perle.* Parıs E. Dentu, 1877.

Tama, Dıogène, ed. *Transactions of the Paris Sanhedrım.* London: C. Taylor, 1807.

Tisserand, E., and Leon Lefébure. *Etude sur l'économie rurale de l'Alsace*. Paris-Strasbourg Vve Berger-Levrault et fils, 1869.

Tourette, [Amédée]. *Discours sur les juifs d'Alsace*. Strasbourg. F.-G. Levrault, 1825

Ulmann, Salomon. *Recueil d'instructions morales et religieuses à l'usage des jeunes israélites français*. Strasbourg. G.-L Schuler, 1843

Weill, Alexandre. *Couronne*. Paris: Poulet-Malassis et de Broise, 1857.

———. *Histoires de village*. Paris: L. Hachette, 1860.

——— *Ma jeunesse*, 2 vols Paris: E. Dentu, 1870.

Secondary Sources

Ackerman, Evelyn B. *Village on the Seine*. Ithaca. Cornell University Press, 1979.

Ackerman, Sune. "Swedish Migration and Social Mobility: The Tale of Three Cities" *Social Science History*, 1 (Winter 1977), 178–209

Albert, Phyllis Cohen. *The Modernization of French Jewry: Consistory and Community in the Nineteenth Century*. Hanover, N.H . University Press of New England, 1977.

———. "Ethnicity and Solidarity in Nineteenth-Century France" In *Mystics, Philosophers, and Politicians: Essays in Jewish Intellectual History in Honor of Alexander Altmann*, ed Jehuda Reinharz and Daniel Swetschinski. Durham, N C Duke University Press, 1982, pp 249–74.

———. "Non-Orthodox Attitudes in Nineteenth-Century French Judaism" In *Essays in Modern Jewish History*, ed Phyllis Albert and Frances Malino East Brunswick, N.J.. Rutgers University Press, 1982, pp. 121–41.

Anchel, Robert. "Contribution levée en 1813–14 sur les juifs du Haut-Rhin." *REJ*, 82 (1926), 495–502.

———. *Les Juifs de France*. Paris. J. B. Janin, 1946

———. *Napoléon et les juifs*. Paris· Presses Universitaires de France, 1928.

Anderson, Michael *Family Structure in Nineteenth-Century Lancashire*. Cambridge Cambridge University Press, 1971.

Anderson, Robert. *Education in France, 1848–1870*. Oxford· Oxford University Press, 1975.

———. "Secondary Education in Mid-Nineteenth Century France: Some Social Aspects." *Past and Present*, 53 (November 1971), 121–46.

Aron, Jean-Paul, Paul Dumont, and Emmanuel Le Roy Ladurie. *Anthropologie du conscrit français*. Paris: Mouton, 1972.

Barkai, Avraham "The German Jews at the Start of Industrialization: Structural Change and Mobility, 1835–60." In *Revolution and Evolution: 1848 in German Jewish History*, ed. Werner E. Mosse, Arnold Paucker, and Reinhard Rürup. Tübingen· Mohr, 1981, pp. 123–56.

Baron, Salo. "Ghetto and Emancipation." *Menorah Journal*, 14 (June 1928), 515–26.

——— "Newer Approaches to Jewish Emancipation." *Diogenes*, 29 (Spring 1960), 56–81.

Ben Simon-Donath, Doris. *Sociodémographie des juifs de France et d'Algérie, 1867–1907*. Paris: POF-Etudes, 1976

Berger, Peter. *The Sacred Canopy*. Garden City, N.Y · Doubleday, 1969.

Berkovitz, Jay "Jewish Educational Leadership in Nineteenth Century France The Role of Teachers." *Proceedings of the Ninth World Congress of Jewish Studies*, division B, vol. 3 The History of the Jewish People (The Modern Times), 47–54.

———. *The Shaping of Jewish Identity in Nineteenth-Century France*. Detroit. Wayne State University Press, 1989

Bloch, Maurice. *L'Alsace juive depuis la Révolution de 1789* Guebwiller: J. Dreyfus, 1907

Blumenkranz, Bernhard, ed *Le Grand Sanhédrin de Napoléon*. Toulouse: Privat, 1979.

———. *Histoire des juifs en France*. Toulouse· Privat, 1972

Boehler, Jean-Michel, Dominique Lerch, and Jean Vogt, ed *Histoire de l'Alsace rurale* Strasbourg· Librairie Istra, 1983

Burns, Michael "Emancipation and Reaction The Rural Exodus of Alsatian Jews, 1791–1848," In *Living with Antisemitism· Modern Jewish Responses*, ed. Jehuda Reinharz Hanover, N H University Press of New England, 1987, pp 19–41.

Cahnman, Werner. "Village and Small-Town Jews in Germany: A Typological Study" *LBIYB*, 19 (1974), 107–31.

Caron, Vicki. *Between France and Germany: The Jews of Alsace-Lorraine, 1871–1918* Stanford· Stanford University Press, 1988

Catane, Moche "Les Communautés du Bas-Rhin en 1809," *REJ*, 120 (1961), 321–43

——— "Le Grand Rabbin Jacob Meyer" *Almanach du KKL* (Strasbourg, 1967), 151–57

——— "The Education and Culture of the Jews of Alsace at the End of the Eighteenth Century and the Beginning of the Nineteenth Century" [Hebrew] In *Proceedings of the Fifth World Congress of Jewish Studies*, vol. 2 Jerusalem, 1972, 308–14.

———. "Les Juifs du Bas-Rhin sous Napoléon I leur situation démographique et économique" Thesis, Université de Strasbourg, 1967

——— "The Library of an Alsatian Jewish Scholar in the Last Century" [Hebrew] *Kirjath Sepher*, 35 (1959–60), 382–86

Catane, Shulamit. "The Local Alsatian Press on the Anti-Jewish Riots in 1848." [Hebrew] *Zion*, 33 (1968), 96–98

Chisick, Harvey. *The Limits of Reform in the Enlightenment. Attitudes toward the Education of the Lower Classes in Eighteenth-Century France*. Princeton Princeton University Press, 1981.

Clément, Roger *La Condition des juifs de Metz dans l'ancien régime*. Paris Imprimerie Henri Jouve, 1903.

Cohen, David "L'Image du juif dans la société française en 1843 d'après les rapports des préfets." *REJ*, 136, nos 1–2 (1973), 163–69.

——— *La Promotion des juifs en France à l'époque du Second Empire, 1852–1870*, 2 vols Aix-en-Provence Université de Provence, 1980

Cohen, Gary B "Jews in German Society· Prague, 1860–1914 " In *Jews and Germans from 1860 to 1933: The Problematic Symbiosis*, ed David Bronsen. Heidelberg. Carl Winter, 1979, pp. 306–37

Crubellier, Maurice *L'Enfance et la jeunesse dans la société française, 1800–1950* Paris. Armand Colin, 1979.

Daltroff, Jean. "Samuel Lévy de Balbronn prêteur d'argent en Basse-Alsace au 18e siècle " *Archives juives*, 24, nos 1–2 (1988), 3–9

Daumard, Adeline. *Les Fortunes françaises au xixe siècle* Paris. Hachette, 1973

Debré, Moses. *The Image of the Jew in French Literature from 1800 to 1908,* trans Gertrude Hirschler New York· Ktav, 1970

Debré, S[imon]. *L'Humour judéo-alsacien.* Paris Rieder, 1933

Delpech, François. *Sur les juifs études d'histoire contemporaine.* Lyon Presses universitaires de Lyon, 1983.

Deux siècles d'Alsace française, 1648, 1798, 1848 Strasbourg. F -X Le Roux, 1948.

Dollinger, Philippe, ed *Histoire de l'Alsace* Toulouse. Privat, 1970

———. *Documents de l'histoire de l'Alsace.* Toulouse Privat, 1972

Dreyfus, François-Georges. *Histoire de l'Alsace* Paris Hachette, 1979

Eliav, Mordechai. *Jewish Education in Germany in the Period of Enlightenment and Emancipation.* [Hebrew] Jerusalem Hasefarim shel ha-sokhnut ha-yehudit l'erez yisrael, 1961

Elkin, Judith Laikin. *Jews of the Latin American Republics.* Chapel Hill: University of North Carolina Press, 1980.

Endelman, Todd *The Jews of Georgian England Tradition and Change in a Liberal Society* Philadelphia· Jewish Publication Society, 1979

Feuerwerker, David *L'Emancipation des juifs en France de l'ancien régime à la fin du Second Empire* Paris. Editions Albin Michel, 1976.

Friedemann, Joë *Alexandre Weill: écrivain contestaire et historien engagé, 1811–1899.* Société savante d'Alsace et des régions de l'est, vol. 29 Strasbourg: Librairie Istra, 1980.

——— "Un Témoin de la vie juive en Alsace au xixe siècle. Alexandre Weill." *Saisons d'Alsace,* nos. 55–56 (1975), 103–18

Furet, François, and Mona Ozouf, ed. *A Critical Dictionary of the French Revolution,* trans. Arthur Goldhammer. Cambridge. Harvard University Press, 1989

Ginsburger, Moïse. "Arrêtés du directoire du département du Haut-Rhin relatifs aux juifs [1er sept 1790–19 brumaire an III]," *REJ,* 75 (1922), 44–73

——— *L'Ecole de Travail israélite à Strasbourg.* Strasbourg Imprimerie du "Nouveau journal," 1935

——— *Histoire de la communauté israélite de Bischheim au Saum.* Strasbourg: Imprimerie du "Nouveau journal," 1937

———. *Les Juifs de Horbourg.* Paris Librairie Durlacher, 1904.

——— "Les Mémoriaux alsaciens " *REJ,* 40 (1900), 231–47, *REJ,* 41 (1900), 118–43

———. "Troubles contre les juifs d'Alsace en 1848 " *REJ,* 64 (1912), 109–17.

Goldscheider, Calvin and Alan S. Zuckerman, *The Transformation of the Jews.* Chicago University of Chicago Press, 1984

Goldstein, Alice "Aspects of Change in a Nineteenth-Century German Village " *Journal of Family History,* 15 (Summer 1984), 145–57.

——— "Urbanization in Baden, Germany Focus on the Jews, 1825–1925." *Social Science History,* 8, no 1 (1984), 43–66

Graetz, Michael *Haperiferya hay'ta l'merkaz.* Jerusalem· Mosad Bialik, 1982.

Graetz, Michael, ed and trans. *The French Revolution and the Jews The Debates in the National Assembly, 1789–1791* [Hebrew] Jerusalem Mosad Bialik, 1989.

Hagani, Baruch. *L'Emancipation des juifs*. Paris. Rieder, 1928.

Hareven, Tamara. "Family Time and Historical Time." *Daedalus* 106 (Spring 1977), 57–70

Harrigan, Patrick. *Mobility, Elites, and Education in French Society of the Second Empire*. Waterloo, Ont. Wilfred Laurier University Press, 1980

————— "Secondary Education and the Professions in France during the Second Empire." *Comparative Studies in Society and History*, 17, no 3 (1975), 349–71

Helfand, Jonathan. "The Contacts between the Jews of France and of the Land of Israel in the First Half of the Nineteenth Century." [Hebrew] *Cathedra*, 36 (1985), 37–54.

—————. "French Jewry during the Second Republic and Second Empire, 1848–1870." Ph.D diss., Yeshiva University, New York, 1979

—————. "Passports and Piety Apostasy in Nineteenth-Century France." *Jewish History*, 3, no. 2 (1988), 59–83.

—————. "The Symbiotic Relation Between French and German Jewry in the Age of Emancipation." *LBIYB*, 29 (1984), 331–50

Hemerdinger, G. "Le Dénombrement des israélites d'Alsace." *REJ*, 42 (1901), 253–64.

Hertzberg, Arthur. *The French Enlightenment and the Jews*. New York Columbia University Press, 1968.

Hildenfinger, Paul. "Les Actes du districte de Strasbourg relatifs aux juifs (juillet 1790–fructidor an III)." *REJ*, 60 (1910), 235–55, 61 (1911), 102–23, 279–84

————— "L'Adresse de la communauté de Strasbourg à l'Assemblée Nationale contre les juifs (avril 1790)." *REJ*, 58 (1909), 112–25

Horowitz, Elliott "The Eve of the Circumcision· A Chapter in the History of Jewish Nightlife." *Journal of Social History*, 23, no 1 (1989), 45–69

Hyman, Paula *From Dreyfus to Vichy The Remaking of French Jewry, 1906–1939*. New York: Columbia University Press, 1979

—————. "Jewish Fertility in Nineteenth-Century France." In *Modern Jewish Fertility*, ed. Paul Ritterband. Leiden E. J. Brill, 1981, pp 78–93

—————. "The Modern Jewish Family. Image and Reality." In *The Jewish Family Metaphor and Memory*, ed David Kraemer. Oxford Oxford University Press, 1989, pp 179–93.

————— "Village Jews and Jewish Modernity The Case of Alsace in the Nineteenth Century." In *Jewish Settlement and Community in the Modern Western World*, ed Ronald Dotterer, Deborah Dash Moore, and Steven M Cohen. Selinsgrove, PA· Susquehanna University Press, in press.

Isser, Natalie, and Lita Linzer Schwartz "Sudden Conversion The Case of Alphonse Ratisbonne." *Jewish Social Studies*, 45 (1983), 17–30

Jardin, André, and André-Jean Tudesq *Restoration and Reaction, 1815–1848*, trans Elborg Forster Cambridge: Cambridge University Press, 1983

Juillard, Etienne *Atlas et géographie de l'Alsace et de la Lorraine (la France rhénane)*. N p.. Flammarion, 1977.

————— *La Vie rurale dans la plaine de Basse-Alsace essai de géographie sociale*. Strasbourg: Editions F.-X Le Roux, 1953.

Kaplan, Marion. "For Love or Money The Marriage Strategies of Jews in Imperial Germany." *LBIYB*, 28 (1983), 263–300

——— "Priestess and Hausfrau. Women and Tradition in the German-Jewish Family" In *The Jewish Family. Myths and Reality*, ed. Steven M. Cohen and Paula E. Hyman New York: Holmes and Meier, 1986, pp. 62–81.

Katz, Jacob. *Emancipation and Assimilation*. Westmead, Eng Gregg International, 1972.

——— *Out of the Ghetto*. Cambridge: Harvard University Press, 1973.

——— "Religion as a Uniting and Dividing Force in Modern Jewish History." In *The Role of Religion in Modern Jewish History*, ed Jacob Katz Cambridge, Mass Association for Jewish Studies, 1975.

Katz, Michael. "Occupational Classification in History" *Journal of Interdisciplinary History*, 3, no 1 (1972), 63–88

——— *The People of Hamilton, Canada West. Family and Class in a Mid-Nineteenth-Century City*. Cambridge: Harvard University Press, 1975

Kleeblatt, Norman, ed. *The Dreyfus Affair· Art, Truth, and Justice* Berkeley University of California Press, 1987.

Klein, Paul. *L'Evolution contemporaine des banques alsaciennes* Paris· Librairie générale de droit et de jurisprudence, 1931

Klein-Zolty, Muriel, and Freddy Raphael. "Jalons pour l'étude de l'humour judéo-alsacien." *Revue des sciences sociales de la France de l'Est*, no 11 (1982), 85–122

Landau, Lazare. "Chrétiens et juifs en Basse-Alsace, de Napoléon Ier à Napoléon III, 1802–1870" *Yod*, no. 6 (1978), 6–15

Laslett, Peter *The World We Have Lost* London Methuen, 1965.

Laslett, Peter, ed *Household and Family in Past Time*. Cambridge. Cambridge University Press, 1972.

Lataulade, Joseph de. *Les Juifs sous l'ancien régime*. Bordeaux, 1906

Leuilliot, Paul. *L'Alsace au début du xixe siècle*, 3 vols Paris. SEVPEN, 1959–60

Lévi, Israël. "Napoléon 1er et la réunion du Grand Sanhédrin." *REJ*, 28 (1894), 265–80

Levinson, Robert. *The Jews in the California Gold Rush*. New York. Ktav, 1978

Lévy, Paul. "Les Ecoles juives d'Alsace et de Lorraine d'il y a un siècle." *La Tribune juive*, nos 32, 33, 34, 36, 38 (1933), 519–20, 540–41, 569, 600, 624.

——— *Histoire linguistique d'Alsace et de Lorraine*, 2 vols Paris. Société d'édition les belles lettres, 1929.

———. *Les Noms des israélites en France* Paris Presses universitaires de France, 1960.

Levylier, Roger *Notes et documents concernant la famille Cerf Berr*, 3 vols. Paris, 1902–6.

Liber, Maurice. "Les Juifs et la convocation des états généraux" *REJ*, 63 (1912), 185–210; 64 (1912), 89–108, 244–77; 65 (1913), 89–133, 66 (1913), 161–212.

———. "Napoléon et les juifs: la Question juive devant le Conseil d'Etat en 1806" *REJ*, 71 (1920), 127–47; 72 (1921), 1–23, 135–62

Liberles, Robert. "Emancipation and the Structure of the Jewish Community in the Nineteenth Century" *LBIYB*, 31 (1986), 51–67.

Liebman, Charles. "Religion, Class and Culture in American Jewish History." *Jewish Journal of Sociology*, 9, no 2 (1967), 227–41.

Loeb, I. "Réflexions sur les juifs." *REJ*, 27 (1893), 1–29, 161–79; 28 (1894), 1–31, 161–85; 29 (1894), 1–26

Lowenstein, Steven M. "The 1840s and the Creation of the German-Jewish Reform

Movement " In *Revolution and Evolution 1848 in German-Jewish History,* ed. Werner Mosse, Arnold Paucker, and Reinhard Rürup. Tübingen. Mohr, 1981, pp 255–97

———— "The Pace of Modernisation of German Jewry in the Nineteenth Century" *LBIYB,* 21 (1976), 41–56

———— "The Rural Community and the Urbanization of German Jewry." *Central European History,* 13, no. 3 (1980), 218–36

Lucien-Brun, Henri *La Condition des juifs en France depuis 1789* Lyon: A. Effantin, 1900.

Malino, Frances. *The Sephardic Jews of Bordeaux: Assimilation and Emancipation in Revolutionary and Napoleonic France* University, Ala.. University of Alabama Press, 1978

Marx, Roland. "Les Juifs et l'usure en Alsace réflexions sur un mythe " *Saisons d'Alsace,* nos 55–56 *(Les Juifs d'Alsace)* (1975), 62–67

———— "L'Opinion publique et les juifs en Alsace sous la Révolution," *Saisons d'Alsace,* no 9 (1964), 84–92

———— *Recherches sur la vie politique de l'Alsace prérévolutionnaire* Strasbourg Librairie Istra, 1966

————. "La Régénération économique des juifs d'Alsace à l'époque révolutionnaire et Napoléonienne " In *Les Juifs et la Révolution française,* ed. Albert Soboul and Bernhard Blumenkranz Toulouse Privat, 1976, pp 105–20

Meiss, Honel *Choses d'Alsace. contes d'avant guerre* Nice L. Barma [1920?]

———— *Traditions populaires alsaciennes à travers le dialecte judéo-alsacien* Nice: Imprimerie du Palais [1929?]

Mevorakh, Barukh. *Napoleon utekufato* Jerusalem. Mosad Bialik, 1968.

Merriman, John, ed *French Cities in the Nineteenth Century* London Hutchinson, 1982

Meyer, Michael *The Origins of the Modern Jew* Detroit Wayne State University Press, 1967

———— *Response to Modernity: A History of the Reform Movement in Judaism* Oxford: Oxford University Press, 1988

Moch, Leslie Page *Paths to the City. Regional Migration in Nineteenth-Century France.* Beverly Hills, Calif.: Sage, 1983

Nahon, Gérard *Les "Nations" juives portugaises du sud-ouest de la France, 1684–1791* Paris Fundacaõ Calouste Gulbenkian, Centro Cultural Portugues, 1981.

Neher, Albert *La Double demeure. scènes de la vie juive en Alsace* Paris. Colbo, 1965

Neher, André. "La Bourgeoisie juive d'Alsace " In *La Bourgeoisie alsacienne, études d'histoire sociale* Strasbourg. Librairie Istra, 1954, pp 435–42

Neher-Bernheim, Renée. "Cerf Berr de Medelsheim et sa famille " *Saisons d'Alsace,* nos 55–56 (1975), 47–61

————. *Documents inédits sur l'entrée des juifs dans la société française, 1750–1850,* 2 vols Tel-Aviv: Diaspora Research Institute, 1977

Nordmann, Achilles. *Der Israelitische Friedhof in Hegenheim in geschichtlicher Darstellung* Basel Wackermagelsche Verlagsanstalt, 1910

Petuchowski, Jacob. "Manuals and Catechisms of the Jewish Religion in the Early Period of Emancipation." In *Studies in Nineteenth-Century Jewish Intellectual History,* ed. Alexander Altmann. Cambridge: Harvard University Press, 1964, pp 47–64

———— *Prayerbook Reform in Europe. The Liturgy of European Liberal and Reform Judaism.* New York: World Union for Progressive Judaism, 1968, pp 105–27

Piette, Christine *Les Juifs de Paris (1808–1840): la marche vers l'assimilation* Québec. Les Presses de l'Université Laval, 1983.

Pinkney, David. *The Decisive Years in France, 1840–1847.* Princeton: Princeton University Press, 1986

Posener, S. "The Immediate Economic and Social Effects of the Emancipation of the Jews in France." *JSS,* 1, no. 3 (1939), 271–326.

———— "Les Juifs sous le Premier Empire." *REJ,* 93 (1932), 192–214; 94 (1933), 157–66.

Price, Roger. *An Economic History of Modern France.* London: Macmillan, 1981.

Prost, Antoine. *Histoire de l'enseignement en France, 1800–1967.* Paris Armand Colin, 1968

Raphael, Freddy "'Dynamique de la tradition' à propos du judaïsme rural d'Alsace." In *Colloques internationaux du Centre National de la Recherche Scientifique,* no. 576, *La Religion populaire* (Paris, Oct. 17–19, 1977), 237–49

————. "La Communauté juive de Haguenau: une destinée exemplaire." *Saisons d'Alsace,* no. 58 (1976), 153–60

———— "Les Juifs d'Alsace et la conscription au xixe siècle." In *Les Juifs et la Révolution française,* ed Albert Soboul and Bernhard Blumenkranz. Toulouse: Privat, 1976, pp 121–42 Reprinted in *Regards nouveaux sur les juifs d'Alsace,* ed Freddy Raphael and Robert Weyl. Strasbourg. Librairie Istra/Editions des Dernières nouvelles, 1980.

———— "Le Mariage juif dans la campagne alsacienne dans la deuxième moitié du xixe siècle." Folklore Research Center Studies, 4 *Studies in Marriage Customs,* ed Issachar Ben-Ami and Dov Noy. Jerusalem, 1974, pp. 181–98.

———— "Rîtes de naissance et médecine populaire dans le judaisme rural d'Alsace." *Ethnologie française,* 1, nos. 3–4 (1971), 83–94

Raphael, Freddy, and Robert Weyl *Juifs en Alsace. Culture, société, histoire.* Toulouse. Privat, 1977.

———— *Regards nouveaux sur les juifs d'Alsace* Strasbourg Librairie Istra/Editions des Dernières nouvelles, 1980

Reuss, Rodolphe. "L'Antisémitisme dans le Bas-Rhin pendant la Révolution, 1790–93 Nouveaux documents inédits." *REJ,* 78 (1914), 246–63.

————. *Histoire d'Alsace* Paris Boivin et cie, 1934.

———— "Quelque documents nouveaux sur l'antisémitisme dans le Bas-Rhin de 1794 à 1799." *REJ,* 59 (1910), 248–76.

Richarz, Monika. "Emancipation and Continuity German Jews in the Rural Economy." In *Revolution and Evolution. 1848 in German-Jewish History,* ed. Werner Mosse, Arnold Paucker, and Reinhard Rürup Tübingen: Mohr, 1981, pp. 95–115

Richarz, Monika, ed. *Jüdisches Leben in Deutschland, 1780–1871* [Stuttgart?] Deutsche Verlags-Anstalt, 1976

———— *Im Kaiserreich.* Stuttgart Deutsche Verlags-Anstalt, 1979

Rodrigue, Aron *French Jews, Turkish Jews.* Bloomington Indiana University Press, 1990.

Rozenblit, Marsha. *Assimilation and Identity: The Jews of Vienna, 1867–1914*. Albany State University of New York Press, 1984.

Rürup, Reinhard *Emanzipation und Anti-Semitismus: Studien zur "Judenfrage" der bürgerlichen Gesellschaft* Göttingen Vandenhoeck and Ruprecht, 1975

——— "The European Revolutions of 1848 and Jewish Emancipation" In *Revolution and Evolution: 1848 in German-Jewish History*, ed Werner Mosse, Arnold Paucker, and Reinhard Rurup. Tübingen: Mohr, 1981, pp. 1–53.

———. "Jewish Emancipation and Bourgeois Society." *LBIYB*, 14 (1969), 67–91.

Sagnac, Philippe "Les Juifs et Napoléon." *Revue d'histoire moderne et contemporaine*, 2 (1900–1901), 461–84; 3 (1901–2), 461–92

Sarg, Freddy. *La Naissance en Alsace*. Strasbourg. Editions Oberlin, 1974

Scheid, Elie *Histoire des juifs d'Alsace*. Paris A. Durlacher, 1887

Schorsch, Ismar. "From Wolfenbüttel to Wissenschaft: The Divergent Paths of Isaak Markus Jost and Leopold Zunz" *LBIYB*, 22 (1977), 109–28

Schwarzfuchs, Simon. *Du juif à l'israélite histoire d'une mutation*. Paris. Librairie Arthème Fayard, 1989.

——— *Les Juifs de France*. Paris: Albin Michel, 1975

——— *Napoleon, the Jews and the Sanhedrin*. London: Routledge and Kegan Paul, 1979

——— "Introduction" to Eliahu Scheid, *Memoirs 1883–1899*. [Hebrew] Jerusalem Yad Yizhak Ben-Zvi, 1983, pp. 7–17.

———. "Les Nations juives de France." *Dix-huitième siècle*, 13 (1981), 127–36

——— "Three Documents from the Life of the Jewish Communities of Alsace-Lorraine" [Hebrew] *Michael*, 4 (1976), 9–31

Scott, Joan W.. and Louise A. Tilly *Women, Work, and Family*. New York. Holt, Rinehart, and Winston, 1978.

Sewell, William, Jr. "Social Mobility in a Nineteenth-Century European City Some Findings and Implications" *Journal of Interdisciplinary History*, 7, no. 2 (1976), 217–33

Shofer, Lawrence "Emancipation and Population Change." In *Revolution and Evolution: 1848 in German-Jewish History*, ed. Werner Mosse, Arnold Paucker, and Reinhard Rurup. Tübingen: Mohr, 1981, pp 63–89.

———. "The History of European Jewry Search for a Method." *LBIYB*, 19 (1979), 17–36.

Siat, P Meyer. "Les Orgues Wetzel dans les synagogues d'Alsace" *Saisons d'Alsace*, nos 55–56 (1975), 245–50

Soboul, Albert "Les Troubles agraires de 1848" In *Problèmes paysans de la Révolution, 1789–1848*. Paris: François Maspero, 1976, pp 293–334.

Soboul, Albert, and Bernhard Blumenkranz, ed. *Les Juifs et la Révolution française*. Toulouse Privat, 1976.

Sorkin, David. *The Transformation of German Jewry, 1780–1840*. New York. Oxford University Press, 1987.

Staehling, Charles *Histoire contemporaine de Strasbourg et de l'Alsace*, 2 vols Nice: Imprimerie Victor-Eugène Gauthier et cie, 1884, and Nancy: Imprimerie Berger-Levrault et cie., 1887

Strauss, Herbert. "Pre-emancipation Prussian Policies towards the Jews, 1815–1847"
LBIYB, 11 (1966), 107–36

Szajkowski, Zosa. *Agricultural Credit and Napoleon's Anti-Jewish Decrees.* New York
Editions historiques franco-juives, 1953.

———— "Anti-Jewish Riots during the Revolutions of 1789, 1830, and 1848." [Hebrew]
Zion, 20 (1955), 82–102

———— *Autonomy and Jewish Communal Debts during the French Revolution of 1789.* New
York: privately printed, 1959

————. *The Economic Status of the Jews in Alsace, Metz, and Lorraine, 1648–1789* New
York Editions historiques franco-juives, 1953

———— *Jewish Education in France, 1789–1939.* New York· Conference on Jewish Social
Studies, 1980.

————. "Jewish Vocational Schools in France in the Nineteenth Century." [Yiddish]
YIVO Bleter, 42 (1962), 81–120.

———— *Jews and the French Revolutions of 1789, 1830, and 1848.* New York Ktav, 1970.

————. "Notes on the Occupational Status of French Jews, 1800–1880." *Proceedings of
the American Academy of Jewish Research*, vols. 46–47 (1979–80), 531–54.

————. *Poverty and Social Welfare among French Jews, 1800–1880.* New York: Editions
historiques franco-juives, 1954.

———— "The Struggle against Yiddish in France" [Yiddish], *YIVO Bleter*, 14, nos 1–2
(1939), 46–77

————. "The Struggle around the Electoral System in the Jewish Communities in
France, 1850–1880." [Yiddish], *YIVO Bleter*, 35 (1951), 139–64.

Szyster, Boruch. *La Révolution française et les juifs.* Toulouse Imprimerie du sud-ouest,
J Castellvi et cie., 1929

Tal, Uriel *Christians and Jews in Germany. Religion, Politics, and Ideology in the Second
Reich, 1870–1914*, trans. Noah Jonathan Jacobs Ithaca· Cornell University Press,
1975.

Thernstrom, Stephen *The Other Bostonians Poverty and Progress in the American Metropolis, 1880–1970* Cambridge Harvard University Press, 1973

Touati, Pierre-Yves. "Le Registre de circoncisions de Moshe et Simon Blum," *REJ*, 142,
nos. 1–2 (1983), 109–31

Toury, Jacob "'Deutsche Juden' im Vormarz." *Bulletin des Leo Baeck Instituts*, 8, no. 29
(1965), 65–82.

————. "Der Eintritt der Juden ins deutsche Burgertum." In *Das Judentum in der
deutschen Umwelt, 1800–1850*, ed Hans Liebeschutz and Arnold Paucker. Tübingen:
Mohr, 1977, pp. 139–242.

————. *Turmoil and Confusion in the Revolution of 1848 The Anti-Jewish Riots in the "Year
of Freedom" and Their Influence on Modern Antisemitism.* [Hebrew] Tel Aviv: Moreshet,
1968.

Treshan, Victor "The Struggle for Integration The Jewish Community of Strasbourg,
1818–1850." Ph D. diss , University of Wisconsin, 1979

———— "The Struggle for Integration· The New Educational System of the Jewish

Community of Strasbourg, 1820–1850 " Paper delivered at the annual meeting of the Association for Jewish Studies, Boston, December 1977

Van de Walle, Etienne. "Marriage and Marital Fertility" *Daedalus,* 97, no. 2 (1968), 486–501

Vidal de la Blache, P *La France de l'est.* Paris Librairie Armand Colin, 1917.

Volkov, Shulamit "Distinctiveness and Assimilation. The Paradox of Jewish Identity in the Second Reich." [Hebrew] In *Crises of German National Consciousness in the Nineteenth and Twentieth Centuries,* ed Moshe Zimmermann. Jerusalem Magnes Press, 1983, pp. 169–85

——— *The Rise of Popular Anti-Modernism in Germany.* Princeton Princeton University Press, 1978.

Wahl, Alfred. *Confession et comportement dans les campagnes d'Alsace et de Bade, 1871–1939 Catholiques, protestants et juifs* 2 vols Metz Université de Metz, 1980

——— *L'Option et l'émigration des Alsaciens-Lorrains, 1871–1872.* Paris. Editions Ophrys, 1974

Wahl, Jean-Jacques "Le Judaïsme rural alsacien au xixe siècle à travers la littérature d'expression française " *Saisons d'Alsace,* n s , nos 55–56 (1975), 91–98.

Weber, Eugen. *Peasants into Frenchmen* Stanford. Stanford University Press, 1976

Weill, Georges. *L'Alsace française de 1789 à 1870* Paris F. Alcan, 1916.

Weill, Georges "Cerf Berr de Medelsheim, militant de l'émancipation " *Nouveaux cahiers,* 45 (1976), 30–42

——— "Les Juifs d'Alsace Cent ans d'historiographie." *REJ,* 139, nos 1–3 (1980), 81–108

——— "Recherches sur la démographie des juifs d'Alsace du xvie au xviiie siècle " *REJ,* 130 (1971), 51–89

Weissbach, Lee Shai "The Jewish Elite and the Children of the Poor. Jewish Apprenticeship Programs in Nineteenth-Century France." *AJS Review,* 12, no 1 (1987), 123–42

Weyl, Robert, and Freddy Raphael. *L'imagerie juive d'Alsace.* Strasbourg Editions des Dernières nouvelles d'Alsace, 1979

Weyl, Robert, Freddy Raphael, and Jean Daltroff "Le Cahier de doléances des juifs d'Alsace " *Revue d'Alsace,* 109 (1983), 65–80

Wilson, Nelly. *Bernard Lazare Antisemitism and the Problem of Jewish Identity in Late Nineteenth-Century France* Cambridge Cambridge University Press, 1978

Wilson, Stephen. *Ideology and Experience Antisemitism in France at the Time of the Dreyfus Affair.* Rutherford, N J. Fairleigh Dickinson University Press, 1982

Zeldin, Theodore *France, 1848–1945* 2 vols Oxford Clarendon Press, 1973

Index

CPSIA information can be obtained
at www.ICGtesting.com
Printed in the USA
BVOW06*0335170817

492140BV00007B/28/P